Financial Stability, Risks, and Ecological Transition

The evolution of capitalist economies through waves of liberalization of markets over the last five decades led to structural changes and greater systemic risks.

This book presents economic research into the roots and remedies of these risks, particularly exploring the key issues of financial stability and the financing of economic activities, on the one hand, and the necessary economic and ecological transition to a more sustainable world, on the other hand. Against a backdrop of these growing global risks – whether economic and financial, ecological or geopolitical – the continuity of financing for innovative activities, transition operations, or investments in regions or countries weakened by conflict is essential to enable economies to generate sustainable wealth to improve living conditions for citizens. Therefore, the contributors to this book explore issues of financial stability in relation to financial regulation, macroprudential policies, the use of digital currencies by central banks, mechanisms for hedging markets against risk and the perception of risk by market players, bank resolution mechanisms, and the role of the insurance sector in a financialized economy. In parallel with this, this book also explores the different ways in which green transition processes can be financed. The role of industrial and fiscal policies in stabilizing markets and encouraging economic activities that would enable sustainable and stable economic development and support the ecological transition in the long term is also highlighted.

This book will be of great interested to readers of green economy and transition, money, finance and banking, and economic and public policy.

Lyubov Klapkiv (PhD) is an Assistant Professor at the University Maria Curie-Skłodowska in Lublin (Institute of Economics and Finance) and a Visiting Professor at the University Grenoble Alpes (2022–2024). She received her PhD degree in Finance from the Kyiv National University of Trade and Economics (Ukraine). She is a graduate of the Line Kirkland Scholarship program 2015/2016. Her main research fields include the economics of insurance, sustainable finance, and financial innovations.

Faruk Ülgen is a Professor of Economics, Head of International Relations and Bachelor Distance Learning Programs within the Department of Economics at the Université Grenoble Alpes, France. He also serves as a Codirector of the Center of Research in Economics of Grenoble (CREG). His current research focuses on the evolution of financial markets and innovations and the evolution of financial regulation and supervision from an institutionalist-evolutionary perspective, drawing on collective action and the economics of the commons.

Routledge Frontiers of Political Economy

Social Inequality and Human Security
Case Studies from Asia
Edited by Christian Ploberger

Rethinking Economic Theories
A New Political Economy for the Biosphere
Tiago Cardao-Pito

Marx's Theory of Value at the Frontiers
Classical Political Economics, Imperialism and Ecological Breakdown
Güney Işıkara and Patrick Mokre

Reinterpreting Libertarianism
New Directions in Libertarian Studies
Edited by Łukasz Dominiak, Igor Wysocki, Stanisław Wójtowicz, and Dawid Megger

The Circular Economy and Institutional Change
Transformation in Theory and Practice
Yılmaz Kaplan

International Economic and Monetary Architecture at the Crossroads
Bretton Woods at 80
Atish Rex Ghosh and Fabio Masini

On Value and Valuation
John Frow

Financial Stability, Risks, and Ecological Transition
Addressing Economic Challenges Under Global Uncertainty
Edited by Lyubov KLAPKIV and Faruk ÜLGEN

For more information about this series, please visit: www.routledge.com/Routledge-Frontiers-of-Political-Economy/book-series/SE0345

Financial Stability, Risks, and Ecological Transition

Addressing Economic Challenges Under Global Uncertainty

Edited by
Lyubov Klapkiv and Faruk Ülgen

Routledge
Taylor & Francis Group
LONDON AND NEW YORK

First published 2026
by Routledge
4 Park Square, Milton Park, Abingdon, Oxon OX14 4RN

and by Routledge
605 Third Avenue, New York, NY 10158

Routledge is an imprint of the Taylor & Francis Group, an informa business

British Library Cataloguing-in-Publication Data
A catalogue record for this book is available from the British Library

ISBN: 978-1-041-12184-8 (hbk)
ISBN: 978-1-041-12188-6 (pbk)
ISBN: 978-1-003-66353-9 (ebk)

DOI: 10.4324/9781003663539

Typeset in Times New Roman
by codeMantra

Contents

Figures

Tables

Contributors

Almawi Andrea is a PhD, temporary lecturer, and researcher at the Université Grenoble Alpes.

Billand Pascal is a Professor at the Université de Lyon, France; CNRS, GATE Lyon Saint-Etienne, France.

Bravard Christophe is a Professor at the Université Grenoble Alpes, UMR 1215 GAEL, France, CNRS, GATE Lyon Saint-Etienne, France.

Dziura Marek is an Associate Professor at the College of Management and Quality Sciences, Krakow University of Economics, Poland.

Dziwok Ewa is a Professor in the Department of Applied Mathematics, Faculty of Finance, University of Economics in Katowice, Poland.

Jaki Andrzej is a Professor of Economics at the College of Management and Quality Sciences, Krakow University of Economics, Poland.

Janowicz-Lomott Marietta is a Professor at the Warsaw School of Economics, Poland.

Klapkiv Lyubov is an Associate Professor at the University Maria Curie-Skłodowska in Lublin, Poland.

Kononovich Inga is a PhD holder and researcher on Climate Change Policy.

Ky Kenneth is a PhD at the Université Grenoble Alpes, France.

Laurent Alain is an Associate Professor at the Université Grenoble Alpes, CREG, France.

Liberadzki Kamil is a Professor at the Warsaw School of Economics, Poland.

Liberadzki Marcin is a Professor at the Warsaw School of Economics, Poland.

Łyskawa Krzysztof is a Professor at the Poznan University of Economics and Business, Poland.

Rojek Tomasz is an Associate Professor at the College of Management and Quality Sciences, Krakow University of Economics, Poland.

Sakovich Marina is a PhD, Research Fellow, Center of Research in Economics of Grenoble, France.

Sarangi Sudipta is a Professor at the DIW Berlin and Department of Economics, Virginia Tech Blacksburg VA, USA.

Shylov Maksym is a PhD student at the Warsaw School of Economics, Poland.

Skibińska-Fabrowska Ilona is an Associate Professor at the University Maria Curie-Skłodowska in Lublin, Poland.

Ülgen Faruk is a Professor of Economics at the Université Grenoble Alpes, CREG, France.

Introduction

Growing challenges under global uncertainty

Lyubov Klapkiv and Faruk Ülgen

Financial Stability, Risks, and Ecological Transition: Addressing Economic Challenges under Global Uncertainty is framed as a platform for a broad cross-section of contributions on transformation processes in the economy and society in the 21st century.

The evolution of capitalist economies through waves of liberalization of markets and related regulation over the last five decades led to structural changes in the way society is organized and markets do function. These changes have also resulted in new ways of organizing economic activities and risen new risks, some of which have turned out to be systemic in nature, insofar as they have triggered instabilities on a societal scale.

"We are witnessing a backsliding in democracy everywhere in the world, even in the most advanced democracy. It is a movement into the bad – in the wrong direction," stated Alain Berset at the World Economic Forum in 2025, a former Swiss president who heads the Council of Europe (Financial Post, 2025).

To date, these risks jeopardize the continuity of our societies and call into question the ability of market economies to cope with growing risks, whether financial (such as the global financial crisis [GFC] of 2007–2009), environmental and humanitarian (climate change and difficulties to achieve the sustainable development goals), health-related (such as the COVID-19 pandemic), or geopolitical (such as the Russia-Ukraine and Israel-Hamas-Palestine wars).

Economic research into the roots and remedies of these risks, which threaten the smooth working of financial markets and economies as well as the viability of life on Earth, is of the utmost importance and requires urgent development and action to address sustainability issues at a global level. From this perspective, the purpose of this book is to examine and address systemic challenges as well as sector-specific issues related to the stabilization of economies mainly through financial stability, risk management and market regulation, green transition, and to point to possible relevant directions toward which the economics profession and economic policies could be directed to find out effective solutions and then enable sustainable practices for viable transition of societies to a more liveable world.

The book offers various chapters that focus on different systemic and specific aspects of economic evolution and financial markets development within the context of rising risks and new challenges such as monetary and financial instabilities, green economy, transition and sectoral risks, and environmental, monetary, and industrial policies and related regulations in the face of growing uncertainties in markets and the global economy.

We believe that two burning issues of our time – financial stability and the financing of economic activities on the one hand, and the necessary transformation of our societies, i.e. the economic and ecological transition to a more sustainable world, on the other – need to be addressed together, since the issues they represent for our future are so intertwined and lie at the heart of the constraints we face today.

DOI: 10.4324/9781003663539-1

Against a backdrop of growing global risks, be they economic and financial, ecological, related to transition, or geopolitical, the continuity of financing for innovative activities, transition operations, or investments in regions or countries weakened by conflict is a prerogative to enable economies to generate sustainable wealth to improve living conditions for citizens. Particular attention is therefore paid to issues related to finance, transition, risk, and stability.

We look at issues of financial stability in relation to financial regulation, macroprudential policies, the use of digital currencies by central banks, mechanisms for hedging markets against risk, and the perception of risk by market players, bank resolution mechanisms, and the role of the insurance sector in a financialized economy.

In parallel with this, we also take an innovative look at the financing of economic activities, focusing on different ways in which the transition process can be financed. The role of industrial and fiscal policies in stabilizing markets and encouraging economic activities that would enable sustainable and stable economic development and support the ecological transition in the long term is also highlighted.

The book includes 14 chapters on a variety of approaches to the functioning of financial markets in relation with the eco-transition process and the financing needs of economic development. It studies the constraints and risks arising in economic and ecological transition that could jeopardize the viability of economies. The chapters, therefore, examine multiple aspects of the evolution of economies over the last decades in an ocean of growing uncertainties and geopolitical concerns.

Chapter 1, *Financial stability and green transition* by Faruk Ülgen, focuses on the financial stability and green transition of our economies as two sides of the same coin, that is, the structural transformation of the market economy into a sustainable societal framework. However, such a transformation encounters an obstacle that stems from the nature of the capitalist economy, which is the opposition between private interest and the common good. This opposition, which is a social dilemma, has been exacerbated by the financialization of economies since the 1990s, leading to the GFC of 2007–2009. This chapter aims to show that the only way to reform market economies to ensure long-term systemic viability is to develop regulatory mechanisms that would enable financial markets to finance ecological transition projects and inclusive green development in a sustainable way. This requires changes not only to the rules governing financial regulation but also to the organization of the energy transition process and, more generally, the economic transition. So such an organization is not possible without tight coordination and cooperation. However, in the context of geopolitical instability, this condition is proving extremely difficult to meet, to the extent that the fight against climate change and design of durable ways to finance the energy transition (the primary objective of the last Conference of the Parties in November 2025 in Baku) prove to be more wishful thinking than an attainable target.

In Chapter 2, *Central bank digital currencies and financial stability*, Alain Laurent discusses the extent to which the Central Bank Digital Currencies (CBDCs) can be developed and used as a relevant way to achieve public policy objectives such as financial stability and stable financial support for innovative economic activities within the eco-transition process. CBDCs represent a major development in the global monetary landscape. By issuing digital currencies, central banks are seeking to modernize payment systems while retaining direct control over the money supply. Their influence on financial stability can be both positive and negative, depending on their design and implementation. CBDCs can strengthen financial stability by offering an alternative to private currencies and decentralized cryptocurrencies. They enable stricter regulation and better traceability of transactions, thereby reducing the risks of fraud and money laundering. In addition, they can facilitate cross-border payments, reducing transaction costs and the risks associated with currency fluctuations. The author provides that CBDCs could also improve the efficiency of monetary policy by strengthening the different channels of monetary policy transmission, contributing then to the stable funding of the transition process along with the required innovations.

Marcin Liberadzki, in Chapter 3, *Use of a bridge institution in the bank resolution: the case of Silicon Valley Bank and Signature Bank*, studies the collapse of Silicon Valley Bank (SVB) in March 2023, which was the second-largest bank failure in U.S. history, after Lehman Brothers in 2008. The collapse of Signature Bank, occurring just two days later, was the third-largest bank failure in the U.S. This time, the Lehman scenario did not repeat – unlike in 2008, the failures of both institutions were carried out in an orderly manner, causing hardly any contagion effect. This chapter describes the use of a bridge bank tool in the resolution of SVB and Signature Bank. A bridge bank is a stabilizing tool designed to temporarily maintain the continuity of critical functions of an institution and its operations until a permanent solution is found. Liberadzki argues that it is one of the resolution tools available, used sporadically in situations where the resolution authority is taken aback by sudden bank failures, mainly due to liquidity problems if not run on a bank.

Chapter 4, *Innovative macroprudential policy for financial stability*, by Marina Sakovich, seeks to analyze how the 2007–2008 GFC brought back into focus the issue of systemic financial instability and the regulation of financial activities at the macroeconomic level. Much work has been done in the decade following the crisis to determine the nature, conditions, and scope of macroprudential regulatory models with a view to strengthening the effectiveness of financial market regulation and supervision mechanisms in parallel with the microprudential regulatory practices that have been implemented for several decades. In the light of the GFC, the latter have proven to have limited capacity to ensure the systemic stability of financial markets. Attention is therefore turned to the possibility of considering innovative combinations of macroeconomic regulatory instruments and modalities that could reduce the occurrence and severity of major financial crises without hampering the dynamism of innovative financial markets. Macroprudential regulation comprises many elements, and the question of choosing the optimal combination of macroprudential policy instruments and their interaction is a critical issue with regard to these observations. In line with this, the main purpose of this chapter is to question whether the financial system is adequately protected from risks, more than 15 years after the GFC.

Inga Kononovich maintains, in Chapter 5, *Economic barriers to green transition*, that the global nature of climate change requires the implementation of actions in favor of a green economy in advanced as well as in developing countries. Delays in designing and implementing appropriate measures in this direction can have very serious and irreparable consequences in the medium and long term, including not only economic problems but severe environmental degradation and negative impacts on population well-being. This chapter provides multiple perspectives on the main economic barriers to the green transition on an international scale. Analysis of barriers to green transition is important while creating the Nationally Determined Contributions (NDCs) and long-term decarbonization strategies. NDCs, as the foundation of the Paris Agreement, represent the commitments of countries to take measures, including green measures, to achieve climate goals, and to report on their progress every five years. This chapter mainly focuses on global economic barriers to green transition with a specific emphasis on the challenges of the green transition in developing countries, which are rooted in unresolved social and infrastructural issues and a high reliance on fossil fuels in sectors that are difficult to decarbonize. This chapter also offers practical recommendations for overcoming these barriers to the green transition in developing economies.

In Chapter 6, *Models of financing energy transition: differences and results*, Andrea Almawi provides a comparative analysis of the financing mechanisms for energy transitions in France,

Germany, and China. It focuses on the alignment between financing strategies, policy declarations, and their actual implementation. Specifically, it examines "pre-project" financing, which involves securing funds before project initiation, and "post-project" financing, which allocates funds after the project's establishment. The primary goal is to evaluate how effectively these countries' announced energy goals and policies have been achieved, analyzing the role of financing mechanisms in this process. By comparing the ambitious declarations with real-world outcomes, this chapter aims to uncover significant discrepancies between policy intentions and practical execution. This analysis seeks to determine whether pre-project financing reduces financial speculation and promotes long-term planning more effectively than post-project financing. By highlighting the importance of political will, economic priorities, and technological advancements, Almawi underscores the need for a diversified approach to financing that addresses the unique challenges faced by each country. It provides valuable insights for policymakers, investors, and stakeholders, emphasizing the necessity of innovative and sustainable financing solutions to accelerate the global transition to renewable energy.

Ewa Dziwok argues, in Chapter 7, *Climate risks, parametric insurance and weather derivatives*, that climate change poses significant risks to financial systems and the broader economy, requiring the engagement of financial institutions. The COVID-19 pandemic has raised investors' awareness of environmental and social issues, further accelerating the move toward sustainable finance. Legal reforms and the emergence of innovative financial instruments, such as green bonds, have played a key role in financing the green transition, and their issuance has grown exponentially in recent years. This study examines the evolution of the green premium ("greenium") over time by estimating the term structure of zero-coupon bonds. While there are many methodologies for defining the green bond premium, it is generally viewed as the price benefit derived from investors' willingness to pay more or accept lower yields in exchange for sustainable impact. Using the Nelson-Siegel-Svensson parametric model, the author estimates zero-coupon yield curves and compares green bonds with their conventional counterparts across selected maturities. Dziwok's findings indicate that green bonds tend to offer slightly lower interest rates; however, the differences are minimal, suggesting that their appeal is primarily driven by non-financial motivations.

Chapter 8, *Climate risks, parametric insurance and weather derivatives*, by Maksym Shylov, maintains that the changing climate is getting increased risk factors for agriculture parties. It brings to logical thought that the above-mentioned losses should be somehow insured (hedged) if they exceed a certain level of loss tolerance. However, traditional insurance does not meet the increasing need for financial protection from the consequences of adverse weather. In response to this, alternative weather risk transfer tools, such as parametric (index) insurance and weather derivatives, are being developed. The author of this article provides an overview of 17 parameters and how such solutions can be distinguished from traditional insurance. Moreover, the genesis and development of weather derivatives and parametric insurance are briefly presented, as well as how these solutions can be applied by food processors in the context of the food supply chain. In addition, the author shows the first results of a survey among food enterprises on how they perceive the frequency and severity of weather-related losses, what impacts such severity and how they protect themselves, what they know about alternative risk transfer tools, and what hinders them from investing into weather derivatives or parametric insurance.

In Chapter 9, *Hybrid capital instruments against risks*, Kamil Liberadzki treats the loss-absorbing capacity of issuers' hybrid debt classified to Restricted Tier 1 (RT1) capital layer as well as Tier 2 and Tier 3 subordinated debt. The characteristics of Solvency II insurers' capital requirements have been presented together with the RT1, Tier 2, and Tier 3 eligibility specifications. Italian life insurer Eurovita S.p.A distress was caused by the interest rate rise, accompanied by the insurer's bonds portfolio value drop and lapse risk materialization. The main shareholder did not inject enough capital into Eurovita, so the insurer had to be placed under the administration of the Italian supervision authority and eventually be taken over (bail-out) by a group of private banks and insurers. Based on his own funds calculus, the author shows that if the potential of Additional Tier 1, Tier 2, and Tier 3 instruments had been exploited by Eurovita, the company would not have breached the required level of Solvency Capital Ratio. The conclusion is that these instruments may effectively increase the institution's resilience while their notional being relatively small to total assets would overburden the issuer.

Lyubov Klapkiv, in Chapter 10, *Entrepreneurs' financial risk perception under the conditions of geopolitical instability*, offers an original analysis of international trade, where the outcome of the contract is highly dependent on the stability of the geopolitical situation in the contractors' country. The complexity of geopolitical mechanisms and their direct and indirect impacts make the forecast tools useless. Geopolitical instability hugely impacts financial stability at both macro and micro scales. In most cases, entrepreneurs' risk management process is based on the subjective evaluation of the unstable situation and choice of approach: avoid or take the financial risk. This chapter develops an analysis of the mechanisms of subjective risk perception of financial risks. Perception of financial risks is dominated by fear of loss. This study is based on behavioral theory, particularly the theory of bounded rationality and prospect theory. The lack of knowledge drives risk-taking as a strategy to find out about the unknowns of the future and to prevent possible harm and/or to develop new opportunities. Based on the survey results, which were conducted among 240 entrepreneurs, the author is trying to identify how financial risk is perceived and which type of risk attitude regarding geopolitical instabilities prevails. The findings from the chapter contribute to the interdisciplinary study of the relationship between financial and geopolitical spheres.

In Chapter 11, *Challenges in financing microenterprises in an unstable economic landscape*, Ilona Skibińska-Fabrowska examines factors determining the choice of sources of financing for business activities, especially investment activities. In the context of contemporary economic challenges, such as financial instability and the need to adapt to a changing economic environment, microenterprises in economies with similar structures and levels of development face specific difficulties in obtaining financing. This study is preliminary about the planned in-depth analysis. The analysis was conducted based on surveys of entrepreneurs. Statistical analysis methods were used to process the results. The findings indicate that the choice of financing sources is more influenced by the owners' experience than by financing costs, and non-financial factors are the main barriers to accessing external capital. The conclusions from the study can be useful for shaping financial policies targeted at microenterprises in economies with comparable economic structures, which is particularly relevant in the context of contemporary economic challenges.

In Chapter 12, *Financialization and the role of the insurance market in the economy*, Marietta Janowicz-Lomott and Krzysztof Łyskawa provide an analysis of the transformation of insurance mechanisms toward clients' needs. Authors agree that, in recent decades, there has been an observable process of growing importance of the financial sector at the expense of the real economy. This process, called financialization, is seen as a deviation in the theoretical view of the basic function of finance as intermediation. Consideration of the scale of financialization inspired the identification of anomalies in the insurance market. This chapter attempts to answer the question of whether it is still possible to speak of an insurance company as an entity that helps its customers cope with the consequences of risk realization or whether insurers already have a different purpose of operation. Are the actions of financial institutions a permanent trend or perhaps a temporary instability? Is this situation a challenge for the policies of states (or supranational organizations, e.g. EU institutions)? Are their actions to date sufficient in this regard? To achieve the goal, the analysis covers insurance products, insurance distribution, and the profitability of insurers.

Marek Dziura, Andrzej Jaki, and Tomasz Rojek, in Chapter 13, *Technology foresight and industrial strategy toward a green and digital future*, summarize that climate neutrality by 2050 will require giant leaps in innovation and a complex technological ecosystem with many interlinked solutions. Artificial intelligence, the Internet of Things, 5G, blockchain, and next-generation computing technologies will help us manage this increased complexity. When technology foresight began to be adopted in industrial countries, it tended to be still somewhat of a marginal activity in developing countries. Today, globalization has radically transformed the range of economic activities that developing countries can perform. Production is fragmented and organized along global value chains. Dense flows of knowledge and technology are available but need to be fully employed in the framework of coherent industrial strategies. This chapter examines how and to what extent technology foresight programs are needed in developing countries, given the new prevailing global context. It is argued that technology foresight and industrial strategy are and must be mutually consistent, and they need to be taken seriously, coherently designed, and implemented in light of their role in shaping economic growth. The authors provide preliminary support to this argument by discussing the theoretical foundations and justification of technology foresight and industrial strategy, and then reviewing some relevant examples from different countries (mainly from Poland, with relations to industrial strategies).

Chapter 14, *Environmental tax policy and R&D innovation networks* by Pascal Billand, Christophe Bravard, Kenneth Ky, and Sudipta Sarangi examines the role of an environmental tax on R&D collaboration networks between firms in the context of developing cleaner production processes. First, three types of innovation networks that can emerge in equilibrium are brought forward. Then, the relationship between the environmental tax and the incentives for firms to add more collaborative links is examined. This shows that an increase in the environmental tax does not always incentivize firms to increase the number of R&D collaborations. Finally, the optimal tax that the public authorities should set in order to maximize social welfare is considered. Given tractability issues, for this problem, the attention is restricted to the case of three firms. This chapter argues that the optimal environmental tax depends on the cost of link formation. The higher the cost of link formation, the lower the environmental tax. Similarly, the optimal environmental tax increases with the number of links that an efficient network contains.

Given the large spectrum of issues and methods of analysis, related to various fields of research and practices such as banking and financial studies, business management, economic development, finance, growth and development, financial innovations and regulation, insurance economics, political economy of financial and economic development, and thanks to the contributors coming from various developing and advanced economies, from Central and Eastern Europe, and from different institutions (scholars and researchers), this book is aimed at a wide audience: policymakers, researchers, faculties, PhD students, and Master's and Bachelor's students.

We hope that this book will be positively welcomed by the readers, and that it will contribute to a deeper understanding of the dynamics of our economies and of the possible solutions to the various problems – including climate change and environmental and resource degradation – that these same dynamics engender in the evolution of society.

Reference

Davos 2025: Some notable quotes from the World Economic Forum meeting (2025, January 23). Financial Post. https://financialpost.com/pmn/davos-2025-some-notable-quotes-from-the-world-economic-forum-meeting

1 Financial stability and green transition

Faruk Ülgen

Introduction

Financial stability and green transition are the two sides of the same global issue, which is the radical transformation of capitalist market economies into sustainable and collectively viable social structures. On the one side, the stability of financial systems is the sine qua non of the smooth working of the economy to lead to economic development. On the other side, the green transition is a matter of survival of life on earth that could allow or not the next generations to have access to (quantitively and qualitatively) appropriate resources and conditions to live decently. Both financial stability and green transition prove to be the essential prerequisites for a livable society. They are not alternatives among multiple choices; they are the only options that we have to hope for a possible collective future. Their linkages and interactions are through the systemic stability of the economy and society but also through the financing process of the transition process. For instance, green finance is studied as a critical component of financial stability, particularly within the context of growing climate-related risks while climate finance is regarded as the way to support mitigation and adaptation actions to address climate change within the United Nations Framework Convention on Climate Change (UNFCCC).

The Economics literature offers many and diverse range of work on the critical role of financial stability, regulation and economic policies for the smooth functioning of economies, and sustainable green transition financing amidst growing risks and geopolitical conflicts. However, the interlinkages between these two concerns are not explicitly studied. This chapter argues that financial stability and green transition are a sine qua non of the transformation of market economies into sustainable societal frameworks. Such a transformation encounters an obstacle that stems from the nature of a capitalist economy: the opposition between private interest and the common/public good. This opposition is a social dilemma that has been exacerbated by the financialization of economies since the 1990s and led to the global financial crisis of 2007–2009.

In light of the weaknesses of liberalized market economies, the only way to make market economies work properly and to ensure long-term systemic viability seems to be linked to the design and implementation of regulatory mechanisms that would enable the financial system to finance green transition projects and inclusive green development in a sustainable way, sheltered from speculative movements in the financial markets, which are mainly driven by speculative, short-term efficiency of operations. This requires changes to the rules governing financial regulation, but also to the organization of the energy transition process, and more generally, the *eco-transition*.

In this vein, the first section brings forward the opposition between private interests and public good as a deep social dilemma that our social organization has to deal with in order to let markets work in a sustainable way. The second section then argues that we should rethink our

DOI: 10.4324/9781003663539-2

economic organization through a twofold stability issue: financial stability and the stability of transition financing to implement the necessary changes regarding environmental and ecological issues to ensure the viability of a livable society. The third section suggests an appropriate regulatory framework to support such a stability scheme. The concluding remarks point to the need for strong coordination and cooperation that such a transformation process does require. In the current context of geopolitical instability, this condition is proving extremely difficult to meet. The fight against climate change and designing durable ways to finance the energy transition that was the primary objective of the last Conference of the Parties in November 2024 in Baku proved to be more wishful thinking than an attainable target.

A deep social dilemma: opposition between private interests and public good

A social dilemma is a situation in which individuals' private interest and the collective well-being of a group are in conflict. Opposed to the invisible hand picture of a market economy that would spontaneously make compatible micro-decisions and goals with macro-objectives and societal coherence, the effective working of decentralized and private interest/private wealth accumulation-based market economies do often generate contradictions between micro-rationality and macro-rationality. Such a situation is usually studied in different frameworks such as cooperative/non-cooperative game-theoretic models or the Economics of the Commons (Capraro, 2013). These models basically bring forward different oppositions between individual interest and collective interest such as "Is the good/best for me the good/best for the group/society" or "Are immediate/short-run benefits I can draw from a given activity consistent with long-run collective advantages that the cooperation could provide society with"?

The basic problem is that

> Though all of the members of the group therefore have a common interest in obtaining this collective benefit, they have no common interest in paying the cost of providing that collective good. Each would prefer that the others pay the entire cost, and ordinarily would get any benefit provided whether he had borne part of the cost or not.
>
> (Olson, 1965, p. 21)

Dealing with societal (common) macro issues requires specific *collective action* mechanisms that could enable people to assess the appropriateness of possible and relevant models of organization to set up sustainable and viable coordination/cooperation frameworks. In the absence of such frameworks, the functioning of society (markets, institutions, policies) becomes weak and subject to recurring crises. Individuals then evolve according to short-sighted, opportunistic strategies, unable to guarantee the long-term viability of their own interests, while society continues to deteriorate. As a result, rational micro-units (citizens) adopt a wait-and-see attitude (*they wait for Godot*); opportunism becomes the dominant choice that rules the world.

Specific cases can be used to illustrate the different facets of the problem:

- With regard to public goods, if individuals can benefit from common resources without contributing to their provision, there will be no rational incentives to push them to be part of the provision process (Table 1.1). While each individual needs these resources to improve their well-being, an efficient and effective provision of these resources by individual, private, and market-led mechanisms is beyond the reach (of the economic and organizational capacity and capabilities) of individuals (*Public goods versus market goods opposition*).

Table 1.1 Social dilemmas as collective action failures

Public goods vs. market goods	Failure of provision of necessary goods
Tragedy of the commons	Depletion of resources – deterioration of living conditions for all
Prisoner's dilemma	Lack of spontaneous viable coordination between private individuals
Free-rider	Opportunism over mutual benefit
Climate change	Failure of collective coordination/cooperation

Source: Author's own work.

- With regard to the depletion of common resources, if individuals have, at their microeconomic level, advantages to overuse shared resources, they will not take care of the reproducibility and future availability of the resources (*The Tragedy of the Commons*).
- With regard to cooperation, people will not cooperate even if cooperation is in their best interest if there is no appropriate coordination environment/institutional structure that would allow them to get access to a collective solution (*Prisoner's Dilemma*).
- With regard to opportunism, people will seek their own interests that could be drawn from others' behavior without contributing to any sort of collective effort process (*Free-rider behavior*).
- With regard to climate change, people or countries will not be effectively committed in a reform process if there is no collective organization and supervision mechanisms that would guarantee the participation of each party by assessing individual/group contributions to efforts to supply public goods, to ensure that they are available to as many people as possible: "I am not going to do good if others are likely to do bad without coming under collective, objective supervision" (*Collective coordination/cooperation failure*).

Overgrazing, overfishing, overconsumption and depletion, pollution, waste, waiting for others to act first (free-rider problem) while society bears the environmental burden, and short-term costs of eco-friendly policies (in terms of resistance from group/lobby interests, political obstacles, personal interests of decision/policymakers, etc.) are the sources of generating "ecological imbalance." Obviously, social dilemmas are very central in ecological economics since they often arise when the pursuit of individual interests comes at the expense of long-term ecological sustainability and collective well-being. Indeed, if everyone only acts in their own self-interest, the group, as a whole, might suffer although a well-designed cooperation would lead to a better situation for each member. Iyer, Reyes and Killingback (2014) remark that:

> From a more formal point of view, a social dilemma can be modeled as a game in which there exists at least one Hicks inefficient Nash equilibrium. It is Hicks inefficient (i.e. socially inefficient) in that there is at least one other outcome in which all individuals would be better off, and since it is a Nash equilibrium there is no incentive for any individual to change their behavior.

In such a situation, the lack of internal or external coordination, that would allow individuals to design common-good-seeking strategies to achieve their own interest in a collective way, prevents society from reaching higher levels of well-being.

The opposition between private interests and the common good is a central issue that reflects a tension between individual (or group) benefits and societal coherence. Since the capitalist market economies are relying on the primacy of individuals over society, matching the market mechanisms with private interest and social coherence requires some specific rules and mechanisms beyond the reach of any individual player. Self-interest and common good become exclusive of each other. At the same time, individuals make society and need social interactions to meet their own goals. That is the *paradox of a market economy*: the first ethical value is private property and individual wealth accumulation while the latter is not possible without the smooth working of society. Climate change is a pressing example of this opposition. In the absence of imposed collective rules, most corporations are prioritizing their private interest (profit, expansion of activities, markets, etc.) over environmental/societal sustainability, which is a common good. Supportive policies follow the same choice and fail to address climate issues or even continue to harm environment and society. Garrett Hardin's *The Tragedy of the Commons* (1968, p. 1244) that points to the depletion of common resources because of individuals' overuse is a well-known version of such a dilemma: "Ruin is the destination toward which all men rush, each pursuing his own best interest in a society that believes in the freedom of the commons. Freedom in a commons brings ruin to all." That is the fundamental collective action issue (incompatibility between individual means and rationality-based strategies and the public/common good provision).

Olson (1965, p. 2) expresses this difficulty in achieving a desired social optimum through the separate strategies of private individuals, acutely:

> (…) even if all of the individuals in a large group are rational and self-interested, and would gain if, as a group, they acted to achieve their common interest or objective, they will still not voluntarily act to achieve that common or group interest.

A relevant and positive direction of analysis can be the management of economic, ecological, and societal constraints by restructuring economic incentives and promoting community-based resource management through cooperation rather than collapse, considering "how to enhance the capabilities of those involved to change the constraining rules of the game to lead to outcomes other than remorseless tragedies" (Ostrom, 1990, p. 7).

Such an orientation may be in line with Commons' institutionalism:

> Collective Action is more than *control* of individual action – it is, by the very act of control, as indicated by the auxiliary verbs, a *liberation* of individual action from coercion, duress, discrimination, or unfair competition, by means of restraints placed on other individuals. And Collective Action is more than restraint and liberation of individual action – it is *expansion* of the will of the individual far beyond what he can do by his own puny acts.
>
> (Commons, 1934, p. 73)

Financial stability and the stability of transition financing

Financial stability, green transition as well as the financing of green transition may be regarded as essential public goods that should be provided within a collective action framework. The basic argument in support of such a statement is that the financial system, ecological and environmental sustainability, and the financing of society-wide actions to achieve sustainability are core factors (and concerns) for the viability of society.

The stability of financial markets (and financial systems) is one of the most crucial issues in market economies, as it is linked to all the other facets of economic evolution, such as growth, development, employment, efficiency, the research and development process, social progress, poverty, inclusion, and so on. This is mainly due to the fact that market economies are first and foremost monetary economies, in which the payments system (the rules, mechanisms, modalities, and institutions that organize and govern the financing of economic activities, household consumption, public spending, and international transactions) is the essential primary framework that determines the conditions and possibilities for the smooth and continuous functioning of the entire economy (and society) (Ülgen, 2013). The payments system includes, among other things, the financial markets (banks and non-bank financial institutions). The entire macroeconomic circuit is made up of financing and settlement relationships and operations between different parties, enabling decentralized private activities to be effectively realized without any collective plan, thanks to the mechanisms of money creation without quantitative constraints that would be imposed beforehand by a central decision process. However, continuous creation of wealth is possible under the guarantee of the lender-of-last-resort, the central bank, as a relevant public anchor. In this way, the payments system and its fixed point, the monetary unit of account, can operate smoothly without calling into question the confidence that every economic agent has in the monetary system in force in a given zone. The presence of public authorities and regulation, under the aegis of the central bank, is sine qua non, a guarantee of confidence and security that allows private debt operations – aimed at private accumulation – to appear as something intended for the public good. The criticality of financial system stability is therefore a structural issue, endogenous to market economies, and concerns not only their characteristics but also their survival expectancy over time. Yet, this stability is not (cannot be) provided by financial market operations although the instability is often an endogenous result of these operations (Minsky, 1986).

As for the green transition, that is an urgent structural change process of the eco-system, a structural transformation of capitalism in relation with the necessary transition to a sustainable and viable society (Figure 1.1). We can call it the *eco-transition*, the economic, ecologic, environmental, and equity-oriented change process.

Green transition is, broadly speaking, a process of moving from a standard capitalist market economy, based on private wealth accumulation (regardless of the social and environmental consequences of the underlying activities), to an alternative model of production, distribution, and consumption that would prioritize and promote sustainability, durability, and viability of the transition (the sustainable, durable and viable [*SDV*] *paradigm*), and then of life on earth, while enabling individuals to make and implement decisions and actions in a free way without undermining the goals and harmony of society. Such an objective does lead to an "Augmented SDV paradigm" that should include social aspects like the acceptability of the transition path framed around common goals such as development and stability, and the achievement of societal utility through the improvement of living conditions (Figure 1.2).

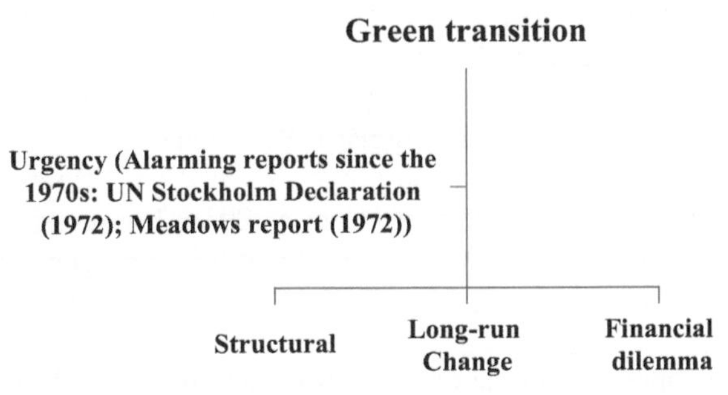

Figure 1.1 Green transition.

Source: Author's own work.

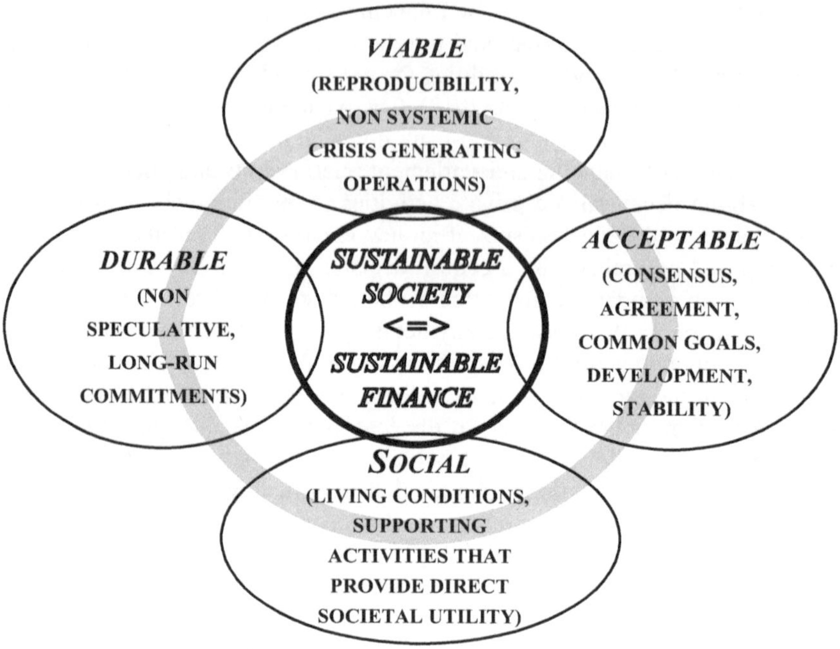

Figure 1.2 Augmented SDV paradigm: conditions for sustainable society with sustainable finance.
Source: Author's own work.

Financial stability and green transition prove to be the essential prerequisites for a livable society. Obviously, effective green transition needs to be financed in a stable and durable way. That calls for collective action to smoothly organize the process in the long run. Collective action is the institutional and visible public hand of coordination and cooperation that would govern the overall framework and give decentralized decisions and actions consistency with stability and effectiveness of the transition. The augmented SDV paradigm argues that the green transition is not an alternative among multiple choices; it is the only option that we have to hope for a possible collective future. It not only relies on the systemic stability of the economy and society but also on the support of financial systems. For instance, green finance is studied as a critical component of financial stability, particularly within the context of growing climate-related risks (Gourdel et al., 2022) while climate finance is regarded as the way to support mitigation and adaptation actions to address climate change within the UNFCCC (United Nations Climate Change), adopted in 1992 at the United Nations Conference on Environment and Development (UNCED), held in Rio de Janeiro, and aimed at preventing human activities from harming the climate system (United Nations, 1992, 2024).

The Economics literature offers a diverse range of work on different issues on the links between financial systems and green transition (Carney, 2015; European Systemic Risk Board, 2021, 2023). These issues are related to various risks that might be generated in the process of transition such as:

- The risks of climate concerns to financial stability such as physical risks (extreme weather and environmental events that may harm different sectors and economic activities), transition risks (regulation aimed at curbing polluting activities can result in economic and financial disruptions in concerned sectors), and liability risks (penalties and legal actions corporations may suffer from if they do not meet changing regulatory constraints).

- The risks within the financial system channels in relation with the soundness of corporations such as market risk (increased asset price volatility), operational risk (due to disruptions to banks and financial institutions), credit risk (loan defaults of vulnerable sectors like coal and oil), liquidity risk (market volatility regarding green and brown assets), environmental, social and governance (ESG) risk (environmental, social, and governance factors that may threat companies' financial and operational performance), and technology risks (technology changes and new rules that may fragilize companies' position in the markets and negatively affect their internal organization and financial situation).

Steele (2020, p. 109) maintains that:

> the climate crisis is, in fact, sowing the seeds of a potential financial crisis. Namely, it will show that climate financial risk is a significant source of vulnerability for the business models of large financial institutions and the financial system as a whole.

All these concerns point to the critical role of financial stability, regulation, and economic policies for the smooth functioning of economies and sustainable green transition financing amidst growing risks and geopolitical conflicts (Bolton et al., 2020; Cardona & Berenguer, 2020; Boneva et al., 2021; Kreibiehl et al., 2022; Braga & Ernst, 2023; Burge, 2023; Deutsche Bank, 2024; Network for Greening the Financial System, 2024a, b; OECD, 2024; IMF, 2025, to quote but a few).

However, the interlinkages between financial stability, green transition, and sustainable green financing are not explicitly studied. In line with another companion work (Ülgen, 2025), I argue that financial stability and green transition are the two sides of the same issue that is the structural transformation of a market economy into a sustainable societal framework. Such a transformation encounters an obstacle that stems from the nature of a capitalist economy: the opposition between private interest and the common/public good. This social dilemma has been transformed into a financial dilemma between financial efficiency (financial markets are rather shaped by and directed toward financial efficiency) and financial stability in the long run, which has been exacerbated by the financialization of economies since the 1990s and led to the global financial crisis of 2007–2009.

The inability of decentralized and non-cooperative market mechanisms to deal with systemic macro concerns is also underlined by M. Carney in his analysis of *The Tragedy of the Horizon* by arguing that climate change generates tremendous risk for financial markets, but these growing risks are ignored by market players because of the market's tendency toward myopia.

In light of the weaknesses of liberalized market economies, the only way to make market economies work properly and to ensure long-term systemic viability seems to be linked to the design and implementation of regulatory mechanisms that would enable the financial system to finance green transition projects and inclusive green development in a sustainable way, sheltered from speculative movements in the financial markets, which are mainly driven by speculative, short-term efficiency of operations. This requires changes to the rules governing financial regulation, but also to the organization of the energy transition process, and more generally, the *eco-transition* (Ülgen & Klapkiv, 2023; Almawi & Ülgen, 2024).

Appropriate regulation for effective transition

Systemic financial stability and long-term financing of eco-transition are interlinked global public goods whose provision would require global regulatory reforms to transform economies into more sustainable socio-economic frameworks.

European Commission (2018) considers, in its taxonomy on climate, environment, and social issues, prudential rules and market regulation as the necessary part of the taxonomy while the private and public investments and policies are regarded as complementary since the regulatory framework constitutes the institutional environment that could enable market and public actors to design and implement strategies and actions consistent with the rules and aims of society. Regulation is the coordination process that is aimed at leading to group coherence for individual decisions and then preventing social dilemmas.

Green transition relies on green financial practices (investments and policies) that could support the implementation of SDV projects, aligning financial resources with transition needs and goals. In this aim, an appropriate organization of markets might promote internalization of environmental costs and ecological limits, promote, if relevant, community-based resource management and reshape economic incentives in line with Ostrom's principles. Under some circumstances, bottom-up, community-driven organization can offer acceptable solutions to resource-related dilemmas. Van Lange et al. (2013, p. 137) argue:

> Likewise, it is often true that relatively small groups in large societies, such as local communities, have enormous potential to organize and manage themselves in ways that promote cooperation and prevent them from depleting natural resources. In small groups people are able to develop rules that match the local circumstances, they are able to monitor one another's behavior, and punish free-riding and reward generosity quite effectively. People care very strongly about their image or reputation in their local community, and so if the norms favouring cooperation are well specified, then often the mere presence of others makes a big difference. These are important virtues of a local organization, formal or informal, relative to a more global authority.

However, financial stability and the global nature of the urgency of green transition have a system-wide scope. They are also complex issues submitted to uncertainty of social evolution and to various risks. Moreover, as climate change presents a significant risk to financial stability and vice versa (financial risk and instability are a source of threat to durable financing operations required for green transition), supervision of institutions' financing of climate-change drivers is essential to regulators' responsibility to support systemic stability. It is also worth noting that the problem of financial and transition stability is a systemic issue and can only be handled at the macro level, through a society-wide collective action framework. Although polycentric schemas can contribute to the efficiency of the overall governance system, the organization, management, and supervision of the provision of global public goods such as financial stability and eco-transition fall under the responsibility and competence of public governance mechanisms (Ülgen, 2025). Central banks and financial regulators play therefore a core role in fostering financial stability and green transition sustainability not only by supervising the market operations but also by promoting sustainable and green finance, assessing and integrating environmental factors into risk models, and ensuring that financial markets support long-term transition projects. Parallel to this, regulatory measures such as climate-related stress tests, integrated into the financial supervision frameworks, and financial disclosure regulations taking into account the exposure of market players to climate-related risks are used by public regulators to monitor financial stability in relation with the transition process.

An essential part of any relevant regulatory framework that aims at dealing with systemic viability issues such as financial stability and green transition with respect to the SDV paradigm is the precautionary principle that is indirectly implemented by the precautionary and preventive decisions of public authorities according to the primacy of public good over private interests: According to the EU Court of Justice,

> the precautionary principle can be defined as a general principle of Community law requiring the competent authorities to take appropriate measures to prevent specific potential risks to public health, safety and the environment, by giving precedence to the requirements related to the protection of those interests over economic interests.
>
> (Bourguignon, 2015, p. 6)

The precautionary principle is not a rigid rule against the market or private initiative. Nor is it a rule for centralizing economic decisions. It is based on the assumption that micro-rationality is highly dependent on the very limited knowledge, means, interests, and judgments of individuals or groups whose main goal is to ensure the profitability of the operations undertaken, without having either the need or the possibility to consider the scope and consequences of the operations on the viability of society (and the economy) as a whole. This observation is objective and general and is not linked to a value judgment. It is part of the same logic that contrasts public and private goods. The latter can be produced by market mechanisms, while the former, necessary to individuals and markets, can only be produced by a collective organization that plays the role of coordinator and harmonizer of the separate and private parties. From this point of view, one can assert that the precautionary principle is the rule of collective action – Global Coordination for the common good that would lead to private good. The ultimate regulatory challenge consists of implementing societal efficiency-seeking public interventions and making decentralized decisions societally consistent according to collective objectives (Ülgen, 2024). The basis of the precautionary principle is, at its simplest meaning: "First, do not harm."

Therefore, certain rules, constraints, and incentives need to be put in place to frame such a coordination mechanism, which would make the Nash equilibrium compatible with the social optimum (which, however, does not fall under the Pareto optimum rule). To summarize, it is possible to list some of the basic rules that would help give eco-transition social meaning and coherence:

1 Strict separation between supervision and market players.
2 Participatory and inclusive organization of discussion and priority-setting bodies in the transition process, free from any consideration of private economic profitability and efficiency.
3 Determination of the most effective means of transforming economic and social dynamics into SDV production, consumption, and technology models.
4 Transparent and independent evaluation and control mechanisms for activities deemed essential to the transition, such as the financial system, research and development projects, transformational investments, etc.
5 Preventing speculative activities in areas critical to transition, and separating transition objectives and resources from other market activities, which requires strict control of the banking system's strategic market orientations.

These points depend closely on society's ability to provide an open democratic environment that would give individuals the will and incentives to contribute to the transformation of the economy and society toward a more livable and decent future.

Concluding remarks: a possible journey to Planet Earth

For financial stability, managing the risks associated with the green transition is crucial. For green transition, stable and durable support of financial systems is crucial. Financial stability and green transition (and its financing) are the two sides of the same coin: a sustainable life on earth. Regulatory frameworks and sustainable finance initiatives can play a central role in guiding the global economy through this shift while ensuring that financial systems remain resilient to emerging environmental risks. In parallel, there is a significant opportunity to foster economic growth by embracing green technologies and investments, which can support long-term financial stability and sustainability if they are supported by stable financial mechanisms. The tautologic statement that financial stability and green transition go hand in hand is related to the very characteristics of capitalist market economies: finance is at the core of the economic engine, and any society-wide transition/transformation process needs huge and stable financial support. However, markets are not able to ensure such a mutual-benefit operation at the macro level. The public goodness of financial stability and eco-transition can prevent a twofold paradox that leads to a terrible social dilemma:

Opposition between public good and private interest (or between micro-rationality and macro-coherence) while both need each other.
Opposition between the efficiency of market operations and the macro-stability of the whole.

The challenge is about creating a system where private interests can thrive but are regulated in a way that does not harm the common good. Ultimately, this debate asks how much individuals, corporations, and governments are willing to sacrifice private benefits in order to secure long-term benefits for society as a whole. It is a dynamic tension that requires constant negotiation and adjustment in response to shifting societal values, economic needs, and technological advancements (Martin, 2023). One of the obstacles to imagine a society-wide compatibility between private interests and the common good might be related to the "theoretical reason" underlined by Hardin (1968, p. 1243): "It is not mathematically possible to maximize for two (or more) variables at the same time." Hic Rhodus, hic salta…

References

Almawi, A. & Ülgen, F. (2024). "Alternative Financing for a Sustainable Energy Transition: An Institutionalist Perspective", *Journal of Economic Issues*, 58(2): 487–495.

Bolton, P., Despres, M., Pereira Da Silva, L.A., Samama, F. & Svartzman, R. (2020). "The Green Swan. Central Banking and Financial Stability in the Age of Climate Change", Bank for International Settlements-Banque de France-Eurosystem, January 2020. https://www.bis.org/publ/othp31.pdf

Boneva, L., Ferrucci, G. & Mongelli, F.P. (2021). "To Be or Not to Be 'Green': How Can Monetary Policy React to Climate Change?", Occasional Paper Series, No. 285, ECB. https://www.ecb.europa.eu/pub/pdf/scpops/ecb.op285~be7d631055.en.pdf

Bourguignon, D. (2015). "The Precautionary Principle: Definitions, Applications and Governance", European Parliamentary Research Service. https://www.europarl.europa.eu/RegData/etudes/IDAN/2015/573876/EPRS_IDA(2015)573876_EN.pdf

Braga, J.P. & Ernst, E. (2023). "Financing the Green Transition. The Role of Macro-Economic Policies in Ensuring a Just Transition", *Frontiers in Climate*, 5: 1192706. DOI: 10.3389/fclim.2023.1192706.

Burge, L. (2023). "101 Sustainable Finance Policies for 1.5°C", Climate Bonds Initiative, March 2023. https://www.climatebonds.net/files/documents/publications/Climate-Bonds_101-Sustainable-Finance-Policies-for-1.5C_Mar-2023.pdf

Capraro, V. (2013). "A Model of Human Cooperation in Social Dilemmas". *PLoS ONE*, 8(8): e72427. https://www.stat.berkeley.edu/~aldous/157/Papers/capraro.pdf

Cardona, M. & Berenguer, M.E. (2020). "What Role for Financial Regulation to Help the Low-Carbon Transition?", Institute for Climate Economics, Paris, June 2020. https://www.i4ce.org/wp-content/uploads/RegulationBasCarbone_VA.pdf

Carney, M. (2015). "Breaking the Tragedy of the Horizon – Climate Change and Financial Stability", Speech by the Governor of the Bank of England, Chairman of the Financial Stability Board, Lloyd's of London, 29 September 2015. https://www.bankofengland.co.uk/-/media/boe/files/speech/2015/breaking-the-tragedy-of-the-horizon-climate-change-and-financial-stability.pdf

Commons, J.R. (1934 [1959]). *Institutional Economics*. Madison: The University of Wisconsin Press.

Deutsche Bank (2024). Sustainable Finance Framework. https://www.db.com/files/documents/csr/sustainability/Sustainable-Finance-Framework.pdf

European Commission (2018). Action Plan: Financing Sustainable Growth, Brussels, 8 March 2018. https://eur-lex.europa.eu/legal-content/EN/TXT/PDF/?uri=CELEX:52018DC0097

European Systemic Risk Board, ESRB (2021). Climate-Related Risk and Financial Stability, July 2021, ECB/ESRB Project Team on Climate Risk. https://www.esrb.europa.eu/pub/pdf/reports/esrb.climateriskfinancialstability202107~79c10eba1a.en.pdf

European Systemic Risk Board, ESRB (2023). Towards Macroprudential Frameworks for Managing Climate Risk, December 2023, ECB/ESRB Project Team on Climate Risk. https://www.esrb.europa.eu/pub/pdf/reports/esrb.report202312~d7881028b8.en.pdf

Gourdel, R., Monasterolo, I., Dunz, N., Mazzocchetti, A. & Parisi, L. (2022). "The Double Materiality of Climate Physical and Transition Risks in the Euro Area", ECB Working Paper Series, n. 2665, May 2022. https://bit.ly/3owzUqf

Hardin, G. (1968). "The Tragedy of the Commons", *Science*, 162(3859): 1243–1248. DOI: 10.1126/science.162.3859.1243.

International Monetary Fund (IMF) (2025). Global Financial Stability Report: Enhancing Resilience amid Uncertainty, Washington, DC, April. https://www.imf.org/en/Publications/GFSR/Issues/2025/04/22/global-financial-stability-report-april-2025

Iyer, S., Reyes, J. & Killingback, T. (2014). "An Application of Evolutionary Game Theory to Social Dilemmas: The Traveler's Dilemma and the Minimum Effort Coordination Game", *PLoS ONE*, 9(4): e93988. DOI: 10.1371/journal.pone.0093988.

Kreibiehl, S., Yong Jung, T., Battiston, S., Carvajal, P. E., Clapp, C., Dasgupta, D., Dube, N., Jachnik, R., Morita, K., Samargandi, N. & Williams, M. (2022). "Investment and Finance", in P.R. Shukla, J. Skea, R. Slade, A. Al Khourdajie, R. van Diemen, D. McCollum, M. Pathak, S. Some, P. Vyas, R. Fradera, M. Belkacemi, A. Hasija, G. Lisboa, S. Luz & J. Malley (eds.), *IPCC, 2022: Climate Change 2022: Mitigation of Climate Change. Contribution of Working Group III to the Sixth Assessment Report of the Intergovernmental Panel on Climate Change*. Cambridge and New York: Cambridge University Press. 1547-1640. DOI: 10.1017/9781009157926.017.

Martin, V. (2023). "Green Finance: Regulation and Instruments", *Journal of Central Banking Theory and Practice*, 2: 185–209. DOI: 10.2478/jcbtp-2023-0019.

Minsky, H.P. (1986 [2008]). *Stabilizing an Unstable Economy*. New York: McGraw Hill.

Network for Greening the Financial System (2024a). "The Green Transition and the Macroeconomy: A Monetary Policy Perspective", NGFS Workstream on Monetary Policy Technical Document, October 2024. https://www.ngfs.net/system/files/import/ngfs/medias/documents/ngfs_the-green-transition-and-the-macroeconomy.pdf

Network for Greening the Financial System (2024b). "Synthesis Report on the Greening of the Financial System. Insights for Financial Actors in Advanced and Emerging Economies", Occasional Paper, November 2024. https://www.ngfs.net/system/files/import/ngfs/medias/documents/ngfs_synthesis_report_on_the_greening_of_the_financial_system.pdf

OECD (2024). *The Role of Economic Regulators in the Green Transition: Driving Sustainable Change in Network Sectors*. The Governance of Regulators. Paris: OECD Publishing. DOI: 10.1787/7d4704c9-en.

Olson, M. (1965). *The Logic of Collective Action*. Cambridge, MA: Harvard University Press.

Ostrom, E. (1990). *Governing the Commons. The Evolution of Institutions for Collective Action*. New York: Cambridge University Press.

Steele, G.S. (2020). "Confronting the "Climate Lehman Moment": The Case for Macroprudential Climate Regulation", *Cornell Journal of Law and Public Policy*, 30: 109–157.

United Nations (1992). United Nations Conference on Environment and Development, Rio de Janeiro, Brazil, 3-14 June 1992. https://www.un.org/en/conferences/environment/rio1992

United Nations (2024). UN Climate Change Conference, Baku, https://unfccc.int/cop29

Ülgen, F. (2013). "Coordination in Economy. An Essay on Money", in F. Ülgen (ed.), *New Contributions to Monetary Analysis: The Foundations of an Alternative Economic Paradigm*. London: Routledge, 172–187.

Ülgen, F. (2024). "Greening Finance? What Institutional Options for a Sustainable Transition?", *Journal of Economic Issues*, 58(2): 642–649.

Ülgen, F. (2025). "Financing the Future: Sustainable Economic and Environmental Transition through Sustainable Regulation", in C.J. Whalen (ed.), *Fashioning Prosperous, Sustainable and Humane Societies: Beyond Precarity*. Cheltenham: Edward Elgar Publishing, 136–153. https://www.e-elgar.com/shop/gbp/fashioning-prosperous-sustainable-and-humane-societies-9781035340255.html

Ülgen, F. & Klapkiv, L. (2023). "An Institutional Framework for a Sustainable Eco-Transition and Financial Regulation", *Journal of Economic Issues*, 57(2): 591–597. DOI: 10.1080/00213624.2023.2202559.

Van Lange, P.A.M., Joireman, J., Parks, C.D. & Van Dijk, E. (2013). "The Psychology of Social Dilemmas: A Review", *Organizational Behavior and Human Decision Processes*, 120(2): 125–141. DOI: 10.1016/j.obhdp.2012.11.003.

2 Central bank digital currencies and financial stability

Alain Laurent

Introduction

Today, central banks issue two types of money (physical cash and electronic central bank deposits, also known as reserves) and provide infrastructure to support a third type of money, private money, principally available through commercial bank deposits. Central banks support commercial bank money in various ways, by allowing commercial banks to settle interbank payments using central bank money; enabling convertibility between commercial and central bank money through banknote provision; and offering liquidity through the lender of last resort function. Importantly, while cash and reserves are a liability of the central bank, commercial bank deposits are not.

Central bank digital currencies (CBDCs) would be a new type of central bank money and as such a liability of the central bank. Physical cash is widely accessible and peer-to-peer. In contrast, central bank reserves are electronic and typically only accessible to qualifying financial institutions. Households and firms would hold CBDC in an account directly or indirectly at the central bank (Group of Central Banks, 2020). In the so-called direct model of CBDC, the central bank keeps its own ledger, executes retail payments, defines the interconnections with private systems, and implements the privacy regime. Interactions with private actors can be managed through application programming interfaces. They can take place at different levels: either wholesale settlements or retail devices such as digital wallets. In this article, we only deal with retail CBDCs. Wholesale CBDCs are nothing new, as bank reserves can be considered as such.

The advent of CBDCs represents a pivotal development in the ongoing transformation of the global monetary and financial landscape. As economies around the world become progressively digitized, the foundational elements of money and banking are undergoing significant reconfiguration. In this context, CBDCs—digital forms of central bank-issued money—have emerged as a central focus in monetary innovation, reflecting a convergence of economic, technological, and strategic imperatives that are reshaping the role of central banks in payments in the digital age (Bank for International Settlements, 2020; see also Brunnermeier et al., 2021, for a broader picture).

Technological advancements further compound the urgency for reform. Innovations in distributed ledger technologies (DLT, a means of saving information through a distributed ledger, i.e., a repeated digital copy of data available at multiple locations), cryptographic security, and real-time payment infrastructure have drastically reduced the costs and frictions associated with transactions. As a result, it is now technically feasible to implement payment systems that are instantaneous and highly efficient. These breakthroughs raise the prospect of a public-sector digital currency that is secure, inclusive, and interoperable across platforms. It may be necessary

DOI: 10.4324/9781003663539-3

to note with Scorer (2017) that several technologies can underlie CBDCs. They do not necessarily need DLT, the technology underlying many cryptocurrencies.

In response to these evolving dynamics, about 100 central banks worldwide—including major economies such as China (with its digital yuan pilot), the European Central Bank (via the digital euro initiative), and Sweden (e-krona)—have initiated research programs, proof-of-concept studies, and pilot deployments. Four smaller economies have adopted their own CBDC: Jamaica (JAM-DEX), the Bahamas (Sand Dollar), Zimbabwe (ZiG), and Nigeria (eNaira). These initiatives vary in scope, design, and objectives but commonly aim to future-proof national monetary systems in the face of technological disruption and shifting economic behaviors. Broadly, CBDCs are envisioned either as complements to physical cash—offering a digital alternative that preserves the public's access to central bank money—or, over the longer term, as full substitutes for banknotes and coins in an increasingly cashless society.

In this chapter, we first present the benefits of CBDCs (section 1) before turning to their main justification: avoiding the fragmentation of monetary space in a context of the disappearance of cash and the proliferation of stablecoins (section 2). However, the implementation of CBDCs is not without substantial risks, particularly concerning financial stability (Bouis et al., 2024; Infante et al., 2022; Panetta, 2022). In section 3, we deal with the risk of bank disintermediation. In a scenario where individuals and firms shift substantial portions of their deposits from commercial banks to CBDCs, especially during times of economic uncertainty, banks could face a significant contraction in their deposit base. This would, in turn, impair their ability to lend and destabilize the traditional two-tiered financial system, where central banks operate through commercial banks to transmit monetary policy. Closely related is the potential for CBDCs to exacerbate liquidity crises (section 4): in periods of financial panic, the perceived safety and liquidity of central bank digital money could precipitate rapid and large-scale withdrawals from commercial banks, effectively enabling "digital bank runs" that could accelerate contagion effects and deepen systemic vulnerabilities.

Pondering the benefits of CBDCs

CBDCs are supposed to offer a range of potential macroeconomic and financial benefits (Bindseil & Pantelopoulos, 2023). One major proposition is the enhancement of monetary policy transmission. By enabling programmable features such as time-based disbursement or targeted transfers, CBDCs could allow central banks to deploy monetary tools with unprecedented precision, particularly during periods of economic distress. If holding CBDCs is remunerated, then the central bank will directly influence the behavior of households, which will increase the efficiency of the bank lending channel. That said, this is not really necessary as, in most developed countries, there is already a very good link between the central bank rate and the bank lending rate.

Moreover, CBDCs are widely seen as a vehicle for improving financial inclusion by providing a universally accessible, low-cost digital payment solution, particularly in regions with limited banking infrastructure or large unbanked populations. However, unbanked households are also more likely to be digitally excluded, which means that endpoint access for a CBDC should not rely solely on a digital wallet via an app or a website. Alternative endpoint solutions, as stored-value cards, should be adopted (Bank for International Settlements, 2021).

From a systemic perspective, CBDCs could modernize payment systems by fostering greater efficiency, lowering transaction costs, enhancing competition, and encouraging innovation within the financial sector. Payment systems are complex markets with multiple participant types (Bank for International Settlements, 2021). Banks and non-banks offer payment services; they offer arrangements to initiate the payment: from the bank account, to the payment instrument, to the technology which connects the payer and the payee to the payment service provider (PSP). Some banks and other PSPs play a key role in processing of payment (identification, authorization, and fee calculation), clearing (transmitting, balancing transactions before settlement), and settlement (transfer of funds). Central banks provide the critical infrastructure (wholesale payments) set and oversee the implementation of standards. In the eyes of many central banks, CBDCs can improve payment systems, especially as payment services may prove very costly (fees on card transactions). As they are direct liabilities of the central bank, they are instant payments with no credit risk whereas, in private payment system, retail payee may receive funds very quickly but underlying wholesale settlements between PSPs may be deferred: short-term loans between PSPs involve underlying credit risk.

There is a great advantage attached to an indirect operational architecture where some functions are entrusted to supervised intermediaries, both banks and non-banks. These intermediaries could be responsible for keeping ledgers and operating payment services, including providing access devices and channels and effecting transactions (Auer & Boehme, 2020).

> It may make it easier to ensure full interoperability between [CBDC] and private forms of money. The whole purpose is to make [CBDC] as fully substitutable to private money as possible. Technical interoperability will be an important determinant. There are many dimensions and requirements to interoperability, including through regulation. It can be achieved at different levels. It is clear, however, that full and easy exchangeability at the user end will help and mimic closely the current perceptions associated with physical cash.
>
> (Brunnermeier & Landau, 2022)

Anyway, there is considerable uncertainty surrounding the extent to which CBDCs will be adopted and the factors that could affect the take-up of CBDCs are thoroughly explored in Group of Central Banks (2021b).

An alternative to cash

Multiple converging forces are driving the global momentum toward the exploration, experimentation, and, in some cases, implementation of CBDCs. One of the most salient is the gradual but steady decline in the use of physical cash, a trend most evident in advanced economies such as Sweden. The decreasing relevance of cash in daily transactions is widely recognized, even if some authors are not so confident in the disappearance of cash (Rösl & Seitz, 2022). This phenomenon has raised concerns about inclusivity, accessibility, and the future role of state-backed legal tender. Simultaneously, the rapid proliferation of private digital currencies—including decentralized cryptocurrencies like Bitcoin and Ethereum (digital assets issued by the private sector, not backed by anyone, that depend primarily on cryptography and distributed ledger or similar technology) as well as more centralized stablecoins (cryptoassets that aim to maintain a stable value relative to a specified asset, or a pool or basket of assets) such as USDC and Tether—poses a potential challenge to the central bank's traditional function as the ultimate anchor of national monetary systems (Bindseil & Pantelopoulos, 2023). These alternative digital assets often operate outside regulatory frameworks and, if widely adopted, could fragment payment systems, reduce the effectiveness of monetary policy transmission, and threaten monetary sovereignty. Some argue that the regulation of digital private money solutions could be an important tool to prevent their proliferation. Anhert et al. (2022), as well as Financial Stability

Board (2022), provide a set of arguments in favor of the need for regulation while pointing at the limits of regulation. True, in recent years, the total market capitalization of asset-backed stablecoins has rapidly increased, nearly tripling in size from around US$ 56 billion in early 2021 to US$ 162 billion in June 2024 (source: Bank for International Settlements), but some believe that the threat of stablecoins is highly exaggerated and, in fact, so far they have not threatened sovereign currencies. First, in 2023, crypto assets accounted for less than 1% of the world's financial assets and 0.19% of e-commerce payments, and the vast majority of their holders used them as investment assets rather than payment instruments (Demertzis & Martins, 2023). Second, from another point of view, others argue that payment platforms do not need their own currency, on the contrary, as PayPal shows. History shows that national currency units do not change easily, and the use of a parallel currency entails transaction and information costs. And although central banks distrust stablecoins, they are all denominated in US dollars (see Bofinger & Haas, 2023).

A collapse in the demand for cash would mean that citizens would no longer have access to central bank money. In this case, confidence in money would depend entirely on confidence in the financial intermediaries that issue and manage bank money. CBDCs make it possible to preserve the advantages of central bank money in the digital age, when the use of cash is becoming increasingly restricted: CBDCs provide an ultimate risk-free means of payment that makes the various private means of payment fungible, without which payments would give rise to a complex network of debts (Bindseil & Pantelopoulos, 2023). Some reject CBDCs because private players can offer highly efficient payment solutions (Cecchetti & Steinholz, 2021), but it is for this very reason that the circulation of cash is threatened, and the existence of CBDCs prevents the payments market from being dominated by a few private players likely to abuse the power conferred by network effects.

From another point of view, CBDCs are supposed to implement «sovereign money». CBDCs would allow to promote a monetary system in which banks would no longer «create» sight deposits and thus means of payment (Benes & Kumhof, 2012; Laina, 2015). For example, banks would no longer be able to force the Treasury, which could let them bear the costs of poor management without having to intervene systematically. In addition, the gains from seigniorage would be increased thanks to the increase in the monetary base. Bindseil (2020) cites Dyson and Hodgson (2016):

> Allowing individuals, private sector companies, and non-bank financial institutions to settle directly in central bank money (rather than bank deposits) significantly reduces the concentration of liquidity and credit risk in payment systems. This in turn reduces the systemic importance of large banks and thereby reduces the negative externalities that the financial instability of banks has on society. In addition, by providing a genuinely risk-free alternative to bank deposits, a shift from bank deposits to digital cash reduces the need for government guarantees on deposits, eliminating a source of moral hazard from the financial system.

Bank disintermediation and CBDCs: understanding the risk

Bank disintermediation refers to the risk that the widespread adoption of CBDCs could lead to a significant withdrawal of deposits from commercial banks. This phenomenon could weaken the traditional role of banks as key credit intermediaries in the financial system.

Commercial banks rely heavily on customer deposits to fund loans. Retail deposits are a primary and relatively stable funding source for banks under normal conditions. However, a widely accessible CBDC introduces a highly liquid and risk-free alternative to traditional deposits, so that households and businesses may permanently reduce their reliance on commercial bank deposits. This alternative becomes particularly attractive during periods of financial uncertainty. If individuals and institutions begin shifting their funds from commercial banks to CBDCs, banks could face substantial funding shortages. To retain deposits, they might be forced to raise interest rates on deposits, increasing their cost of funding, or to reduce their supply of credit. They might also resort to wholesale funding sources, which are generally more volatile than customer deposits. A heavy dependence on wholesale funding during crises could thus heighten the risk of a system-wide liquidity freeze, as it was experienced during the 2008–2009 financial crisis.

If deposit-taking is decoupled from lending, the synergies between these two activities (described in Brunnermeier & Payne [2021]) are lost, making them riskier (Infante et al., 2022). Banks could raise spreads and increase transaction fees in order to maintain profitability. Commercial banks' business model would have to adapt. Services that are currently subsidized by deposits would need to become viable by themselves (Committee on Payments and Market infrastructures, 2018).

As shown by the Committee on Payments and Market infrastructures (2018), the introduction of CBDCs affects patterns of financial intermediation. If households only substitute banknotes for CBDCs, nothing is really changed, but if households substitute retail deposits for CBDCs, banks have to provide reserves to credit households' CBDC account. However, if banks have unlimited access to liquidity, then the loss of deposits would not be a problem (Brunnermeier & Niepelt, 2019).

In order to maintain the adequate level of reserves to implement monetary policy, the central bank needs to buy bonds or provide additional credit to banks. Banks use the central bank's funds to compensate for the loss of deposits: the central bank's balance sheet makes it possible to avoid deleveraging. There is only a shift in intermediation as the central bank intermediates between households and banks. In this case, the central bank would have to expand its balance sheet and its footprint in the banking system and on the financial markets, as increased recourse by banks to central bank refinancing would imply an increase in banks' collateral requirements. There would therefore be higher needs for safe and liquid securities such as Treasury bills, unless the central bank revised its operational framework and agreed to reduce its requirements with lower quality collateral.

Intermediated CBDC models, where commercial banks or other financial institutions act as intermediaries in distributing CBDCs, can help preserve their role in the financial system, but, to address the risks of bank disintermediation, several policy tools have been proposed. In a two-tier remuneration system, as proposed by Bindseil (2020), CBDC holdings above a certain threshold would receive a maximum remuneration of 0. A negative interest rate could disincentivize large CBDC holdings and discourage excessive shifts from bank deposits. However, it is not certain that a zero return would prevent the accumulation of CBDCs, as the absence of a return could be interpreted as an insurance premium in return for holding a perfectly safe asset (Bofinger & Haas, 2023). And a negative return might not be a sufficient deterrent in the event of a severe banking crisis.

Other mitigation measures could limit the scope of CBDCs in payments or prevent using CBDC as a store of value. For instance, low transfer limits could be imposed to make CBDCs impractical for use in large-value payments. Similarly, holding limits on CBDCs could be set to cap the amount that individuals and institutions are allowed to store in digital currency (Bank for International Settlements, 2020). The European Central Bank proposes, for example, to limit the holding of digital euros to €3,000 per person and to impose a negative interest rate above that figure. One might well ask what point there is in deploying such a system to create a mini-CBDC. What is more, this solution would have the major disadvantage of causing a payment to be rejected if the beneficiary exceeded the authorized limit. To avoid such uncertainty, it would be possible to provide a mechanism for transferring the surplus in the CBDC portfolio to an associated conventional bank account.

Bank runs

CBDCs are direct liabilities of central banks, and, as such, they are considered risk-free. In contrast, commercial bank deposits are only partially backed by reserves and inherently subject to credit and liquidity risks. During a financial crisis or amid rumor-driven panic, depositors may prefer the security of holding CBDCs, which offer a superior combination of safety, liquidity, and convenience over conventional bank deposits. If CBDCs are broadly accessible and easily convertible from deposit accounts, this preference could trigger an immediate and widespread shift of fund, a rapid "flight to safety" from commercial banks to CBDCs.

Historically, bank runs have been constrained by physical and institutional frictions, such as limited banking hours, ATM withdrawal limits, and delays in interbank transfer processing. However, the advent of CBDCs introduces a fundamentally different dynamic. CBDCs enable instantaneous, frictionless, and risk-free transfers of funds from commercial banks to a central bank-issued digital currency, thereby significantly increasing the speed and severity of potential runs.

In traditional bank runs, depositors physically queue at bank branches or ATMs to withdraw cash, and digital transfers between banks involve inherent processing delays. These frictions slow the pace of outflows. CBDCs, however, eliminate these constraints. Digital wallets that support CBDC transactions enable 24/7 access and instant conversion of bank deposits into central bank currency. App-based interfaces further facilitate high-speed transfers, increasing the likelihood and potential severity of panic-induced reactions. In a highly digitized financial environment characterized by mobile banking, fintech applications, and real-time information flows, CBDC conversions could be triggered automatically. Algorithms, smart contracts, or user-defined rules might initiate mass withdrawals from commercial banks the moment certain market conditions or news events are detected. Furthermore, social media-fueled panic could propagate rapidly across the digital economy, resulting in systemic, high-speed "auto-withdrawals" that accelerate the pace of digital bank runs to unprecedented levels. For instance, in 2023, in the US, Silicon Valley Bank faced deposits outflow which was remarkable in terms of scale and scope when compared with other episodes of banking stress: in the case of Silicon Valley Bank, it took only two days in March 2023 for losing 85% of deposits (around $140 billion) whereas, during the financial meltdown experienced in Iceland in 2008, the local bank Icesave lost 20% of its deposits over 75 days (Basel Committee on Banking Supervision, 2023), and in Japan, in the middle of a huge banking crisis at the end of 1990s, it took a week or so for the deposits of failed banks to fall by 10% (Group of Central Banks, 2021a).

As a result, commercial banks could experience rapid and large-scale deposit withdrawals. Should this result in acute liquidity shortages, banks may be compelled to liquidate assets at unfavorable prices or to seek emergency funding from the central bank. In fact, researchers have stressed the distinctive feature of central banks as lender of last resort, which represents the ultimate bulwark against financial instability and the risk of bank runs.

Kumhof and Noone (2018) propose several mechanisms that could eliminate the risk of runs on deposits in CBDCs and allow the central bank to retain control over the amount of monetary base present in the banking system and therefore control over the interest rate. These authors envisage a type of CBDC, a CBDC held by both banks (wholesale CBDC) and households, whereas in this article, we have restricted the analysis to retail CBDCs. These mechanisms are as follows: CBDCs are remunerated at an adjustable interest rate in order to allow the CBDC market to balance. The second principle prohibits the convertibility of CBDCs into reserves (if customers seek to convert deposits into CBDCs, this will deplete the banks' reserves and make it impossible for the central bank to control the amount of reserves). The third principle is that bank deposits are not automatically convertible into CBDCs. Kumhof and Noone explain that this will not undermine confidence in bank deposits (it is rather bank liquidity, capitalization, and the existence of deposit insurance that are important), and that it will not threaten the parity between bank deposits and central bank money, as long as the central bank undertakes to balance the supply of and demand for CBDCs. However, as Bindseil (2020) puts it,

> it would need to be explained further why one core feature of overnight deposits with banks –i.e. convertibility on demand at any time into central bank money – would apply to central bank money in the form of banknotes, but not in the form of CBDC. Moreover, what if banknotes would eventually cease to exist, as it may be forecast at least for some countries like Sweden? This would seem to imply that banks would no longer promise unconditionally the convertibility of sight deposits into central bank money.

Another stream of research draws on the canonical Diamond and Dybvig model: Diamond and Dybvig (1983) develop a model to explain why banks choose to issue deposits that are more liquid than their assets and to understand why banks are subject to runs. Bank runs typically occur when depositors lose confidence in the banking system and rush to withdraw their funds in large numbers. Fernandez-Villaverde et al. (2021) present such a model where depositors arbitrate between CBDCs and bank deposits in period 1 and show that a run on the central bank cannot occur at the following periods. The authors assume that, first, the central bank cannot default and, second, that it has recycled deposits into loans to the economy via investment banks. These investments are not redeemable and therefore not subject to liquidation in a subsequent period.

Last example, if we take the basic assumptions of the model presented by Brunnermeier and Niepelt (2019), the central bank underlies financial intermediation:

> When households expand their CBDC holdings and lower their deposit holdings, then the central bank's liabilities expand correspondingly. In exchange for the CBDC, the central bank acquires claims vis-a-vis the banking sector. That is, the central bank automatically provides substitute funding for banks, effectively intermediating between non-banks and banks.

Conclusion

The impact of the introduction of CBDCs on financial stability depends first and foremost on their successful dissemination to the general public. It is likely that banks will be able to manage the appearance of this new liquid asset without difficulty if mitigating measures accompany the introduction of CBDCs. But if circulation has to be restricted, what is the point of implementing a complex process for designing and disseminating this new form of central bank money? And are we sure that the general public wants it? A survey of media sentiment toward CBDCs reveals a certain reserve, if not outright hostility (Ozili & Náñez, 2024). While financial inclusion is an important objective, there are alternatives for providing access to a payment system run by the Central Bank, as shown by the example of the PIX platform in Brazil (Duarte et al., 2022).

In addition, according to good specialists in the field, the efficiency gains that CBDCs would provide are far from proven:

> It still has to be shown that underlying IT data base and consensus/data validation mechanisms are really gamechangers that allow the efficiency of payments [and even so] is it a reason to assume that also functionally we are entering a new world with such technologies?
>
> (Bindseil & Pantelopoulos, 2023)

In the context of the disappearance of cash, there remains the need to offer access to a perfectly secure and perfectly liquid instrument and not to allow stablecoins and other cryptocurrencies to monopolize the payments space. From an analytical point of view, the study of the introduction of CBDCs shows the power of the Central Bank, its ability to adapt to technological developments, and, if it so wishes, to adapt its balance sheet to absorb financial instability.

References

Anhert, T., Assenmacher, K., Hoffman P., Leonello, A., Monnet, C. & Porcellacchia, D. (2022, August). The Economics of Central Bank Digital Currencies. ECB Working Paper Series n° 2713. https://www.ecb.europa.eu/pub/pdf/scpwps/ecb.wp2713~91ddff9e7c.en.pdf

Auer, R. & Boehme, R. (2020, March). The Technology of Retail Central Bank Digital Currency. *BIS Quarterly Review*, 85–100. https://www.bis.org/publ/qtrpdf/r_qt2003j.pdf

Bank for International Settlements (2020). Annual Report. (Chapter 3: Central Banks and Payments in the Digital Era). https://www.bis.org/publ/arpdf/ar2020e3.htm

Bank for International Settlements (2021). Annual Report. (Chapter 3: CBDCs: An Opportunity for the Monetary System). https://www.bis.org/publ/arpdf/ar2021e3.htm

Basel Committee on Banking Supervision (2023, October). Report on the 2023 Banking Turmoil. Bank for International Settlements. https://www.bis.org/bcbs/publ/d555.pdf

Benes, J. & Kumhof, M. (2012, August). The Chicago Plan revisited. IMF Working Paper WP/12/202. International Monetary Fund. https://www.imf.org/external/pubs/ft/wp/2012/wp12202.PDF

Bindseil, U. (2020, January). Tiered CBDC and the Financial System. ECB Working Paper Series n° 2351. https://www.ecb.europa.eu/pub/pdf/scpwps/ecb.wp2351~c8c18bbd60.en.pdf

Bindseil, U. & Pantelopoulos, G. (2023). *Introduction to Payments and Financial Market Infrastructures*. Springer. https://doi.org/10.1007/978-3-031-39520-8

Bofinger, P. & Haas, T. (2023, April). The Digital Euro (CBDC) as a Monetary Anchor of the Financial System. Suerf Policy Notes n°309. https://www.suerf.org/publications/suerf-policy-notes-and-briefs/the-digital-euro-cbdc-as-a-monetary-anchor-of-the-financial-system/

Bouis, R., Gelos, G., Miettinen, P., Nakamura, F., Nier, E. & Soderberg, G. (2024). Central Bank Digital Currencies and Financial Stability: Balance Sheet Analysis and Policy Choices. IMF Working Paper WP/24/226. International Monetary Fund. https://www.imf.org/en/Publications/WP/Issues/2024/10/11/Central-Bank-Digital-Currencies-and-Financial-Stability-Balance-Sheet-Analysis-and-Policy-556246

Brunnermeier, M., James, H. & Landau, J.P. (2021, May). The Digitalisation of Money. BIS Working Paper n°941. https://www.bis.org/publ/work941.pdf

Brunnermeier, M. & Landau, J.P. (2022). *The Digital Euro: Policy Implications and Perspectives*. Publication for the Committee on Economic and Monetary Affairs, Policy Department for Economic, Scientific and Quality of Life Policies, European Parliament, Luxembourg. https://www.europarl.europa.eu/RegData/etudes/STUD/2022/703337/IPOL_STU(2022)703337_EN.pdf

Brunnermeier, M. & Niepelt, D. (2019). On the Equivalence of Private and Public Money. *Journal of Monetary Economics*, 106, 27–41.

Brunnermeier, M. & Payne, J. (2021). CBDC, FinTech, and Private Money Creation. In Niepelt, D. (Ed.), *Central Bank Digital Currency: Considerations, Projects, Outlook*. CEPR Press, Paris & London, 65–71.

https://cepr.org/publications/books-and-reports/central-bank-digital-currency-considerations-projects-outlook

Cecchetti, S. & Steinholz, K. (2021). Central Bank Digital Currency: The Battle for the Soul of the Financial System. VoxEU. https://cepr.org/voxeu/columns/central-bank-digital-currency-battle-soul-financial-system

Committee on Payments and Market Infrastructures (CPMI) (2018, March). Central Bank Digital Currencies. https://www.bis.org/cpmi/publ/d174.htm

Demertzis, M. & Martins, C. (2023). The Value Added of Central Bank Digital Currencies: A View from the Euro Area. Policy Brief 13/2023, Bruegel. https://www.bruegel.org/policy-brief/value-added-central-bank-digital-currencies-view-euro-area

Diamond, D.W. & Dybvig, P.H. (1983). Bank Runs, Deposit Insurance, and Liquidity. *Journal of Political Economy*, 91(5), 401–419. https://www.jstor.org/stable/1837095#metadata_info_tab_contents

Duarte, A., Frost, J., Gambacorta, L., Koo Wilkens, P., Shin, H.S. et al. (2022, March). Central Banks, the Monetary System and Public Payment Infrastructures: Lessons from Brazil's Pix. BIS Bulletin n°52. https://www.bis.org/publ/bisbull52.pdf

Dyson, B. & Hodgson, G. (2016). Digital Cash: Why Central Banks Should Start Issuing Electronic Money. Positive Money. https://positivemoney.org/uk/publications/digital-cash/

Fernandez-Villaverde, J., Sanches, D., Schilling, L. & Uhlig, H. (2021, July). Central Bank Digital Currencies: Central Banking for All? *Review of Economic Dynamics*, 41, 225–242. https://doi.org/10.1016/j.red.2020.12.004

Financial Stability Board (2022). Regulation, Supervision and Oversight of Crypto-Asset Activities and Markets. https://www.fsb.org/uploads/P111022-3.pdf

Group of Central Banks (2020). Central Bank Digital Currencies: Foundational Principles and Core Features. https://www.bis.org/publ/othp33.pdf

Group of Central Banks (2021a, September). Central Bank Digital Currencies: Financial Stability Implications. BIS. https://www.bis.org/publ/othp42_fin_stab.pdf

Group of Central Banks (2021b, September). Central Bank Digital Currencies: User Needs and Adoption. BIS. https://www.bis.org/publ/othp42_user_needs.pdf

Infante, S., Kim, K., Orlik, A., Silva, A.F. & Tetlow, R.J. (2022). The Macroeconomic Implications of CBDC: A Review of the Literature. Finance and Economics Discussion Series 2022–076. Washington, DC: Board of Governors of the Federal Reserve System. https://www.federalreserve.gov/econres/feds/files/2022076pap.pdf

Kumhof, M. & Noone, C. (2018, May). Central Bank Digital Currencies – Design Principles and Balance Sheet Implications. Bank of England Staff Working Paper n°725. https://www.bankofengland.co.uk/-/media/boe/files/working-paper/2018/central-bank-digital-currencies-design-principles-and-balance-sheet-implications

Laina, P. (2015). Proposals for Full-Reserve Banking: A Historical Survey from David Ricardo to Martin Wolf. *Economic Thought*, 2(4), 1–19.

Ozili, P.K. & Náñez, S. (2024). Central Bank Digital Currency Adoption Challenges, Solutions, and a Sentiment Analysis. *Journal of Central Banking Theory and Practice*, 13(1), 133–165. https://doi.org/10.2478/jcbtp-2024-0007

Panetta, F. (2022). More Than an Intellectual Game: Exploring the Monetary Policy and Financial Stability Implications of Central Bank Digital Currencies. Speech given to the IESE Business School Banking Initiative Conference on Technology and Finance, Frankfurt am Main. https://www.ecb.europa.eu/press/key/date/2022/html/ecb.sp220408~980e39957b.en.html

Rösl, G. & Seitz, F. (2022). Central Bank Digital Currency and Cash in the Euro Area: Current Developements and One Specific Proposal. *Credit and Capital Markets – Kredit und Kapital*, 55(4), 523–551.

Scorer, S. (2017, June). Central Bank Digital Currencies: DLT or Not DLT? That Is the Question. Bank Underground. https://bankunderground.co.uk/2017/06/05/central-bank-digital-currency-dlt-or-not-dlt-that-is-the-question/

3 Use of a bridge institution in the bank resolution

The case of Silicon Valley Bank and Signature Bank

Marcin Liberadzki

Introduction

A bridge bank is a licensed national bank that operates under a board appointed by the resolution authority. It assumes deposits and certain other liabilities and acquires certain assets of the failing bank. The structure of a bridge bank is intended to "bridge" the gap between a bank's failure and the time when the resolution authority can stabilize the institution and implement an orderly resolution. It is typically used when the resolution authority is caught off guard by a sudden failure, such as due to a loss of liquidity. The temporary and stabilizing nature of a bridge institution is recognized by restructuring and orderly liquidation authorities. Usually law stipulates that a bridge institution can operate for a definite period of time. The resolution authority transfers insured deposits, other key liabilities, and most assets to the bridge bank until a buyer is found. Shares and subordinated debt remain for liquidation. The residual entity is, in principle, to be wound up under "normal" insolvency proceedings (Schillig, 2016). For instance, under the EU's Bank Recovery and Resolution Directive (BRRD), a bridge institution is created to maintain critical functions and to assume and hold parts or all of the shares and assets of the institution under resolution. The BRRD also provides for a two-year term with the possibility of a one-year extension. The bridge bank tool also appears as a central instrument in the single point of entry (SPOE) strategy developed by the Federal Reserve and the Federal Deposit Insurance Corporation (FDIC) for the restructuring and orderly liquidation of systemically important financial institutions (SIFIs) under Title II of the Dodd-Frank Act in the U.S.. Under SPOE, the FDIC can transfer the assets of the failed SIFI, short-term debt, and secured debt of the financial institution's holding company in distress to a newly created bridge institution, leaving the shares and long-term debt to absorb losses and support the functioning of critical subsidiaries. By combining the bail-in tool with the bridge, SPOE aims to ensure that the significant entities of the bank remain well-capitalized and operational, thereby minimizing disruption and spillover effects (Peihani, 2023). Given the strong balance sheet of the bridge financial company, the FDIC expects it to be able to obtain funding privately by accessing financial markets. In order to overcome any temporary liquidity problems, the FDIC would provide funding through the Orderly Liquidation Fund for a brief transitional period (FDIC, 2013).

Resolution of Silicon Valley Bank

Description of the resolution tool

The FDIC was the first to act on March 10, 2023, announcing that Silicon Valley Bank (SVB) was closed and placed into receivership. The insured deposits were transferred to the "Deposit

DOI: 10.4324/9781003663539-4

Insurance National Bank of Santa Clara", where the deposits were guaranteed up to the statutory maximum of $250,000 per account (FDIC, March 10, 2023).

On Sunday, March 12, the FDIC took over another failing institution, Signature Bank. To prevent the problems of SVB spreading to the banking system, public authorities extended depositor protection beyond the statutory maximum set within the existing U.S. deposit guarantee mechanism of $250,000 per depositor from Monday, March 13. Since over 90% of SVB's deposit liabilities were concentrated in accounts above this maximum limit, the FDIC's intervention secured a significant portion of SVB's uninsured deposit volumes (FDIC, March 13, 2023). This "systemic risk exception" contained in the 1991 Act allowed the FDIC to take immediate action without spending time looking for the least costly way to resolve the bank's problem.[1] All deposits – both insured and uninsured – and essentially all assets and all Qualified Financial Contracts of SVB were transferred to the newly created bridge bank, Silicon Valley Bridge Bank National Association (FDIC, March 13, 2023).

German and British authorities responded to SVB's events on an international level. The German financial supervisory authority announced on March 13 that a "moratorium" had been imposed on the German subsidiary of SVB, created under German corporate law, with assets worth €789 million. SVB UK was acquired by HSBC for £1.

The following weekend, the Federal Reserve announced the creation of an emergency lending tool, the "Bank Term Funding Program" (BTFP), from which all eligible depository institutions could borrow, provided there was "good collateral". The Federal Reserve invoked its authority to act in "unusual and urgent circumstances", considered in the 1935 revision of the Federal Reserve Act, and created an innovative emergency lending program on generous terms. Historically, the Federal Reserve would have accepted the market value of securities as the collateral value and allowed banks to borrow only up to that market value minus a small cushion. For BTFP, the collateral value was increased to the nominal value of government securities. As a result, five-year government bonds issued in 2021, which were then trading at about $0.85 on the dollar, would still count as full $1 collateral from the discount window.[2]

By Thursday, March 16, a joint statement from the Fed and the Treasury Department confirmed that a group of 11 private banks had committed to supporting one of their counterparts, First Republic Bank (FRC), by depositing $30 billion in the bank. Due to ongoing equity losses characteristic of the institution, press reports from March 21 indicated discussions in the private sector about organizing a capital injection for FRC. Overall, these policy actions helped slow the deposit outflow, delaying the final collapse of FRC in May but did not prevent it. With assets worth $213 billion, FRC was even larger than SVB.[3]

Incorporation of SVB assets and liabilities into First-Citizens Bank & Trust Company

On March 26, 2023, the FDIC entered into a purchase and assumption agreement for all deposits and loans of Silicon Valley Bridge Bank National Association with First-Citizens Bank & Trust Company, Raleigh, North Carolina. On Monday, March 27, 2023, 17 former branches of Silicon Valley Bridge Bank National Association opened under the name First-Citizens Bank & Trust Company. As of March 10, 2023, Silicon Valley Bridge Bank had total assets of approximately $167 billion and total deposits of approximately $119 billion. The March 26 transaction included the purchase of the Silicon Valley Bridge Bank's loan portfolio worth approximately $72 billion in exchange for deposit liabilities of $56.5 million (FDIC, March 26, 2023). The difference between the acquired assets and liabilities was $16.5 billion, strengthening First Citizens' regulatory capital.

According to SEC (Securities and Exchange Commission) documents, First Citizens received a five-year $35 billion loan from the FDIC at a fixed interest rate of 3.5% to finance the transaction (SEC, 2025). Approximately $90 billion in securities and other assets remained under receivership, available to the FDIC. During this process, the administration assured investors in a call that under the terms of the transaction, there would be no need to take over any of the securities held to maturity, estimated at $151 billion less than their book value in SVB's books, according to the bank's own 2022 report. Additionally, the FDIC obtained the right to an equity appreciation agreement with First Citizens BancShares Inc., Raleigh, North Carolina, with a potential value of up to $500 million. On March 28, 2023, the FDIC informed the bank of exercising this right, setting a deadline of five business days for payment. This happened because Citizens' shares rose by 54% due to optimism about how the acquisition would improve the bank's finances. The absorption of SVB transformed First Citizens into one of the 15 largest American banks (Dickson, 2023).

The FDIC and First-Citizens Bank & Trust Company entered into a loss-sharing agreement regarding commercial loans acquired from the former Silicon Valley Bridge Bank National Association, ensuring that the FDIC would cover First Citizens' losses exceeding $5 billion on commercial loans over the next five years. The FDIC, as the receiver, and First-Citizens Bank & Trust Company would share losses and potential recoveries from loans covered by the loss-sharing agreement. The transaction was expected to maximize recovered amounts from assets by keeping them in the private sector. It was also expected that the transaction would minimize disruptions for credit customers (Dickson, 2023).

As a result, the FDIC determined the cost of SVB's failure to its Deposit Insurance Fund (DIF) to be $178,200,260,000 (almost $17.9 billion). SVB's total deposits amounted to $175,378,000,000, and total assets amounted to $209,026,000,000 (FDIC, BankFind Suite: Bank Failures & Assistance Data). Additionally, the city of New York filed a lawsuit against the FDIC regarding overdue taxes from SVB amounting to over $21 million. By law, it is now required to collect funds from member banks. FDIC Chairman Martin Gruenberg told Congress that his government agency has discretionary authority to order larger lenders to contribute disproportionately higher premiums to the DIF and pledged to consider their concerns (Hetzner, 2023).

This isn't the first time the chairman has crossed swords with the board of the holding. "First Citizens has finalized more FDIC transactions than almost any other bank since 2009", the CEO told investors during an April conference call, hailing the acquisition as "significant" in scale and "financially, strategically, and operationally compelling". It appears that the holding is increasingly adept at securing the most favorable terms for its bank's shareholders. As for the government, testimony from Gruenberg and Fed Vice Chairman Michael Barr, as well as comments from Treasury Secretary Janet Yellen, show that U.S. financial authorities were primarily focused on quickly resolving the SVB crisis, which they feared would trigger a domino effect and undermine broader confidence in banks (Hetzner, 2023). Gruenberg admitted that an earlier takeover of SVB would have been preferable, but given the short time needed to properly conduct due diligence, the only offer made in the first weekend after taking over the lender on March 10 was more expensive than liquidation. As a result, it was decided to extend the process, leading to 18 parties submitting concrete bids. "These were negotiations, Congressman, and this is what we were able to work out", Gruenberg told lawmakers, trying to explain why he couldn't negotiate better terms with First Citizens. Asked by Representative John Rose of Tennessee whether he thought he did well in negotiations, the FDIC chairman allowed himself a chuckle. "Maybe we could have done better", he replied. "I don't know" (Hetzner, 2023).

The acquisition of SVB involved an unusual provision: a $70 billion credit line courtesy of the FDIC. The financing was meant to help First Citizens meet liquidity needs that would arise over the next two years due to incorporating SVB into its operations, Raleigh, North Carolina lender said in its application (Reyes, 2023). The credit line was granted for five years, and the agency charges interest equal to the secured overnight financing rate plus 25 basis points.

Utilization of a Bridge Institution in the resolution of Signature Bank in March 2023

Description of the resolution tool

The collapse of Signature Bank was the third-largest bank failure in U.S. history, occurring just two days after the collapse of SVB, the second-largest bank failure in the U.S.

On Sunday, March 12, 2023, Signature Bank, New York, NY, was closed by the New York State Department of Financial Services, which appointed the FDIC as the receiver. To protect depositors, the FDIC transferred all deposits and essentially all assets of Signature Bank to Signature Bridge Bank National Association, a full-service bank that was to be operated by the FDIC while promoting the institution to potential bidders (FDIC, March 12, 2023). As the receiver, the FDIC operated Signature Bridge Bank, N.A., to maximize the value of the institution for future sale and to maintain banking services previously provided by Signature Bank.

To prevent the problems at SVB from spreading to the banking system, public authorities extended depositor protection beyond the statutory maximum set under the existing U.S. deposit guarantee mechanism of $250,000 per depositor on the same day. This "systemic risk exception" contained in the 1991 Act allowed the FDIC to take immediate action without spending time looking for the least costly way to resolve the bank's problem. According to the FDIC, over 99% of bank accounts in the U.S. held less than $250,000, but large sums of cash deposited into high-dollar accounts still left large amounts of money uninsured. M. Gruenberg (head of the FDIC) stated that, in 2021, nearly 47% of all money deposited in U.S. banks was in accounts that were not insured (Reimann, 2023).

A week later, on March 19, the FDIC entered into a purchase and assumption agreement for essentially all deposits and certain loan portfolios of Signature Bridge Bank, N.A. with Flagstar Bank National Association, Hicksville, New York, a wholly-owned subsidiary of New York Community Bancorp Inc., Westbury, New York (hereinafter: NYCB). On Monday, March 20, 2023, 40 former Signature Bank branches were to operate under the name Flagstar Bank, N.A., owned by New York Community Bancorp. Branches would open during normal business hours. Depositors of Signature Bridge Bank, N.A., other than those associated with digital asset activities, would automatically become depositors of the acquiring institution (Flagstar Bank's offer did not include approximately $4 billion in deposits related to the digital assets of the former Signature Bank). The FDIC provided these deposits directly to customers whose accounts were linked to digital asset banking (FDIC, March 19, 2023).

As of December 31, 2022, the former Signature Bank held deposits totaling $88.6 billion and assets valued at $110.4 billion (the 20th largest bank in the U.S.). By comparison, New York Community Bancorp's total assets in December 2022 were $90 billion, ranking it 35th among the largest commercial banks in the U.S. The transaction included the purchase of Signature Bridge Bank's, N.A., assets valued at approximately $38.4 billion, including loans worth $12.9 billion and $2.5 billion in cash purchased at a discount of $2.7 billion. Approximately $60 billion in loans remained under receivership for later disposition by the FDIC.

The transaction also included Signature's wealth management and broker-dealer activities and 40 branches, including 30 offices in the New York metropolitan area and several others in California.

Investors seemed to approve the transaction: New York Community's shares rose more than 30% on Monday following the announcement (Kline, 2023). The FDIC obtained the right to equity appreciation in New York Community Bancorp Inc. common shares, with a potential value of up to $300 million when the price exceeds the "strike price" of $6.65 per share (FDIC, 19 March 2023). On May 16, 2023, the FDIC announced its intention to sell NYCB shares. The FDIC was to sell approximately 39 million NYCB shares in a guaranteed public offering. NYCB reported that the company would not be selling any shares and that all proceeds from the offering would be directed to the FDIC. The FDIC planned to sell its bank shares no later than June 8 (Taub, 2023).

Exclusions of assets from acquisition by NYCB

The transaction announced on Sunday did not include any multifamily loans or commercial real estate loans, largely secured by multifamily buildings subject to regulations limiting landlords' ability to raise rents. NYCB had a goal of diversifying and moving away from such a heavy emphasis on multifamily loans (Kline, 2023). NYCB was already one of the largest multifamily lenders in the New York area, where it specializes in financing rent-regulated buildings. Public records analyzed by Maverick Real Estate Partners, a commercial real estate loan investment firm, indicate that Signature held rent-stabilized loans worth more than $11 billion. The loans had higher debt-to-value ratios than comparable portfolios owned by JPMorgan Chase & Co., NYCB itself, and other banks. The analysis found that "Signature's loan portfolio has higher leverage than most other similar companies", said Ted Martell, co-founder of Maverick. "This comes with higher risk" (Clark et al., 2023). According to NYCB's fourth-quarter 2022 earnings presentation, as of December 31, multifamily loans accounted for 55.3% of New York Community's loan portfolio, while commercial real estate loans accounted for 12.3%. The Signature deal, which includes credit lines for law firms and entertainment companies, allowed NYCB to expand into new businesses (Kline, 2023).

NYCB acquired $34 billion in deposits, representing only about 38% of the $88.6 billion in deposits reported as of the last day of December 2022. Adding these deposits to NYCB's existing balance sheet reduced the loan-to-deposit ratio, which measures the total number of loans to total deposits, from 118% to 88%. Importantly, the agreement excludes any Signature deposits related to cryptocurrencies, which reportedly amount to about $4 billion. The FDIC said it expects Signature's failure to cost the DIF approximately $2.5 billion.

Disposition of remaining assets

Subsequently, on April 3, 2023, the FDIC announced its intention to seek a buyer for the remaining assets (FDIC, April 3, 2023). The agency announced that about $60 billion in assets remained for sale. "The portfolio consists primarily of commercial real estate (CRE) loans, commercial loans, and a smaller pool of single-family residential loans. The CRE loans include a concentration of multifamily properties located primarily in New York", the agency said in a press release. The agency made it clear that it was paying particular attention to commercial real estate loans secured by multifamily buildings with rent stabilization or control, as these are an important source of affordable housing in New York. "The FDIC has a statutory obligation, among other things, to maximize the protection of the availability and affordability of residential properties for low- and moderate-income individuals", the FDIC stated in its report (FDIC, April 3, 2023). The FDIC planned to begin the sale process in the summer and partnered with Newmark & Company Real Estate Inc. for sales advisory services. The agency noted that the loans would be sold "as is" and without guarantees to eligible buyers only.

On June 16, 2023, Customers Bancorp Inc. purchased $631 million in loans belonging to Signature Bank. The purchase from the FDIC was 85% of the portfolio's book value, the West Reading, Pennsylvania-based bank said in a statement. In July 2023, the FDIC reported that it was seeking buyers for a loan portfolio valued at $18.5 billion from Signature related to major private equity firms and investment firms (Wong & Clark, 2023). On September 5, 2023, the FDIC began seeking buyers for $3.3 billion in commercial real estate loans made by Signature Bank. Most of the loans were secured by multifamily properties, primarily in New York. About $1.5 billion in loans were related to properties where rent was stabilized or controlled (Wong & Clark, 2023). The most difficult assets to dispose of were about $1.27 billion in bonds tied to project loans backed by Ginnie Mae. These are bonds secured by pools of Ginnie Mae Project Loans. The loans underlying the bonds are taken out by developers from banks and other lenders, often to build or renovate housing. The resulting homes are typically intended for low- or moderate-income families, and the loans are subject to prepayment penalties. The FDIC likely did not want to hold assets on its books until maturity. The government agency is tasked with stabilizing the banking system and has no mandate to hold investments indefinitely. Restructuring mortgage bonds is possible but has its drawbacks. By bundling the bonds and changing their cash flows, the FDIC could create derivative securities that might attract investors. However, the base pool would remain the same, so making some securities safer for money managers could make the remainder riskier (Carpenter & Brush, 2023).

The FDIC considered alternatives to bond price cuts, including potentially converting debt into new securities. According to people who requested anonymity due to non-public information, BlackRock held preliminary discussions with investors about the bonds. However, the securities proved difficult to sell in part because the bonds were likely to yield coupons below market value for years. The loans secured by them were taken out before the Federal Reserve began raising rates and often carry high penalties if refinanced within the first ten years, with repayment potentially taking decades (Carpenter & Brush, 2023). When the FDIC disposes of assets, it conducts a competitive sales process to ensure it receives the maximum possible value. It also aims to preserve affordability and availability of homes for low- and moderate-income individuals.

In October 2023, PNC Financial Services Group Inc. purchased a $16.6 billion portfolio of capital-commitment facilities, mainly for private equity sponsors, arranged by the failed Signature Bank. The portfolio included $9 billion in capital loans (Taub, 2023). The price of the Signature portfolio transaction was not disclosed, but PNC stated that the deal was financed with available cash. Official data shows the bank had approximately $6.2 billion in cash at the end of the second quarter. Unlike other transactions involving parts of failed banks, PNC's agreement with the FDIC does not include loss-sharing guarantees (McCaffrey, 2023). The FDIC often uses such agreements, where the agency agrees to share losses with the acquiring institution, to encourage healthy banks to bid on parts of failed banks.

A joint venture involving Blackstone Inc. and the Canada Pension Plan Investment Board agreed to buy $1.2 billion in stakes in a nearly $17 billion commercial real estate loan portfolio from Signature. Separately, Associate Fund Management, an investment manager affiliated with Steve Ross's Associated Cos., teamed up with two non-profit organizations to acquire stakes in ventures holding a total of $5.8 billion in loans tied to rent-controlled and rent-stabilized residential buildings (Wong & Clark, 2023).

On December 20, 2023, the FDIC sold 20% of a venture holding approximately $9 billion in loans to an entity controlled by Santander Bank, N.A. (SBNA). The SBNA Investor entity paid $1.1 billion. The FDIC retained an 80% stake in the venture, which holds loans secured by apartment properties with rent stabilization or control. The transaction marked the final step in the FDIC's plan to divest about $33 billion in commercial real estate loans held by Signature Bank (Wong & Clark, 2023).

Transaction costs

In a data report on its website, the FDIC listed the cost of Signature Bank's failure to its DIF at $884,248 million. The cost of SVB's failure to its DIF was $17.82 billion (FDIC, BakFind Suite: Bank Failures & Assistance Data). As reported by Bloomberg on November 17, 2023, the FDIC estimated that covering all uninsured depositors at Signature Bank and SVB in March 2023 cost the fund around $16.3 billion (Johnson, 2023). At the beginning of the year, the fund held over $128 billion (Meghjani, 2023). To cover these costs, large banks were expected to pay higher fees – an annual rate of about 13.4 basis points instead of 12.5 basis points as proposed, to be collected over eight periods. Lenders with less than $5 billion would still not have to pay anything, the FDIC noted. The DIF is typically replenished by all insured banks through quarterly assessments calculated using specific formulas (Meghjani, 2023). In May 2023, the FDIC had estimated that the resolution of SVB, Signature Bank, and First Republic would likely drain $35 billion from DIF. The sale of First Republic included a cost-sharing agreement between JPMorgan and the FDIC for certain loans from First Republic's previous portfolio, which the agency estimated would draw $13 billion from DIF. Combined with the then-estimated $22.5 billion in losses from the failures of Silicon Valley and Signature, DIF was expected to shrink by about $35 billion annually, and the FDIC would have to pass these costs onto banks in some manner.

In January 2024, New York City sued the FDIC, acting as receiver for Signature Bank's estate, alleging that the U.S. regulatory agency owed approximately $44 million in unpaid municipal taxes. According to the lawsuit filed in federal court in Manhattan, the shortfalls for 2015–2021 were related to unreported income allocations and adjustments to investment and capital income (Bakewell, 2024).

Rise in subordinated bond prices of Signature Bank

Bonds tied to the now-defunct Signature Bank showed unexpected value, causing securities prices to surge from near zero. The two-tranche subordinated bonds, a $375 million 4% due 2030 tranche and $200 million 4.125% due 2029 tranche, were priced at 39 at the beginning of January 2024 (ION Analytics, 2024). In early December 2023, the price of the 4% subordinated bonds maturing in 2030 rose to about 13 cents on the dollar after trading at a quarter of a penny in November, according to Trace (Basu, 2023). The 4.125% subordinated bonds maturing in 2029 also traded at 13 cents in December, compared to a penny in November. The surge in bond activity – which had been minimal since the FDIC's takeover of the New York bank in March 2023 – came after investors noted from Signature Bridge Bank's balance sheet that, as of September 30, 2023, it had a positive net asset value of $446 million.[4] Approximately $575 million in subordinated bonds is tied to Signature Bank, and any surplus in the bridge bank should theoretically be returned to creditors by the FDIC (Basu, 2023).

Conclusions

Once a bank is formally declared to be in resolution, a resolution authority can: (i) transfer a portion of its assets and liabilities into a bridge bank, so that they can be protected there, (ii) it can sell off parts of the business or separate some of the assets out into a special-purpose vehicle for wind-down, as well as it can (iii) unilaterally impose write-down or converting into shares bank 'eligible liabilities' or to require an institution in resolution to issue new shares or other capital instruments (bail-in) (Liberadzki & Liberadzki, 2019). A bridge bank is a stabilizing tool designed to temporarily maintain the continuity of critical functions of an institution and its operations until a permanent solution is found. In general, the bridge bank tool has been used only sporadically, and its contribution to restructuring and orderly liquidation seems twofold:

1 Maintaining financial stability through the continuity of critical functions and
2 The restructuring and orderly liquidation authority gains additional time to plan the resolution (Peihani, 2023).

The first factor appears particularly significant in the context of larger institutions, where the size of the balance sheet and operational complexity may hinder a quick sale and where closing the bank could also trigger a domino effect and instability. The second factor may be more important in the resolution of smaller institutions, where the restructuring and orderly liquidation authority needs more time to plan an orderly exit in the face of insolvency. In case of SVB and Signature, the resolution authority was taken by surprise by a sudden failure due to liquidity risk.

The success of the exit strategy will ultimately depend on various factors, such as current market conditions, depositor confidence, and finding a viable buyer. The latter factor is especially important. It may happen that residual bank is to be liquidated because a credible buyer could not be found, despite authorities searching for months after the establishment of a bridge bank.

Notes

1 This exception cannot be invoked casually: it requires a positive vote from the boards of the FDIC and the Federal Reserve, as well as the approval of the U.S. Secretary of the Treasury. Invoking the exception also triggers careful scrutiny from the FDIC, especially since Silicon Valley Bank was not previously classified as systemically important.
2 The bank's periodic funding program marked a significant departure from the Fed's previous practices and required invoking the "extraordinary and urgent circumstances" clause from Section 13(3) of the Federal Reserve Act. This extraordinary authority, granted by Congress in 1935, had not been used for over 70 years before it was first activated during the global financial crisis of 2008–2009. Since then, the Fed has determined that "extraordinary and urgent circumstances" occurred twice more: first during Covid-19 and again during the panic of 2023.
3 This delay provided the FDIC with enough time to organize an orderly auction, and the winning "cheapest" bid, submitted by J.P. Morgan, and included the full assumption of all uninsured deposits. Thus, the FDIC did not have to invoke the systemic risk exception to make a decision regarding First Republic.
4 Sixty point eight billion dollars in assets under liquidation and 60.3 billion dollars in liabilities.

References

Bakewell, S. (2024, January 29). New York Sues FDIC over $44 Million in Unpaid Taxes by Failed Signature Bank. *Bloomberg*. https://www.bloomberg.com/news/articles/2024-01-30/new-york-sues-fdic-over-44-million-in-unpaid-taxes-by-failed-signature-bank

Basu, R. (2023, December 12). Traders Eye Potential Windfall in Defunct Signature Bank's Bonds. *Bloomberg*. https://www.bloomberg.com/news/articles/2023-12-12/traders-eye-potential-windfall-in-defunct-signature-bank-s-bonds

Carpenter, S., Brush, S. (2023, September 12). US Is Looking to Offload Nearly $13 Billion of MBS Seized from SVB and Signature Bank. *Bloomberg*. https://www.bloomberg.com/news/articles/2023-09-12/us-looking-to-sell-unusual-mbs-seized-from-svb-and-signature

Clark, P., Gittelsohn, J., Epstein, J. (2023, March 21). After Signature Bank Deal, FDIC Is Left With $11 Billion in 'Toxic Waste' Loans. *Bloomberg*. https://www.bloomberg.com/news/articles/2023-03-21/after-signature-deal-fdic-is-left-with-11-billion-in-toxic-waste-loans

Dickson, S. (2023, March). First Citizens' Stock Surge From SVB Deal Gives $500 Million to FDIC. *Bloomberg*. https://search-1ebscohost-1com-1o8h9l06e0077.han.sgh.waw.pl/login.aspx?direct=true&db=bsu&AN=162845992&lang=pl&site=bsi-live

Federal Deposit Insurance Corporation (FDIC). (2013). *Resolution of Systemically Important Financial Institutions: The Single Point of Entry Strategy*. 78 Federal Register 76617. https://www.federalregister.gov/documents/2013/12/18/2013-30057/resolution-of-systemically-important-financial-institutions-the-single-point-of-entry-strategy

FDIC. (2023, March 10). *FDIC Creates a Deposit Insurance National Bank of Santa Clara to Protect Insured Depositors of Silicon Valley Bank, Santa Clara, California* [Press release]. https://www.fdic.gov/news/press-releases/2023/pr23016.html

FDIC. (2023, March 13). *FDIC Acts to Protect All Depositors of the former Silicon Valley Bank, Santa Clara, California* [Press release]. https://www.fdic.gov/news/press-releases/2023/pr23019.html

FDIC. (2023, March 19). *Subsidiary of New York Community Bancorp, Inc., to Assume Deposits of Signature Bridge Bank, N.A., From the FDIC* [Press release]. https://www.fdic.gov/news/press-releases/2023/pr23021.html

FDIC. (2023, April 3). *FDIC Announces Upcoming Sale of the Loan Portfolio from the Former Signature Bank, New York, New York* [Press release]. https://www.fdic.gov/news/press-releases/2023/pr23026.html

Hetzner, C. (2023, April). FDIC chair takes heat from lawmakers over cut-price deal that gave Silicon Valley Bank to First Citizens: "Maybe we could have been better." *Fortune*. https://search-1ebscohost-1com-1o8h9l06e0070.han.sgh.waw.pl/login.aspx?direct=true&db=bsu&AN=162837522&lang=pl&site=bsi-live

ION Analytics. (2024, January 4). *Signature Bank Securities Vault Higher Despite Questions on Recovery*. https://ionanalytics.com/insights/debtwire/signature-bank-securities-vault-higher-despite-questions-on-recovery/

Johnson, K. (2023, November 16). Big Banks Saddled with Steep Tab for SVB, Signature Depositors. *Bloomberg*. https://www.bloomberg.com/news/articles/2023-11-16/big-banks-to-be-saddled-with-tab-for-svb-signature-depositors

Kline, A. (2023, March 22). New York Community's Challenge: Keeping Signature's Remaining Deposits. *American Banker*. https://www.americanbanker.com/news/new-york-communitys-challenge-keeping-signatures-remaining-deposits

Liberadzki, M., Liberadzki, K. (2019). *Contingent Convertible Bonds, Corporate Hybrid Securities and Preferred Shares*. Springer Books, Springer.

McCaffrey, O. (2023, October 3). PNC Becomes the Latest Bank to Take Advantage of Regional Bank Failures. *American Banker.* https://www.americanbanker.com/news/pnc-becomes-the-latest-bank-to-take-advantage-of-regional-bank-failures

Meghjani, T. (2023, August 4). Wall Street Giants Expect $8.9 Billion Hit from Bank Failures. *Bloomberg*. https://www.bloomberg.com/news/articles/2023-08-04/wall-street-giants-expect-8-9-billion-hit-from-bank-failures

Peihani, M. (2023). Resolution of Small and Medium-Sized Deposit-Taking Institutions: Back to Basics? *American Business Law Journal*, 60, 419–475. https://doi.org/10.1111/ablj.12225

Reimann, N. (2023, May 1). FDIC Suggests Scrapping $250,000 Bank Account Insurance Limit - But Just for Businesses. *Forbes*. https://www.forbes.com/sites/nicholasreimann/2023/05/01/fdic-suggests-scrapping-250000-bank-account-insurance-limit-but-just-for-businesses/

Reyes, M. (2023, March). FDIC Grants First Citizens Rare Credit Line for SVB. *Bloomberg*. https://search-1ebscohost-1com-1o8h9l02g0003.han.sgh.waw.pl/login.aspx?direct=true&db=bsu&AN=162701105&lang=pl&site=bsi-live

SEC. (2025, April 7). Form 8-K Current Report First Citizens BancShares, Inc. https://www.sec.gov/Archives/edgar/data/798941/000079894125000016/fcnca-20250407.htm

Schillig, M. (2016). *Resolution and Insolvency of Banks and Financial Institutions.* Oxford University Press. https://doi.org/10.1093/oso/9780198703587.001.0001

Taub, D. (2023, October 3). PNC Buys Book of Signature Bank's Private Equity Loans from FDIC. *Bloomberg.* https://www.bloomberg.com/news/articles/2023-10-03/pnc-buys-book-of-signature-bank-s-private-equity-loans-from-fdic

Wong, N., Clark, P. (2023, September 5). FDIC Starts Marketing $33 Billion of Signature Property Debt. *Bloomberg.* https://www.bloomberg.com/news/articles/2023-09-05/fdic-starts-marketing-33-billion-of-signature-property-debt

4 Innovative macroprudential policy for financial stability

Marina Sakovich

Introduction

The 2007–2008 Global Financial Crisis (GFC) has highlighted the need to regulate not only individual financial institutions but also the system as a whole. Since then, the concept of macroprudential regulation has been actively promoted. Various macroprudential policy (MaP) tools have been developed and the channels through which MaPs could affect the economy have been explored over time. However, questions about the effectiveness of MaPs still remain open.

There is a variety of tools that can be used by national authorities to maintain financial stability. Instruments interact with each other in a complex way. The question of choosing a relevant set of tools and their calibration is one of the main issues to be considered in financial regulation frameworks. The balance between the cost of regulation and the benefits of financial stability is particularly relevant in a context of economic and financial turmoil but also under the constraints of energy transition and sustainable development since financial market are at the heart of economic and societal evolution. In this aim, it seems to be suitable to determine the nature, conditions, and scope of possible macroprudential frameworks with a view to strengthening the effectiveness of financial markets regulation and supervision along with the microprudential regulatory practices that are in force since the 1990s in financial systems. In the light of the GFC, microprudential regulation alone has not proven to be apt to ensure systemic stability of markets since it was only focusing on the resilience of individual institutions to external (and limited) shocks. Therefore, attention can be turned to the possibility of considering innovative combinations of macroeconomic regulatory instruments and ways that could reduce the occurrence and severity of major financial crises without hampering the dynamism of innovative financial markets. Assessing financial stability through early warning indicators (Early Warning Signals, EWS) or stress-testing models seems to be an important element in maintaining financial stability (or containing financial instability).

The concept of MaP is quite broad and includes various elements such as the instruments, the channels through which these instruments affect the economy, the evaluation of the effectiveness of the measures applied, and the assessment of the financial stability of the economy. An important issue is the interaction between macroprudential and monetary policies. The question remains whether the financial system is adequately protected from risks at the current moment. This chapter seeks to answer to this critical question.

The first section points to a plethora of definitions about financial stability and financial crisis. The second section is devoted to a review of the evolution of the regulatory framework from micro to macroprudential regulation. It details the ways of risk identification from EWS to stress testing for further application of MaP instruments. The third section considers the effectiveness of MaP, including channels of implementation and tools. The fourth section provides an overview of the interaction between monetary policy and MaP. The last section concludes.

DOI: 10.4324/9781003663539-5

Financial stability, financial crisis, and leading indicators

The concepts of financial stability and financial crises are inherently opposite. The issues of determining financial stability have been disclosed in studies of various authors for quite a long time. Particular attention had been drawn to the definition of financial stability from the 2000s and especially over 2003–2006 (Table 4.1). However, these various and developed research studies could not prevent the GFC that redirected again the attention of scholars and policy makers towards the systemic fragilities and weaknesses of financial markets and to the need to strengthen financial stability at macro level. The attention to various elements of financial stability is increasing, and these variables and factors are being studied separately. However, there is almost no definition of financial stability in later papers. This shows that financial stability is a complex concept with many elements. There is no accurate definition of financial stability. Although in most cases, the stability is related to the ability of financial systems to function smoothly (mainly) as an intermediation process between loanable funds and financial needs.

Even though there is no a universal definition of financial stability, the stability of financial markets can be defined opposite to financial instability and financial crisis, the former pointing to the ability of financial markets to allow the economy to work smoothly while the latter

Table 4.1 Definition of financial stability

Definition	*Authors*
Ability of the financial system to cope with a run of a single bank	Fecht (2003)
The financial system's ability: (a) to facilitate both an efficient allocation of economic resources – both spatially and especially intertemporally – and the effectiveness of other economic processes (such as wealth accumulation, economic growth, and ultimately social prosperity); (b) to assess, price, allocate, and manage financial risks; and (c) to maintain its ability to perform these key functions – even when affected by external shocks or by a build up of imbalances – primarily through self-corrective mechanisms.	Schinasi (2004)
Condition in which an economy's mechanisms for pricing, allocating, and managing financial risks (credit, liquidity, counterparty, market, etc.) are functioning well enough to contribute to the performance of the economy.	Schinasi (2004) A broader definition
Stems from the prevalence of a financial system that is able to provide on a durable basis, and without major disruptions, an efficient allocation of savings to investment opportunities.	Das et al. (2004)
Smooth functioning of the components of the financial system (financial institutions, markets, payments, settlement, and clearing systems).	Cihak (2006)
Situation when the efficiency of financial intermediation between ultimate borrowers and ultimate lenders is not subject to significant adverse shocks.	Cihak (2006) Aggregated from several Financial Stability Reports
A condition in which the financial system works smoothly with all of its key components satisfactorily performing their roles: financial institutions carrying out their financial intermediary functions, market participants maintaining a high level of confidence in their financial market, and the financial infrastructure being well developed.	Heath and Goksu (2017)
Financial stability is a society-wide concern and should be addressed at macro level as a social dilemma through collective action to ensure a continuous/stable provision of monetary/financial operations.	Ülgen (2022a)

reflecting a state of ill-working of markets regarding their role of financing economic activities of different people and institutions in a durable way. In most cases, the same indicators are used to assess financial stability or financial crisis. As Čihák (2007, p. 7) argues:

> some financial stability reports define financial stability as the antithesis of financial crises: system-wide episodes in which the financial system fails to function and the institutional underpinnings of a monetary economy – payments and settlements systems, the acceptability of bank deposits as money—are disrupted.

At the same time, the financial stability may be defined as a public good (Ülgen, 2020; Ülgen, 2022a). Ülgen (2021, p. 536) emphasizes that financial stability as an essential public good should be produced, distributed, managed, and controlled by public authorities to guide the behaviour of private actors towards globally compatible economic actions to achieve the common good. Financial stability should be considered a public good (Ülgen, 2022b, p. 330) because it is a systemic need that cannot be satisfied by market mechanisms. In fact, since economic relations are based on the possibility of continuous payment and settlement transactions, monetary and financial services can be considered part of the vital infrastructure of the capitalist economy. Financial stability is a public concern that links the viability of the whole with the consequences of the monetary and financial decisions of a few. Thus, the financial system exhibits the characteristics of a basic infrastructure common to the whole of society, and financial stability exhibits the characteristics of a public good. This underlines the importance of financial stability for the functioning of the entire economy. Variants of financial stability definition may include micro and macro levels. This determines the emergence of different levels of regulation: micro and macroprudential regulation. At the micro-level, we can define financial stability as the resilience of the financial system to shocks and disequilibria and to continue smoothly functioning (settlements, credit, payments) in the case of a failure of a single financial institution or in case of a systemic crisis. More broadly, at the macro level, financial stability is connected with monetary policy issues such as inflation, GDP growth, interest, and currency rates. That is why prudential policy, which is responsible for financial stability, is often interconnected with monetary policy of central banks.

Due to the complexity of the financial system and to the recurrence of system wide crises, a large number of institutions are involved in ensuring financial stability at both international and national levels. International level mainly includes G20 Forum, Financial Stability Board, International Monetary Fund, and Bank for International Settlements. At the national level, one may find national central banks and other national regulatory and supervision agencies.

The financial crisis is also a very broad concept. We can segment a crisis according to the area in which it occurs or the vulnerabilities that are behind it. For example, Adrian et al. (2013) document that vulnerabilities can emerge in four areas: (1) systemically important financial institutions (SIFIs),[1] (2) shadow banking, (3) asset markets, and (4) the non-financial sector. The mechanism of a financial crisis is usually associated with a wave-like economic development:

> During expansionary booms, funding constraints are loose, and intermediaries can build up leverage and maturity mismatch. The high effective risk appetite of intermediaries in those times leads to a compression in the pricing of risk and an increase in asset price valuations.
>
> (Adrian et al., 2013, p. 8)

This analysis is very close to the Financial Instability Hypothesis (FIH) of Minsky. According to Minsky (1992), financial instability arises from within, as a result of the functioning of markets especially when government/public regulation is loosened. This means that instability is rather endogenous than caused by external shocks, as assumed in standard market (equilibrium) approaches. According to FIH, without appropriate government regulation and continuous supervision, markets can go through three stages:

1 Hedge finance: debt obligations are covered by expected profits; this situation pushes actors to further risky operations;
2 Speculative finance: the situation worsens, profits are not high enough to cover debt obligations, and new loans are required to repay debts;
3 Ponzi finance: no profit, debt obligations do not generate enough money to repay debts, debtor actors must borrow again to pay interest and dividends, but cannot repay capital. If the debt chain is interrupted, the debtor entities go bankrupt and can pull the whole banking system down with them. This would be the case when large institutions (too-big-to-fail or SIFIs) are involved in the crisis. This is a systemic crisis, which requires extra-market intervention, usually by central banks and governments.

High costs of financial crises are one of the reasons for the authorities' increased attention to supporting financial stability. Adrian et al. (2013), Aikman et al. (2013), and Grigaite et al. (2020) notice that fire sales and adverse feedback loops can result in material disruptions in financial and economic activity when adverse shocks hit, due to connections between the real and financial sectors. The cost of financial crisis also includes GDP drop and social costs.

A crisis arising in one financial or industrial sector may easily spread to the entire market due to the high interconnection between different sectors and institutions (see Figure 4.1). Therefore, most local crises can be seen as potential triggers for a systemic crisis. Consequently, modern regulation is largely aimed at preventing local crises as well as limiting system interconnections.

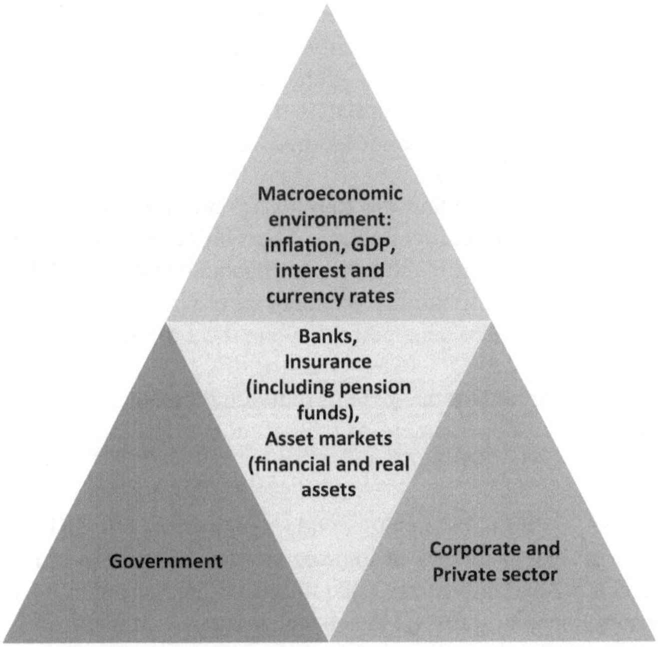

Figure 4.1 Financial system interlinkages (by the author).

Since there is no single definition of financial stability, there are also very different approaches to defining financial stability indicators. Given the conceptual complexity of financial stability, developments in financial stability cannot be summarized in a single quantitative indicator (Schinasi, 2004, p. 11). Financial stability is difficult to define through a simple variable, due to the complex interdependence of different elements that could affect stability within the financial system as well as within the real economy (Dattels et al., 2010, p. 6).

However, as financial stability is inherently the opposite value of a financial crisis, the indicators of the financial crisis can be used to define financial stability. Several examples of groups of indicators that are used to assess financial stability as well as indicators for assessing financial crisis (instability) can be put forward.

In addition to defining the indicators of financial stability or stress, it is important to define a benchmark. Borgioli et al. (2013, p. 19) argue that by analysing the behaviour of some relevant financial stress indicators as compared to their benchmark behaviour, it is possible to identify periods and countries where deviations are significant. The choice of the indicators, on the one hand, and of the benchmark, on the other hand, is therefore crucial for the results. Tables 4.2 and 4.3 provide some examples of indicators:

Confronting financial stress remains one of the major policy issues of the day. In the next section, we consider regulatory approaches that are intended to enhance financial stability.

Regulation structures: from microprudential to macroprudential

The regulation of individual financial institutions emerged long before the GFC. Basel Committee (The Internal Ratings-Based Approach. Consultative Document, 2001, p. 1) offered proposals for an internal ratings based approach (the IRB approach) to capital requirements for credit risk:

> The Committee believes that such an approach, which relies heavily upon a bank's internal assessment of its counterparties and exposures, can secure two key objectives consistent with those which support the wider review of The New Basel Capital Accord. The first is additional risk sensitivity, in that a capital requirement based on internal ratings can prove to be more sensitive to the drivers of credit risk and economic loss in a bank's portfolio. The second is incentive compatibility, in that an appropriately structured IRB approach can provide a framework which encourages banks to continue to improve their internal risk management practices.

Microprudential policies help maintain the stability of individual financial institutions, but do not provide insight into the systemic situation. The GFC demonstrated that microprudential policies were necessary but not sufficient to ensure financial stability. MaPs help to smooth the financial cycle and reduce the probability of financial crisis. This helps protect the economy from potential losses from a macro perspective beyond the individual concerns and then ensures stability at systemic level.

Financial risks may arise both at the level of individual financial institutions and at the level of the financial system. The development of regulation evolves in tandem with the increasing complexity of financial instruments and transactions.

> Micro-prudential supervision and market conduct regulation, etc., existed well before the global financial crisis and as indeed, in some economies, did macro-prudential policy. But the global financial crisis demonstrated that micro-prudential policy is necessary but not sufficient to ensure financial stability; hence the emergence of macro-prudential policy to complement micro-prudential policy with a more systemic perspective.
>
> (Heath and Goksu, 2017, p. 8)

Table 4.2 Examples of financial stability indicators

Borgioli et al. (2013)	*Heath and Goksu (2017)*	*Dattels et al. (2010)*
Profitability and efficiency • Return on equity (ROE)	1 Increasing the resilience of the financial system Financial institutions: - Deposit-takers - Non-bank financial institutions (with domestic/foreign and state/private breakdowns) Financial markets: - Money markets, securities, and derivatives markets - Interest rates and FX rates - Infrastructure and financial inclusion	A Monetary and financial conditions The availability and cost of funding linked to global monetary and financial conditions. i G-7 real short-term interest rate ii G-3 excess household and corporate liquidity iii Goldman Sachs global financial conditions index iv Growth of custodial reserve holdings at the Federal Reserve Bank of New York v G-3 bank lending conditions
Asset quality • Non-performing and doubtful loans and debt securities (percentage of total loans and debt securities) (NPL)	2 Containing the build-up systemic vulnerabilities: credit, debt, and asset prices Credit-related: - Credit growth - Type of credit - Connected, concentrated, and directed lending Debt-related: - Outstanding debt levels - Leverage ratios - Non-financial corporations, households, and governments Asset prices: - Real estate - Equity and bond prices	B Risk appetite The willingness of investors to take on additional risk by adjusting exposure to riskier asset classes, the consequent potential for increased losses, and implication for the functioning of broader financial markets i Merrill Lynch investor survey of risk appetite ii State street investor confidence index iii Total net inflows into emerging market bond and equity funds
Capital adequacy • Tier 1 (T1)	3 Structural vulnerabilities within the financial system: financial interconnections and spillovers Domestic and cross-border: - Financial interconnections within economies and across borders - Capital flows - Spillover analysis - International environment	C Macroeconomic risks Macroeconomic shocks with the potential to trigger a sharp market correction, given existing conditions in capital markets i Projection of global real GDP growth in the world economic outlook ii G-3 confidence indicators iii OECD composite leading indicators iv Implied global trade growth v Global breakeven inflation rate index vi Cost of protection against default on mature market sovereign debt

(*Continued*)

Table 4.2 (Continued)

Borgioli et al. (2013)	*Heath and Goksu (2017)*	*Dattels et al. (2010)*
Liquidity • Loans-to-deposits ratio		D Emerging market risks Risks to global financial stability stemming from emerging market asset classes, looking specifically at fundamentals in emerging markets and vulnerabilities to external risks i Estimated fundamental emerging market external debt spreads ii Emerging market sovereign credit quality iii Emerging market private sector credit growth iv Inflation volatility v Corporate credit spreads
Leverage • Assets-to-equity ratio		E Credit risks Credit exposures creating the potential for defaults that could produce losses in systemically important financial institutions as well as the corporate and household sectors i Merrill Lynch global high yield index spread ii Share of low-quality corporate debt iii Moody's speculative grade default rate iv Banking stability index v Loan delinquency rate vi Household obligation payment ratio F. Market and liquidity risks Market exposures of SIFIs and the potential for consequent mark-to-market losses, and the extent to which markets may be underpricing risk i Hedge fund leverage proxy ii Average net speculative positions in U.S. futures markets iii Estimated common component in asset class returns iv Equity risk premia v Composite volatility vi Funding and market liquidity index

Table 4.3 Examples of risk (instability) indicators

Adrian et al. (2013)	*Eidenberger (2014)*	*Pouvelle (2012)*
Standard measures of some of these factors for bank holding companies considered to be systemically important include regulatory capital and leverage ratios, asset liquidity, and wholesale short-term funding	Excessive credit growth	Stock market volatility
Market indicators, such as CDS premiums, equity prices, and expected default probabilities based on estimates of asset volatilities and liabilities	High returns of bank stocks	Bank stock price index volatility
Conditional Value at Risk is an estimate of the value at risk of the financial system conditional on a firm's distress, based on co-movement of equity prices in the lower tail of the firm's and market return distributions		Government bond yield spread
Network measures map interlinkages between firms, helps to identify key nodes or clusters, and can be used to simulate how a shock, such as the distress of a firm, could be amplified through the network		Libor-OIS spread

Table 4.4 Comparison of macro- and microprudential approaches (by Borio, 2003)

	Macroprudential	*Microprudential*
Proximate objective	Limit financial system-wide Distress	Limit distress of individual institutions
Ultimate objective	Avoid output (GDP) costs	Consumer (investor/depositor) protection
Characterization of Risk	Seen as dependent on collective behaviour ("endogenous")	Seen as independent of individual agents' behaviour ("exogenous")
Correlations and common exposures across institutions	Important	Irrelevant
Calibration of prudential controls	In terms of system-wide risk; top-down	In terms of risks of individual institutions; bottom-up

Therefore, Adrian et al. (2013, p. 2) note: "Macroprudential policies are designed to reduce vulnerabilities to mitigate the amplification of negative shocks, and also to pre-position institutions so that they can absorb shocks".

The different approaches to regulation at the micro and macro levels are not opposed to each other; indeed, they complement each other. Heath and Goksu (2017, p. 9) suggest that "it became increasingly obvious that micro-prudential analysts need macro data and macroprudential analysts need granular micro data, and they potentially benefit from each other's insights in order to identify emerging systemic risks and vulnerabilities". A comparison of micro- and macro-level approaches to financial regulation is presented by Borio (2003) and summarized in Table 4.4.

Recurring systemic crises require consideration of alternative sustainable models of financial regulation. The opposition between regulation associated with state power and market activity associated with private decisions leads to an opposition between regulation between micro-rational behaviour and macro-rational governance (Ülgen, 2022b). A compromise approach to regulation that ensures private and public interests may be polycentric market governance between tight government control and loosely regulated free markets. Ülgen (2022a) notes that in a decentralized regulatory system, the constituent entities should be governed by a comprehensive set of rules aimed at aligning the information and incentives of individual actors with broader social goals such as financial stability; these rules should be supported by mutually agreed monitoring procedures. Voss and Schroth (2018) argue that polycentric governance perspective acknowledges that, in addition to nation states, other initiatives contribute to the shaping of collective orders; they involve local governments, businesses, civil society organizations, and social movements. Thus, regulation/supervision of financial systems as a whole (macroprudential) is the responsibility of public authorities, in addition to markets/private actors. In some specific cases, elements of governance may be delegated to local institutions in order to increase the flexibility and speed of regulatory action (Ülgen, 2022a). Regulation is based on the identification of risk points, so the assessment of systemic risk is a critical component of choosing how to proceed with a regulatory approach. Systemic risk-generating activities are at the root of financial system vulnerabilities. Systemic risk can be defined as the probability of failures in financial institutions caused by asset impairments, potentially leading to serious negative consequences for the economy. Identifying vulnerabilities that could lead to a financial crisis is an important part of MaP. It is necessary to monitor not only individual financial institutions but also the financial system as a whole. Tools for identifying such risks include stress testing and EWS.

An important task is to react in advance to rising risks in the financial system. The use of EWS allows the timing of macroprudential measures to be optimal. There are challenges in the application of existing indicators. Researchers are also making proposals for new indicators to identify systemic risk. An important parameter for the effectiveness of an early warning signal is its ability to signal increased risk within a time frame sufficient to apply MaP measures.

There is no consensus on what exactly constitutes a warning signal of an upcoming systemic crisis. Early warning indicators include credit and asset price growth (Biljanovska et al., 2019), property price growth (Deghi et al., 2020), credit-to-GDP ratio (Drehmann and Yetman, 2020), exchange rate (Nier et al., 2020), and liquidity and interconnections between financial market participants (Heijmans and Wendt, 2020).

Biljanovska et al. (2019) found that asset price bubble accompanied with credit imbalance indicate financial crisis. They show that credit imbalances were excessive both before the 1987 and the 2008 systemic crises, but only in the latter case were they accompanied by overvalued asset prices, and asset price overvaluations can emerge even when credit is subdued, such as before the dot-com bubble in the early 2000s and – more strikingly – since 2014. Credit imbalance is measured by credit-to-GDP ratio. Asset price bubbles by themselves are also driven by credit.

Deghi et al. (2020) use nonlinear dynamic stochastic general equilibrium model with occasionally binding housing collateral constraints to offer a new methodology to predict downside risk to house prices and find it to be a useful early-warning indicator that can be used for financial stability surveillance. Drehmann and Yetman (2020) research credit-to-GDP ratio and find that credit gaps based on linear projections in real time perform poorly when based on country-by-country estimation, but as a panel, and impose the same coefficients on all economies, linear projections perform marginally better than the baseline credit-to-GDP gap.

Nier et al. (2020) use a sample of 62 economies over the period of 2000: Q1–2016: Q4, build dynamic panel regressions, and show that an appreciation of the local exchange rate is associated with a subsequent increase in the domestic credit gap. Heijmans and Wendt (2020) develop a composite risk indicator that combines data on liquidity risk and systemic impact through interconnections among participants in order to determine the criticality of individual participants.

The results of the studies reviewed suggest that early warning indicators are an important part of MaP, including influencing the choice of MaP instruments. There is much scope for research in this area, as existing indicators can be improved. And there is scope to propose new indicators that can be used as EWS.

Stress testing is a prudential policy tool. Typically, it is "what if" analysis. Stress testing is based on building of scenarios and is related with market discipline. Scenario must be plausible and should take into account procyclical behaviour. Different types of scenarios are correlated to different objectives. Results of stress tests are used for macro- and microprudential policy calibration. Macrofinancial imbalances include leverage, liquidity risk, risk mispricing, and maturity mismatch. Although the concept of stress testing is well developed, the authors still see certain directions for improving the quality of stress testing conducted by financial institutions. At the same time, some of the works are devoted to a review of existing stress-testing systems in various countries.

Jobst and Oura (2019) discuss four major steps in assessing the system-wide impact of sovereign risk: scope, loss estimation, shock calibration, and capital impact calculation. Górnicka and Valderrama (2020) present a semi-structural model of default risk. Authors use this model to simulate bank credit losses for stress-testing purposes and to calibrate borrower-based macroprudential tools. Budnik (2020) presents a new Banking Euro Area Stress Test model for assessing system-wide resilience while accounting for interactions between the financial sector and the real economy. Study group established by the BIS (2020) compares the stress-testing methodologies then used by the seven Latin American central banks that participated in the study group. Gross et al. (2020) present an integrated tool suite for IFRS 9 and Current Expected Credit Losses compatible estimation in top-down solvency stress tests. The research carried out and the suggestions made show that stress testing can offer options for improvement in order to provide a clear picture of the financial risks of institutions and the system as a whole.

Micro- and macroprudential regulation complement each other. The application of macroprudential approaches does not exclude dealing with risks at the level of individual financial institutions. To justify the use of a particular regulatory tool, a system for identifying potential risks must be developed. In the case of macroprudential regulation, such risk identification tools are EWS and stress testing. These methods are often not formalized by regulators and have a wide range of possibilities for suggestions for improvement.

Channels, tools, and effectiveness of macroprudential policy

MaPs are central bank policies aimed at ensuring systemic financial stability and increasing the resilience of the financial sector in face of macro shocks that could threaten the viability of monetary and financial structure, by building special capital buffers or covering losses in the event of a stress scenario. An important component of MaP is to resist the formation of market bubbles and to limit systemic risk-taking by financial institutions.

MaPs are designed to reduce vulnerabilities to mitigate negative system-wide shocks. For example, MaPs limit systemic risks by limiting credit growth in a particular sector of the economy when the evolution of markets could lead to systemic concerns. The accumulated experience in this area suggests that MaPs are a combination of risk-containment measures aimed at containing systemic risk.

The availability of diversified macroprudential tools to contain excessive systemic risk appears to be an important development trend of regulation. Numerous MaP instruments have now been developed, including countercyclical buffers, conservation capital requirements, leverage limits, loan loss provisions, limits on credit growth, loan restrictions, limits on foreign currency, limits on the loan-to-value (LTV) ratio, limits on the debt-service-to income ratio, liquidity requirements, limits on the loan-to-deposit ratio, limits on foreign exchange positions (LFX), reserve requirements, concept of SIFIs, and others. The interaction of MaP instruments deserves particular attention. This issue is the subject of research and is often interlinked with the issue of the effectiveness of measures. A consequence of this is the question of choosing the optimal set of MaP instruments by authorities.

Most of MaP working papers justify the effectiveness of MaP. There are studies that focus on the impact of MaPs on economic growth and compare the effectiveness of macroprudential and monetary policies as there is currently a wide range of MaP tools available; accordingly the studies and their results often differ with respect to the use of a particular instrument.

Basu et al. (2020) develop a model of optimal monetary policy, capital controls, foreign exchange intervention, and MaP. The authors built a model of a small open economy and mentioned that it is essential that instruments are considered jointly. Budnik (2020) studies 28 European Union countries from 1995 to 2017 and argues that the optimal choice of MaPs depends on the phase of the business cycle and on monetary policy stance. Ultimate effect of a macroprudential instrument on credit depends on monetary policy. This is an area that could be extensively researched, as the current set of MaP instruments is quite large. Cozzi et al. (2020) also draw attention to the interaction and effectiveness of macroprudential and monetary policies and find that MaP diminishes the frequency and severity of financial crises, thus eliminating the need for extremely low interest rates. Counter-cyclical capital measures reduce the neutral real interest rate in normal times.

Araujo et al. (2020) using meta-analysis techniques find that a tightening of MaP has statistically significant effects on credit. For instance, tightening limits on LTV or debt-service-to-income (DSTI) ratios produce similar average effects on reducing household credit but have weaker effects on house prices. A result of the paper is to point to stronger effects from tightening than loosening actions. Bergant et al. (2020) study emerging markets and note that tighter level of regulation reduces the sensitivity of GDP growth to VIX (CBOE Volatility Index) movements and capital flow shocks. It also constrains economic activity when global financial conditions are buoyant.

Researchers draw attention to the positive results in increasing financial sustainability, while at the same time having a negative impact on economic growth and activity. Belkhir et al. (2020) argue that the application of MaPs has a statistically and economically direct negative effect on the probability of banking crises and the same time depress economic growth and confirm this in the study. It seems to us important to continue research into the identification of signals for the optimal moment to apply MaP instruments. The moment at which it is possible to prevent an emerging financial crisis and at the same time to minimize the negative impact on economic growth.

Brandao-Marques et al. (2020) compare the effectiveness of macroprudential and monetary policy using cost-benefit analysis. The paper evaluates the net benefits of policies using quadratic loss functions, estimating policy effects on the full distribution of future output growth and inflation with quantile regressions. Tightening MaP is beneficial in net terms. By contrast, tightening monetary policy entails net losses. Buying foreign exchange or tightening capital controls has small net benefits.

The application of MaP instruments does not always achieve the intended effect. Galati et al. (2020) study the effects of credit restrictions on the balance sheet structure of banks and other financial institutions. Banks mainly respond to credit restrictions by making adjustments to the liability side of their balance sheets, particularly by increasing the proportion of long-term funding rather than cutting lending. Cappelletti et al. (2020) argue that higher capital buffers have a positive disciplinary effect by reducing banks' risk-taking while having an adverse impact on the real economy through a decrease banks' lending activity.

The issue of efficiency of MaP is being widely discussed; Xu et al. (2019) analyze how bank profitability impacts financial stability. Author concludes that "effective and timely implementation of the Basel III framework, the need for well-calibrated macroprudential tools, and to ensure that banks' reliance on wholesale funding and leverage remains prudentially manageable". Poghosyan (2019) assesses the effectiveness of lending restriction measures, such as LTV and DSTI ratios, assesses their dynamic association with house prices, and credit for up to 16 quarters. He finds an association between lending restrictions and target variables and argues that "macroprudential measures can be more effective if they are supported by monetary policy actions" (Poghosyan, 2019, p. 14).

Ferreira et al. (2019, p. 8) highlight common weaknesses that can undermine the effectiveness of the supervisory process, such as inappropriate institutional setting, lack of skilled resources, insufficient forward-looking analysis, lax credit risk standards, inappropriate liquidity risk standards and monitoring, weak corporate governance, and weak enforcement. The paper provides recommendations on how countries that are not members of the Basel Committee could incorporate capital and liquidity standards into their frameworks.

A large set of MaP instruments has been developed. Different instruments impact financial stability through different channels, based on capital requirements, liquidity-based, and borrower-based. The question of the choice of MaP instruments[2] and their effectiveness is relevant. Each paper reviewed above (Araujo et al., 2020; Basu et al., 2020; Belkhir et al., 2020; Brandao-Marques et al., 2020; Cappelletti et al., 2020; Ferreira et al., 2019; Galati et al., 2020; Poghosyan, 2019; Xu et al., 2019) discusses different MaP policy tools. This shows the diversity of the tools and the importance of each of them. At the same time, none of the papers considers the interaction of the different MaP instruments.

Macroprudential policy and monetary policy interaction

The interaction of macroprudential and monetary policy is one of the most popular issues studied. Both policies use similar variables and channels connected with credit. There is limited experience in the use of MaP to compare with monetary policy. Monetary policy is wider and focuses on price stability, inflation, and output gap, and covers all sectors of the economy. MaP is concentrated on the financial system's stability, smoothing the credit boom, and increasing the resilience of the financial system and covers mostly banking sector.

Before the GFC, the monetary authorities (central banks) predominantly focused on monetary policy (through inflation targeting, i.e. maintaining price stability) without acting on systemic financial stability as a policy objective of the regulation framework. The GFC has pointed out the weaknesses of such a policy path and brought forward the role of authorities in monetary and financial stability as an integrated framework. The question then arises: if monetary authorities focus now on systemic financial stability issues through MaP, what should the appropriate monetary policy be? Should the authorities still prioritize anti-inflationary monetary policy, while the core issue is not the inflation anymore but rather depression and uncovered financial crisis? Researchers show that the two policies have a reciprocal influence on each other. Applying the policies together means that the right balance between them has to be determined.

Adrian et al. (2020) argue that monetary policy that focuses purely on inflation and output-gap stabilization can lead to instability. Macroprudential measures can mitigate the intertemporal risk-return tradeoff created by the vulnerability channel. Authors extend the New Keynesian model to include endogenous risk. Corradin et al. (2020), using aggregate data, document that, prior to 2015, heightened financial market volatility coincided with worsening money market conditions, while higher central bank liquidity provision was associated with reduced money market stress. After 2015, the evidence is consistent with central bank asset purchases inducing scarcity effects in some money market segments and with active securities lending supporting money market functioning.

Altavilla et al. (2020) argue that there are strong complementarities between monetary policy and MaP in shaping the evolution of bank credit. Further research in this area would be interesting in order to identify specific points in time when the policy instruments should be applied so that they can support each other's effectiveness as much as possible. Hoerova et al. (2020, p. 35) find that liquidity tools are beneficial but cannot completely remove the need for Lender of Last Resort interventions by the central bank. Even if European banks had fully complied with the Basel III liquidity standards, they would have still required very substantial central bank liquidity assistance.

Some studies point to higher efficiency of MaP compared to monetary policy to provide financial stability. Martinez-Miera and Repullo (2019, p. 3) argue that MaP should be the primary tool for addressing risks to financial stability. Kockerols and Kok (2019, p. 1) suggest that an active use of MaPs targeting financial stability risks would alleviate the burden on monetary policy to "lean against the wind" and find that "MaP has net marginal benefits in addressing risks to financial stability in the euro area, whereas monetary policy has net marginal costs". Aikman et al. (2019, p. 2) show how deploying the countercyclical capital buffer to adjust bank capital requirements in response to changing risks substantially improves outcomes relative to when the interest rate is the only cyclical policy tool.

Raising interest rates does not always reduce the risk of financial institutions. Tightening monetary policy may increase the risks of the financial system. Experts (Adrian et al., 2020; Aikman et al., 2019; Altavilla et al., 2020; Hoerova et al., 2020) agree that joint modeling of the two policies is important because there is certainly an interaction of policies and each of them, individually and together, influence macroeconomic variables. In addition, their interaction is not completely understood at the moment. For example, Takáts and Temesvary (2019) argue that tighter MaP mitigates the lending impact of monetary policy (irrespective whether monetary policy tightens or eases) – whereas easier MaP amplifies the lending impact of monetary policy. Kim and Mehrotra (2019) argue that MaP shocks have effects on real GDP, the price level and credit that are very similar to those of monetary policy shocks, but the detailed transmission of the two policies is different. The response may vary from country to country.

Papers reviewed point to interaction between monetary and MaPs. Both policies use similar variables and channels connected with credit. There is no clear understanding of the joint use of these two policies. This is also due to limited experience in the use of MaP to compare with monetary policy. We can say that the ultimate goal of both policies is targeting systemic financial stability that is a necessary condition for the smooth functioning of the economy. Monetary policy is wider, focuses on the price stability, inflation, and output gap and covers all sectors of the economy, while MaP is concentrated on smoothing the credit boom, increasing the resilience of the financial system and covers banking sector. However, the aim of the MaP is to allow markets to function properly to support economic development. Therefore, MaPs are often considered as complementary to monetary policy. There is no doubt that macroprudential and monetary policies influence each other. The design and application of policy instruments should take account this mutual interaction.

Conclusion

Despite the fact that elements of counteraction to systemic financial crises have been applied for quite a long time, the issues of increasing financial stability still remain under multi-facet research programs. This is partly due to the change and complexity of the financial system and the emergence of new risks. Moreover, the systems that existed before 2008 have proved to be imperfect, and there is no evidence that the MaP measures used are definitely effective. Thus, the first Basel Accords to support financial stability (developed by the Bank for International Settlements) were developed in the 1980s; Basel II appeared in the late 1990s, developing approaches to supporting financial stability (capital requirements, supervisory process, disclosure of information). Despite the indicated developments in the field of financial stability regulation, Lehman Brothers went bankrupt in 2008 and the subsequent GFC occurred.

In response to the GFC, financial stability regulation was developing; in particular, more attention is paid to controlling the liquidity of financial institutions, and stress testing. The question remains whether the financial system is adequately protected from risks at the current moment, and whether MaP is effective enough. Some studies point to the costs of MaPs in terms of reduced credit supply to the business sector (Laeven et al., 2022), increased financial sector stability through reduced efficiency in the non-financial sector (Belkhir et al., 2022), increased risks in the non-banking sector (Adrian et al., 2022), and reduced economic growth potential (Laeven et al., 2022). Financial stability and financial crisis are opposite concepts, so the same indicators are used to measure financial stability or crisis. Due to the broad interpretation of the concept of financial stability, many indicators can be used to determine it. The absence of a single indicator of financial stability makes it difficult to assess the effectiveness of MaP measures.

Most researchers agree on the effectiveness of MaPs. However, many note the costs of such policies in terms of curbing credit, economic activity, and economic growth. At the same time, monetary policy faces a number of difficulties, and many researchers agree that MaP can largely complement monetary policy. Although these are two different policies, they mutually influence each other.

To increase the effectiveness of MaP, it is necessary to determine the spectrum by the criterion of financial stability/crisis and also adjust the calibration of MaP measures depending on the magnitude of the potential risk. It is obvious that both monetary and MaPs are necessary for balanced economic development and protection from financial crises.

Notes

1 A SIFI is a bank, insurance company, or other financial institution whose failure might trigger a financial crisis. They are colloquially referred to as "too big to fail".

2 A classification of macroprudential instruments can be provided following Alam et al. (2019, 25): Countercyclical Buffers, Conservation, Capital Requirements, Leverage Limits, Loan Loss Provisions, Limits on Credit Growth, Loan Restrictions (LoanR), Limits on Foreign Currency, Limits on the LTV Ratio, Limits on the DSTI Ratio, Tax Measures, Liquidity Requirements, Limits on the Loan-to-Deposit Ratio, LFX, Reserve Requirements, SIFI, and other.

References

Adrian, T., Covitz, D., & Liang, N. (2013). *Financial Stability Monitoring. Federal Reserve Bank of New York Staff Reports*. Staff Report No. 601. https://www.newyorkfed.org/medialibrary/media/research/staff_reports/sr601.pdf

Adrian, T., Duarte, F., Liang, N., & Zabczyk, P. (2020). *Monetary and Macroprudential Policy with Endogenous Risk*. IMF WP/20/236. https://www.imf.org/en/Publications/WP/Issues/2020/11/13/Monetary-and-Macroprudential-Policy-with-Endogenous-Risk-49885

Adrian, T., Natalucci, F. M., & Gureshi, M. S. (2022). *Macro-Financial Stability in the COVID-19 Crisis: Some Reflections*. IMF Working Paper WP/22/251. https://www.imf.org/en/Publications/WP/Issues/2022/12/16/Macro-Financial-Stability-in-the-COVID-19-Crisis-Some-Reflections-525739

Aikman, D., Giese, J., Kapadia, S., & McLeay, M. (2019). *Targeting Financial Stability: Macroprudential or Monetary Policy?* ECB 2278. https://www.ecb.europa.eu/pub/pdf/scpwps/ecb.wp2278~a3eb7fea61.en.pdf

Aikman, D., Haldane, A. G., & Kapadia, S. (2013). *Operationalising a Macroprudential Regime: Goals, Tools and Open Issues*. mfm.uchicago.edu/wp-content/uploads/2020/04/Aikman_Haldane_Kapadia_OPERATIONALISING-A-MACROPRUDENTIAL-REGIME-GOALS-TOOLS-AND-OPEN-ISSUES.pdf

Alam, Z., Alter, A., Eiseman, J., Gelos, G., Kang, H., Narita, M., Nier, E., & Wan, N. (2019). *Digging Deeper - Evidence on the Effects of Macroprudential Policies from a New Database*. IMF 1966. https://www.imf.org/en/Publications/WP/Issues/2019/03/22/Digging-Deeper-Evidence-on-the-Effects-of-Macroprudential-Policies-from-a-New-Database-46658

Altavilla, C., Laeven, L., & Peydró, J.-L. (2020). *Monetary and Macroprudential Policy Complementarities: Evidence from European Credit Registers*. ECB No. 2504. https://www.ecb.europa.eu/pub/pdf/scpwps/ecb.wp2504~2ea8ce96ed.en.pdf

Araujo, J., Patnam, M., Popescu, A., Valencia, F., & Yao, W. (2020). *Effects of Macroprudential Policy: Evidence from Over 6,000 Estimates*. IMF WP/20/67. https://www.imf.org/en/Publications/WP/Issues/2020/05/22/Effects-of-Macroprudential-Policy-Evidence-from-Over-6-000-Estimates-49440

Basu, S., Boz, E., Gopinath, G., Roch, F., & Unsal, F. (2020). *A Conceptual Model for the Integrated Policy Framework*. IMF WP/20/121. https://www.imf.org/en/Publications/WP/Issues/2020/07/07/A-Conceptual-Model-for-the-Integrated-Policy-Framework-49558

Belkhir, M., Ben Naceur, S., Candelon, B., & Wijnandts J.-C. (2020). *Macroprudential Policies, Economic Growth, and Banking Crises*. IMF WP/20/65. https://www.imf.org/en/Publications/WP/Issues/2020/05/22/Macroprudential-Policies-Economic-Growth-and-Banking-Crises-49264

Belkhir, M., Naceur, S. B., Candelon, B., & Wijnandts, J.-C. (2022). *Macroprudential Regulation and Sector-Specific Default Risk*. IMF Working Paper WP/22/141. https://www.imf.org/en/Publications/WP/Issues/2022/07/15/Macroprudential-Regulation-and-Sector-Specific-Default-Risk-520865

Bergant, K., Grigoli, F., Hansen, N.-J., & Sandri, D. (2020). *Dampening Global Financial Shocks: Can Macroprudential Regulation Help (More Than Capital Controls)?* IMF WP/20/106. https://www.imf.org/en/Publications/WP/Issues/2020/06/26/Dampening-Global-Financial-Shocks-Can-Macroprudential-Regulation-Help-More-than-Capital-49516

Biljanovska, N., Górnicka, L., & Vardoulakis, A. (2019). *Optimal Macroprudential Policy and Asset Price Bubbles*. IMF 19184. https://www.imf.org/en/Publications/WP/Issues/2019/08/30/Optimal-Macroprudential-Policy-and-Asset-Price-Bubbles-48591

BIS. (2020). *Stress Testing in Latin America: A Comparison of Approaches and Methodologies*. No. 108. https://www.bis.org/publ/bppdf/bispap108.htm

Borgioli, S., Gouveia, A. C., & Labanca, C. (2013). *Financial Stability Analysis Insights Gained from Consolidated Banking Data for the EU*. ECB. https://www.ecb.europa.eu/pub/pdf/scpops/ecbocp140.pdf

Borio, C. (2003). *Towards a Macroprudential Framework for Financial Supervision and Regulation?* BIS Working Papers No. 128. https://www.bis.org/publ/work128.pdf

Brandao-Marques, L., Gelos, G., Narita, M., & Nier, E. (2020). Leaning against the Wind: A Cost-Benefit Analysis for an Integrated Policy Framework. IMF WP/20/123. https://www.imf.org/en/Publications/WP/Issues/2020/07/07/Leaning-Against-the-Wind-A-Cost-Benefit-Analysis-for-an-Integrated-Policy-Framework-49554

Budnik, K. (2020). The Effect of Macroprudential Policies on Credit Developments in Europe 1995–2017. ECB No. 2462. https://www.ecb.europa.eu/pub/pdf/scpwps/ecb.wp2462~e8ceacd6b0.en.pdf

Cappelletti, G., Ponte Marques, A., Salleo, & Martín, D. V. (2020). How Do Banking Groups React to Macroprudential Policies? Cross-border Spillover Effects of Higher Capital Buffers on Lending, Risk-Taking and Internal Markets. ECB No. 2497. https://www.ecb.europa.eu/pub/pdf/scpwps/ecb.wp2497~4442c0a2d8.en.pdf

Cihak, M. (2006). How Do Central Banks Write on Financial Stability? IMF Working Paper. WP/06/163. https://www.imf.org/external/pubs/ft/wp/2006/wp06163.pdf

Čihák, M. (2007). *Central Banks and Financial Stability: A Survey*. IMF.

Corradin, S., Eisenschmidt, J., Hoerova, M., Linzert, T., Schepens, G., & Sigaux, J.-D. (2020). Money Markets, Central Bank Balance Sheet and Regulation. ECB No. 2483. https://www.ecb.europa.eu/pub/pdf/scpwps/ecb.wp2483~24d0fb56ec.en.pdf

Cozzi, G., Darracq Pariès, M., Karadi, P., Körner, J., Kok, C., Mazelis, F., Nikolov, K., Rancoita, E., Van der Ghote, A., & Weber, J. (2020). Macroprudential Policy Measures: Macroeconomic Impact and Interaction with Monetary Policy. ECB No. 2376. https://www.ecb.europa.eu/pub/pdf/scpwps/ecb.wp2376~7e9a0cae47.en.pdf

Dattels, P., McCaughrin, R., Miyajima, K., & Puig, J. (2010). Can You Map Global Financial Stability? IMF Working Paper. WP/10/145. https://www.imf.org/en/Publications/WP/Issues/2016/12/31/Can-You-Map-Global-Financial-Stability-23947

Das, U. S., Quintyn, M., & Chenard, K. (2004). Does Regulatory Governance Matter for Financial System Stability? An Empirical Analysis. IMF Working Paper. WP/04/89. https://www.imf.org/external/pubs/ft/wp/2004/wp0489.pdf

Deghi, A., Katagiri, M., Shahid, S., & Valckx, N. (2020). Predicting Downside Risks to House Prices and Macro-Financial Stability. IMF Working Paper. WP/20/11.

Drehmann, M., & Yetman, J. (2020). Which credit gap is better at predicting financial crises? A comparison of univariate filters. BIS Working Papers No 878 . https://www.bis.org/publ/work878.pdf

Eidenberger, J. (2014). What Predicts Financial (In)Stability? A Bayesian Approach. Deutsche Bundesbank. No. 36/2014. https://www.bundesbank.de/resource/blob/703882/a3a26bf1c3175b30f01db43406378bbd/mL/2014-12-18-dkp-36-data.pdf

Fecht, F. (2003). On the Stability of Different Financial Systems. Economic Research Center of the Deutsche Bundes Bank. Diskussian Paper 10/03. https://www.bundesbank.de/resource/blob/703112/84ac2f7207a9aeca62c68fd3888dce1b/mL/2003-05-14-dkp-10-data.pdf

Ferreira, C., Jenkinson, N., & Wilson, C. (2019). From Basel I to Basel III: Sequencing Implementation in Developing Economies. IMF 19127. https://www.imf.org/en/Publications/WP/Issues/2019/06/14/From-Basel-I-to-Basel-III-Sequencing-Implementation-in-Developing-Economies-46895

Galati, G., Kakes, J., & Moessner, R. (2020). Effects of Credit Restrictions in the Netherlands and Lessons for Macroprudential Policy. BIS No. 872. https://www.bis.org/publ/work872.htm

Górnicka, L., & Valderrama, L. (2020). Stress Testing and Calibration of Macroprudential Policy Tools. IMF WP/20/165. https://www.imf.org/en/Publications/WP/Issues/2020/08/14/Stress-Testing-and-Calibration-of-Macroprudential-Policy-Tools-49677

Gross, M., Laliotis, D., Leika, M., & Lukyantsau, P. (2020). Expected Credit Loss Modeling from a Top-Down Stress Testing Perspective. IMF WP/20/111. https://www.imf.org/en/Publications/WP/Issues/2020/07/03/Expected-Credit-Loss-Modeling-from-a-Top-Down-Stress-Testing-Perspective-49545

Heath, R., & Goksu, E. B. (2017). Financial Stability Analysis: What Are the Data Needs? IMF Working Paper. WP/17/153. https://www.imf.org/en/Publications/WP/Issues/2017/07/10/Financial-Stability-Analysis-What-are-the-Data-Needs-45013

Heijmans, R., & Wendt, F. (2020). Measuring the Impact of a Failing Participant in Payment Systems. IMF Working Paper No. 20/81. https://papers.ssrn.com/sol3/papers.cfm?abstract_id=3652500#

Hoerova, M., Mendicino, C., Nikolov, K., Schepens, G., & Van den Heuvel, S. (2020). Benefits and Costs of Liquidity Regulation. ECB No. 2169. https://www.ecb.europa.eu/pub/pdf/scpwps/ecb.wp2169.en.pdf

Jobst, A. A., & Oura, H. (2019). Sovereign Risk in Macroprudential Solvency Stress Testing. IMF 19266. https://www.imf.org/en/Publications/WP/Issues/2019/12/06/Sovereign-Risk-in-Macroprudential-Solvency-Stress-Testing-48768

Kim, S., & Mehrotra, A. (2019). Examining Macroprudential Policy and Its Macroeconomic Effects – Some New Evidence. BIS 825. https://www.bis.org/publ/work825.htm

Kockerols, T., & Kok, C. (2019). Leaning against the Wind: Macroprudential Policy and the Financial Cycle. ECB 2223. https://www.ecb.europa.eu/pub/pdf/scpwps/ecb.wp2223.en.pdf

Laeven, L., Maddaloni, A., & Mendicino, C. (2022). Monetary Policy, Macroprudential Policy and Financial Stability. ECB Discussion Papers. No. 2647. https://www.ecb.europa.eu/pub/pdf/scpwps/ecb.wp2647~0a0b3030e1.en.pdf

Martinez-Miera, D., & Repullo, R. (2019). Monetary Policy, Macroprudential Policy, and Financial Stability. ECB 2297. https://www.ecb.europa.eu/pub/pdf/scpwps/ecb.wp2297~934ae5f81a.en.pdf

Minsky, H. (1992). The Financial Instability Hypothesis. The Jerome Levy Economics Institute of Bard College. Working Paper No. 74. https://www.levyinstitute.org/pubs/wp74.pdf

Nier, E. W., Olafsson, T. T., & Gao Rollinson, Y. (2020). Exchange Rates and Domestic Credit - Can Macroprudential Policy Reduce the Link? IMF WP/20/187. https://www.imf.org/en/Publications/WP/Issues/2020/09/11/Exchange-Rates-and-Domestic-Credit-Can-Macroprudential-Policy-Reduce-the-Link-49725

Poghosyan, T. (2019). How Effective Is Macroprudential Policy? Evidence from Lending Restriction Measures in EU Countries. IMF 1945. https://www.imf.org/en/Publications/WP/Issues/2019/03/01/How-Effective-is-Macroprudential-Policy-Evidence-from-Lending-Restriction-Measures-in-EU-46640

Pouvelle, C. (2012). Evidence from French Banks. IMF Working Paper. WP/12/103. https://www.imf.org/external/pubs/ft/wp/2012/wp12103.pdf

Schinasi, G. J. (2004). Defining Financial Stability. IMF Working Paper. WP/04/187. https://www.imf.org/external/pubs/ft/wp/2004/wp04187.pdf

Takáts, E., & Temesvary, J. (2019). How Does the Interaction of Macroprudential and Monetary Policies Affect Cross-Border Bank Lending? BIS 782. https://www.bis.org/publ/work782.pdf

The Internal Ratings-Based Approach. Consultative Document (2001). Basel Committee on Banking Supervision. https://www.bis.org/publ/bcbsca05.pdf

Ülgen, F. (2020). Public Good, Public Action and Financial Regulation. *Annals of Public and Cooperative Economics*, vol. 92(1), pp. 147–167. DOI: 10.1111/apce.12308.

Ülgen, F. (2021). Financial Regulation: From Commodification to Public Action. *Journal of Economic Issues*, 55:2, 531–538. DOI: 10.1080/00213624.2021.1913379.

Ülgen, F. (2022a). From the Crisis of Financialization to the COVID Crisis: In Search of a Collective Action between Market and State. *Journal of Economic Issues*, 56:2, 584–591. DOI: 10.1080/00213624.2022.2065859

Ülgen, F. (2022b). *From Public Choice to Minskyan Collective Action: The Case for Macro Rationality-Based Financial Regulation. A Modern Guide to Post-Keynesian Institutional Economics*, edited by C. J. Whalen, 321–338. Edward Elgar Pubishing.

Voss, J. P., & Schroth, F. (2018). *The Politics of Innovation and Learning in Polycentric Governance. Governing Climate Change. Polycentricity in Action?* Cambridge University Press.

Xu, T. T., Hu, K., & Das, U. S. (2019). Bank Profitability and Financial Stability. IMF 1905. https://www.imf.org/en/Publications/WP/Issues/2019/01/11/Bank-Profitability-and-Financial-Stability-46470

5 Economic barriers to green transition

Inga Kononovich

Introduction

For the last 50 years, growing production capacities and energy consumption worldwide have been one of the factors contributing to increased greenhouse gas (GHG) emissions[1] and other pollutants globally. These issues have negative impacts on climate and economic and social well-being worldwide. According to the Intergovernmental Panel on Climate Change (IPCC) Sixth Assessment Report, human-caused climate change has increased the frequency and intensity of extreme weather events globally. The estimated cost of extreme events partly or wholly attributable to climate change is $143 billion per year over the past two decades (IPCC, 2023). The implementation of green economy elements is essential for the future vitality of national economies. In response to the growing challenges, some countries have started to implement "green" tools for reducing carbon emissions and improving energy efficiency. These tools have become part of national climate policies, which are closely linked to the green transition. Nowadays, the most effective climate policies are concentrated in developed economies (UN Environment Programme [UNEP], 2024a). Nevertheless, both developing and developed countries still face specific economic barriers to the green transition.

Another important issue is the coordination of the green transition at the international level. There are many international environmental, sustainable, and climate agreements, but they do not fully meet the needs of all countries. Although the agreements promote various instruments for green transition and set climate, ecological, and sustainable goals, they are often not met; the agreements themselves tend to be more symbolic than truly effective.

This chapter lists the main economic barriers to the green transition, with special attention paid to emerging market economies that possess significant natural and human capital. Analyzing these barriers is important for creating national and international development strategies, climate policies, and regulations.

Review of related studies

Currently, issues related to climate change, energy efficiency, regulation of GHG emissions, and the development of the green economy are receiving increasing attention from both scientific communities and international organizations and governments. A growing number of countries are incorporating various aspects of the green economy into their long-term strategies and plans. In 2024, over 140 countries, covering 88% of global emissions, have made national net-zero commitments (United Nations, n.d.-a). Despite this, there is still a lack of consensus on the definition of the green economy and a unified approach to the green transition concept.

DOI: 10.4324/9781003663539-6

Despite the fact that the concept of the green economy is relatively "young," its evolution has been quite rapid and complex. One of the earliest studies on the green economy was conducted by Pierce D., Marcandya A., and Barbier E. in their work "The Green Economy Project" (Pearce, 1989) published in 1989. The concept of "green growth" (United Nations, 2005), introduced in 2005 during the Fifth Ministerial Conference on Environment and Development in Asia-Pacific in Seoul, for the first time included aspects of the relationship between social issues and climate change.

Among other theories that have significantly contributed to the development of social and infrastructure aspects of the green economy concept, the theory of sustainable development is worth mentioning. This theory was developed and presented as part of the major research program "Research for Sustainable Development" (United Nations, 1987).

In current research, scientists view the interconnection between environmental, social, and economic factors as the "green economy." With regard to the development of the green economy, international organizations and scholars examine a variety of green obstacles or barriers. These barriers primarily have economic and social characteristics and are mostly concentrated in emerging markets (International Finance Corporation, n.d.).

Two fundamental principles are laid in the formation of green economic systems. They are that prices more accurately reflect environmental values and guarantee that all individuals have access to fundamental amenities and means of livelihood (Khor, 2010). To establish the green economy, it is essential to transition to a new model of economic development. This is referred to as the green transition. The concept of "green transition" is highly ambiguous. This transition implies a transformation of all economic activities and sectors. Nowadays, the green transition has effectively started to be launched in most countries through the Paris Agreement and the Agenda 2030 with its Sustainable Development Goals (SDGs).

Climate policy is a public administration tool for implementing measures for this green transition. The problem is that the gap between current climate policies and demand has widened. Despite the rapid introduction of regulatory measures in many countries, there is no unified set of green principles. The economic, social, and environmental challenges faced by different countries vary greatly. Some countries incorporate more social considerations into their policies, while others prioritize economic and environmental factors. In this context, addressing the barriers to the green transition is a pressing issue.

Global deregulations during the green transition

This chapter lists the main economic barriers to the green transition, with special attention given to the growing emerging market economies. Economic barriers to achieving the goals set by international climate and environmental agreements frame the future green development of national economies.

NDCs should be more sufficient to achieve the goals of the Paris Agreement. Among the international treaties, the most significant agreement that obligates countries to implement certain aspects of the green economy is the Paris Agreement. The Paris Agreement strengthens the global response to the threat of climate change by pursuing three main objectives: limiting the increase in global average temperature, enhancing adaptation to climate impacts, and aligning financial flows with low-emission development pathways (International and Comparative Law Research Center, 2024). All the goals mentioned above are subject to ongoing discussions within the context of climate negotiations. To achieve the goals of the Paris Agreement, countries (each Party of the Agreement) need to record their commitments in the form of a Nationally Determined Contribution (NDC). In NDCs, countries outline the planned measures for reducing

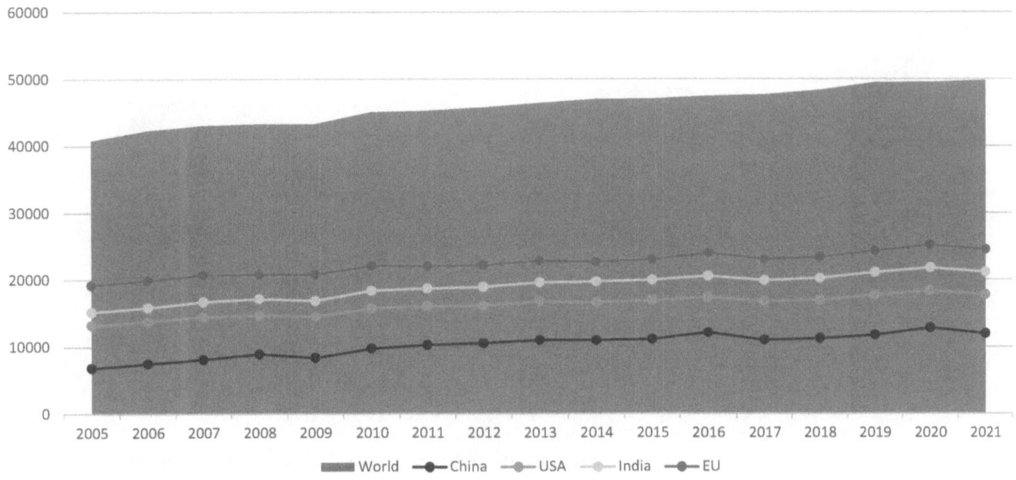

Figure 5.1 GHG emissions, 2005–2021.

Source: Climate Watch (n.d.).

GHG emissions, which should be updated every five years and be more ambitious than the previous ones (United Nations, 2015).

To achieve the Paris Agreement goal of 1.5°C, the necessary reduction of GHG emissions is estimated at 45% from 2019 emission levels by 2030 and by 85% in 2050; to achieve the goal of below 2°C above pre-industrial levels, it is necessary to reduce GHG emissions by 20% from 2019 emission levels by 2030 and by 65% in 2050 (IPCC, 2023). However, over the past 20 years, there has been only an increase in global GHG emissions. Global GHG emissions rose by more than 22% until 2005, with the fastest growth occurring in large developing countries (India and China), which saw an increase of more than 70% until 2005 (see Figure 5.1).

The UNEP estimates confirm that, by 2030, only CO_2 emissions will exceed 23 billion tons. This is the maximum amount that can be emitted in order to limit global warming to 2°C above pre-industrial levels (UNEP, 2024a).

One of the economic barriers to the green transition regarding the achievement of the aims of the Paris Agreement is that **countries' NDCs, even if fully implemented, are not sufficient to limit the increase in global average temperatures to 1.5°C**. According to UNEP assumptions, the continuation of the mitigation effort implied by current policies is estimated to limit global warming to a maximum of 3.1°C over the course of the century. These projections highlight the crucial impact of immediate action on likely temperature outcomes and the need for enhanced support to enable countries to achieve their NDCs (UNEP, 2024a).

In this respect, it is essential not only to increase additional efforts to address global warming but also to enhance existing mechanisms and strategies for implementing climate policies. The most effective examples of climate measures can be found as a combination of policy instruments, mostly in developed countries within the construction and industrial sectors (see Figure 5.2) (Stechemesser et al., 2024).

The problem is that the largest increase in GHG emissions has been observed in developing countries. Their governments have not yet sufficiently utilized the potential of NDCs and Long-Term Low Emission Development Strategies (LT-LEDS) to communicate plans and

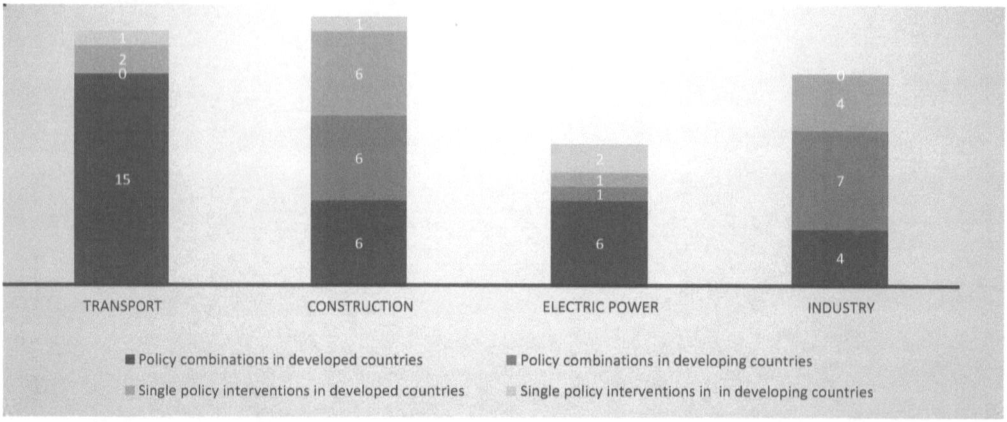

Figure 5.2 Evaluation of the climate policies' impact in developed and developing countries.
Source: Stechemesser et al. (2024).

targets supporting a transition away from fossil fuels due to the specifics of their economies (Jones et al., 2023). Moreover, most industries could abate only between 10% and 60% of their carbon emissions without incurring additional costs (World Economic Forum, 2024). Deregulations in the markets for fossil fuels and other natural resources are slowing down the process of transitioning to a more sustainable economy. To achieve the Paris Agreement's goals, a sharp decline in fossil fuel emissions is also necessary. Fossil CO_2 emissions account for approximately 68% of current GHG emissions, which are mostly driven by the combustion of coal, oil, and gas in the energy sector, as well as industrial processes associated with the manufacture of metals, cement, and other materials (UNEP, 2024b). Additionally, the energy transition is changing the materials landscape.

One of the economic barriers to green transition is the **deregulation of markets for fossil fuels and other natural resources**. This means that the global use of natural resources is characterized by fundamental inequalities, with a disproportionate environmental burden shifting to lower-income countries. According to the Global Resources Outlook 2024 (UNEP, 2024b), the environmental impact of high-income countries on climate change is ten times greater than that of lower-income nations. Developed countries continue to negatively impact climate, biodiversity, and water resources in developing countries through their importation of goods. Developed countries consume more than 40% of the annual world volume of mineral raw materials but produce less than 20% of the world volume (McKinsey & Company, 2024). Some developed countries are solely dependent on other countries' natural resources. For instance, China provides 100% of the EU's supply of heavy rare earth elements, Turkey provides 98% of the EU's supply of boron, and South Africa provides 71% of the EU's needs for platinum (European Council, n.d.). To protect industries and hedge against risks of supply disruption, some developed countries are enacting new policies, which will also impact the global materials landscape. For example, in November 2023, the EU reached a provisional agreement on a European Critical Raw Materials Act. It aims to regionalize extraction, processing, and recycling for more than 15 strategic raw materials by setting targets for local production and limiting single-country dependency to 65% for imports of each strategic raw material (McKinsey & Company, 2024).

The BRICS countries have an advantage in terms of their share in the world production of metals necessary for high technologies: 79% of aluminum production and 77% of palladium production, 44.35% of the world's oil reserves (Robson, 2023). Supply chains continue to be geographically concentrated. A handful of regions dominate mining (China, South Africa, Indonesia, and Chile), while China is the leader in refining (McKinsey & Company, 2024). Fossil fuels and materials mining are not only the main source of revenue for these countries but also create a significant number of employment opportunities in developing countries. For example, in South Africa, most jobs are provided by the coal-fired electricity industry, and due to the high dependence on coal production in many areas, the energy transition is seen not only as a necessity but also as a potential social threat. In addition to the net flow of material, energy, and natural resources from these countries, environmental and debt burdens are also transferred to regions that are extracting natural resources. Therefore, many developing countries possess natural resources and face the urgent need to decarbonize their industries, which entails both financial investments and the training of a substantial portion of their population. At the same time, many developed countries are widening their technological lead and implementing measures to protect their national economies. Therefore, in order to achieve the green transition, it is essential to strike a balance such that the elimination of climate change-related systemic risk does not exacerbate systemic risks related to inequality and poverty in developing countries.

Financial gap remains a major barrier to the green transition. Although annual investment flows in energy are predicted to rise fivefold by 2050 (International Renewable Energy Agency, 2023), there is an emerging trend: the exclusion of "polluting" companies from sustainable investment portfolios. For example, the French government implemented a standard in March 2024 that will prohibit fossil fuel companies from being part of investment funds labeled as "socially responsible investments" (Verney & Verney, 2023). The current topic of discussion is whether the exclusion of "polluting" companies may actually worsen the situation regarding decarbonization efforts. After all, it is possible to decarbonize such industries, but this requires global modernization and financial support; thus, the development of the concept of "transition finance" is necessary. This decision will provide support for high-emission sectors during their green transition process.

For the first time, the concept of transition finance was proposed by the second Sustainable Finance Working Group during the G20 Summit in Indonesia in 2022. This new concept aims to improve sustainable financial instruments to strengthen accessibility and affordability, including access to sustainable financial markets globally (Indonesia Economic Forum, 2022). Currently, the concept of transition finance has been incorporated into some national and regional plans for net-zero in mostly developed economies, although there is no active promotion of this approach in developing countries. The lack of consensus on how to define and approach sustainable, green, and transition finance creates the potential for greenwashing, which can ultimately hinder the successful implementation of green initiatives. Banks and other financial institutions could support businesses by providing green transition loans. Developing the market for transition finance would benefit not only institutional investors but also the general public, as transition finance instruments could facilitate the implementation of challenging green infrastructure projects and attract additional investors.

Finance is a driver of the green transition, but not only in the energy sector. There is a new trend towards reallocating financial resources from investments in fossil fuels to investments in green technologies. According to the McKinsey Global Energy Perspective 2023, between 0.5% and 0.8% of GDP in 2040 will be deployed in fossil fuels, while more than 0.8% of GDP will be concentrated in green and decarbonization technologies (McKinsey & Company, 2023). According to the International Energy Agency's Net Zero Roadmap for the Global Energy Sector, investments in fuel production and fossil fuel technology are predicted to decline by more than half by 2050. Total capital spending on green technologies and traditional oil and gas operations averages $650 billion per year over 2021–2050, just less than the annual investment in oil and gas projects between 2016 and 2020 (International Energy Agency, 2021). Currently, there is an increase in green investment flows worldwide, and there are positive trends in their growth. 17 advanced green technologies could create a market worth more than $9.5 trillion by 2030, about three times the current size of the Indian economy (United Nations Conference on Trade and Development [UNCTAD], 2023). The market value of green technologies is expected to increase fourfold by 2030, and the market value of electric vehicle production will increase fivefold by 2030 (UNCTAD, 2023). There is a significant need for technological development in the least developed and developing countries. The total exports of green technologies from developed countries jumped from around $60 billion in 2018 to over $156 billion in 2021. In the same period, exports from developing nations rose from $57 billion to only about $75 billion. In three years, developing countries' share of global exports fell from over 48% to under 33% (UNCTAD, 2023). Thus, the barrier is that investments in green technologies are mostly concentrated in developed countries and China.

Carbon pricing could serve as a tool for accelerating the green transition. Carbon pricing is another effective way to incorporate the costs of climate change into economic decision-making. Robust carbon trading could cut the cost of implementing NDCs by more than half—by as much as $250 billion—by 2030 (InvestCorp, 2024). Since its introduction, carbon markets have significantly grown to an estimated aggregate trading volume of $978 billion in 2022, compared with the 2012–2017 average size of approximately $55 billion annually. The Global Carbon Markets are expected to reach $2.7 trillion by 2028 (McKinsey & Company, 2023). Emissions Trading Systems and carbon taxes are implemented or under consideration in 75 countries in 2024, covering about 24% of global emissions (World Bank Group, 2024a). In 2024–2025, Brazil, India, Chile, Colombia, and Türkiye are making strides in carbon pricing implementation.

Furthermore, analysts forecast that the carbon assets market will expand to $100 billion by the year 2030, revealing that a $100 billion carbon market could protect 150 million hectares of land, equivalent to the size of Peru, and drive $700 billion in annual investments in carbon projects. Analysts also estimate that such a market could support 12.4 million jobs in forestry, nearly 3 million in sustainable agriculture, 310,000 in renewables, and 50,000 in adjacent industries. The implied price of CO_2 will be more than $180/t$CO_2$ to achieve the 1.5°C trajectory in time, and it will be more than $150/t$CO_2$ to achieve net-zero commitments by leading economies at a slower pace (McKinsey & Company, 2023). Article 6 mechanisms of the Paris Agreement provide the framework for international carbon markets and the interstate exchange of outcomes from climate projects (United Nations Framework Convention on Climate Change [UNFCCC], 2025). Nevertheless, there remains ambiguity regarding the equilibrium between supply and demand for carbon assets. The uncertainties surrounding international carbon markets' regulations and standards have become another economic barrier to the green transition. Different regional- and state-level compliance markets in developing and developed countries have led to deregulation and slowed down the achievement of global climate goals.

Sectoral initiatives could be a tool for improving global carbon market regulations and Article 6 carbon mechanisms. An example of this is the Carbon Offsetting and Reduction Scheme for International Aviation (CORSIA). CORSIA uses a baseline year and requires international flights to either align with the baseline through technological improvements, operational improvements, and sustainable aviation fuels, or to offset any emissions above the baseline. To ensure environmental integrity, CORSIA has an approved list of criteria that must be met for offsets to be eligible. While more ambitious goals are needed to bring aviation in line with the Paris Agreement, it is an important first step for the sector (International Civil Aviation Organization, n.d.). Despite the fact that CORSIA envisages the use of carbon units within the framework of Article 6 of the Paris Agreement under the UNFCCC, the mechanisms for system interconnection have yet to be developed.

Specific green barriers for emerging market countries

Emerging market countries are large, developing economies. These countries possess significant reserves of natural resources and have vast territorial areas and populations. Their impact on the green transition is considerable, as their share of GHG emissions from fossil fuel combustion has exceeded 50%. Additionally, these countries experience rapid economic growth. These countries account for about 30% of global GDP and 45% of the global population. They serve as a model for other developing nations. As a result, addressing barriers to the green transition in these nations can significantly expedite the overall process of transitioning towards a more sustainable future.

However, given the high rates of population growth and the numerous unresolved infrastructure challenges, these economies also require financing for infrastructure development. Infrastructure challenges in most developing countries include a lack of access to basic healthcare and educational services for the majority of the population, as well as a shortage of skilled workers and inadequate access to clean water and sanitation. According to World Bank data, the percentage of vulnerable employment (defined as employment in informal sectors) in many developing countries was more than 50% in 2022, compared to less than 15% in developed countries. Additionally, the availability of basic infrastructure, such as electricity, roads, and telecommunications, was less than 75% in developing countries in 2022, while it was more than 95% in most developed countries (World Bank Group, 2024b).

The SDGs (United Nations, n.d.-b) are of particular relevance to developing countries. These goals officially came into force on 1 January 2016 and comprise 17 objectives to be achieved by 2030, most of which address current challenges faced by developing nations in terms of development. Goals 12 and 13, in particular, are directly linked to the green transition and climate policies. The drop in international project finance will exacerbate the $4 trillion gap in investment needed to meet the SDGs in developing countries (World Bank Group, 2024b). Developing countries will need to invest about $2.5 trillion annually until 2030 to develop infrastructure (electricity, transport, water supply, and sanitation); this is equivalent to 4.5%–8% of the GDP of developing economies (World Bank, 2023). The financial need for infrastructure modernization in developing countries is significant. This can negatively impact the development of innovative industries, science and technology, and green economy sectors. Thus, for many developing countries, the green transition is accompanied by infrastructure growth and development. The integration of the SDGs with the green transition represents a viable solution, particularly in terms of financing this transition. Individual countries that reduce GHG emissions can also experience significant immediate benefits by advancing several SDGs (International Monetary Fund et al., 2024).

In 2023, the UN established a special group (the Expert Group on Climate and SDG Synergy) to assess the critical interconnections between the SDGs and climate agendas (United Nations Department of Economic and Social Affairs, n.d.). According to the report of the expert group, only 15% of the SDGs will have been achieved by 2030 (United Nations, 2024). The report emphasizes the need for further development of measures to enhance the synergy between the SDGs and climate. Despite the assessment of the potential of the green transition pathway by international organizations through regulatory frameworks, this pathway has not yet been fully developed. For developing economies, this represents a significant barrier to the green transition, given their specific socio-economic circumstances and infrastructure challenges. Thus, a specific barrier to the green transition for developing economies is **the absence of coordinated implementation of climate tools related to the SDGs** in these countries. Additionally, it is important to note the significance of measures that consider the unique development contexts.

Conclusion

The green transition is an essential stage in the further socio-economic development of nations. However, the new policy instruments, which include environmental aspects, have not yet been effective enough and require coordination at both the national and international levels. Climate policy is an important new element in most long-term strategies for countries' development. Effective implementation of climate policies will allow countries to transition to a green economy with minimal economic losses. This chapter provides an analysis of barriers to the green transition and proposes measures to address them. Table 5.1 is provided below, outlining these barriers and suggesting relevant actions at both international and national levels.

Summing up all the previous points, the main barriers to the green transition are concentrated in developing countries. These countries have not yet fully exploited the potential of their national development plans. The shutdown of fossil fuel companies may have irreversible socio-economic consequences for many of them. In addition, a significant part of green investment is concentrated in developed countries, while investment needs are in developing countries, with the specificities of linking these financial flows to infrastructure. That's why the green transition of them requires accelerated cooperation between the international scientific

Table 5.1 Actions for overcoming economic barriers to green transition and their potential risks

Economic barriers to green transition	*Most vulnerable group*	*Proposed solutions, measures*	*Risks*
Countries' NDCs, even if fully implemented, are not sufficient to limit the increase in global average temperatures to 1.5°C	All countries	The establishment of international expert and analytical platforms for: 1 Monitoring the progress of countries towards achieving the goals of the Paris Agreement; 2 Assessing the effectiveness of climate policies, including the identification of combinations of measures for their further implementation in NDCs 3.0	Serious environmental issues and climate change will impact not only the environment but also the socio-economic development of countries. This could lead to a significant rise in healthcare costs, decreased productivity among the population, and mass migration.
Deregulation in markets for fossil fuels and other natural resources	Mostly countries that extract natural resources	1 The creation of an international database on global resource use. 2 Enhancing energy efficiency in infrastructure. 3 Facilitating and promoting transition finance among institutional, national, and foreign investors as an effective way to accelerate the decarbonization of "polluting" industries.	1 Slowing down the transition to a more sustainable and environmentally friendly society in countries that extract natural resources. 2 Serious depletion of natural resources and environmental degradation. 3 Decline in the standard of living for the majority of people around the world.

(*Continued*)

Table 5.1 (Continued)

Economic barriers to green transition	*Most vulnerable group*	*Proposed solutions, measures*	*Risks*
Investments in green transition are mostly concentrated in developed countries and China	Developing countries	1 The development of a concept for financing the synergy between the SDGs and climate change, including the creation of recommendations, roadmaps, standards, and standards, with a particular focus on banks and insurance companies. 2 The development of financial instruments and mechanisms by MDBs to finance NCQG and achieve financial objectives set at COP-29 in Baku.	1 Economic, political, and technological uncertainties. 2 Focus on short-term investment plans. 3 Increased levels of public debt in developing countries and growing energy demands, as well as conflicting environmental concerns arising from the energy transition. 4 Serious environmental issues and climate change will impact not only the environment but also the socio-economic development of countries. This could lead to a significant rise in healthcare costs, decreased productivity among the population, and mass migration.
The uncertainties of common carbon markets' regulations and standards	All countries	1 Updating international databases with consolidated data on all carbon markets, including voluntary carbon markets. 2 Conducting annual reviews and reports by the UN analyzing all transactions under Article 6 of the Paris Agreement and voluntary carbon markets to expand the market under Article 6 of the Paris Agreement and improve the quality of carbon credits in voluntary carbon markets.	1 Increased levels of public debt in developing countries. 2 Numerous greenwashing operations. 3 Economic, political and technological uncertainties.
The absence of coordinated implementation of climate tools related to the SDGs in developing countries	Mostly developing countries	The establishment of a collaborative partnership between the scientific community and governmental authorities to conduct research aimed at determining the effectiveness of integrating the SDGs with climate change, as well as to develop appropriate tools for its implementation.	Serious environmental issues and climate change will have an impact not only on the environment but also on the socio-economic development of countries. This could lead to a significant rise in healthcare costs, decreased productivity among the population, and mass migration.

community and government agencies to develop practical recommendations, principles and standards for decarbonisation of developing countries without harming their economies. The creation of international analytical platforms and databases to support the green transition is also an important step.

Note

1 This includes carbon dioxide (CO_2) emissions from fossil fuels and industry (fossil CO_2), CO_2 emissions and removals from land use, land-use change and forestry (LULUCF CO_2), methane (CH_4), and nitrous oxide (N_2O) emissions.

References

Climate Watch. (n.d.). Data explorer. https://www.climatewatchdata.org/data-explorer/historical-emissions?historical-emissions-data-sources=climate-watch&historical-emissions-end_year=2021&historical-emissions-gases=all-ghg&historical-emissions-regions=All%20Selected&historical-emissions-sectors=total-including-lucf%2Ctotal-including-lucf&historical-emissions-start_year=1990&page=1

European Council. (n.d.). An EU critical raw materials act for the future of EU supply chains. https://www.consilium.europa.eu/en/infographics/critical-raw-materials/

Indonesia Economic Forum. (2022). G20 encourages development of framework for financial transition. https://www.indonesiaeconomicforum.com/g20-encourages-development-of-framework-for-financial-transition/

Intergovernmental Panel on Climate Change. (2023). Climate change 2023: Synthesis report. Contribution of Working Groups I, II and III to the sixth assessment report of the Intergovernmental Panel on Climate Change. https://www.ipcc.ch/report/ar6/syr/downloads/report/IPCC_AR6_SYR_LongerReport.pdf

International and Comparative Law Research Center. (2024). HOW TO COP: Climate change, the United Nations Framework Convention on Climate Change, and the multilateral negotiation process. https://iclrc.ru/en/publications/113

International Civil Aviation Organization. (n.d.). Carbon offsetting and reduction scheme for international aviation (CORSIA). https://www.icao.int/environmental-protection/CORSIA/Pages/default.aspx

International Energy Agency. (2021, May). Net zero by 2050: A roadmap for the global energy sector. https://iea.blob.core.windows.net/assets/deebef5d-0c34-4539-9d0c-10b13d840027/NetZeroby2050-ARoadmapfortheGlobalEnergySector_CORR.pdf

International Finance Corporation. (n.d.). Challenges of green finance: Private sector perspectives from emerging markets. https://www.ifc.org/en/insights-reports/2023/challenges-of-green-finance

International Monetary Fund, Organisation for Economic Co-operation and Development, United Nations, World Bank and the World Trade Organization. (2024). Carbon pricing, policy spillovers, and global climate goals. https://www.wto.org/english/res_e/booksp_e/climate_action_e.pdf

International Renewable Energy Agency. (2023). World energy transitions outlook 2023. https://www.irena.org/Digital-Report/World-Energy-Transitions-Outlook-2023

InvestCorp. (2024, April). "Greasing the wheels" of decarbonization: A primer on the global carbon markets. https://www.investcorp.com/wp-content/uploads/2024/04/The-Global-Carbon-Markets-April-2024-vF.pdf

Jones, N., Verkuijl, C., Cabré, M. M., & Piggot, G. (2023). Connecting the dots: Mapping references to fossil fuel production in national plans under the UNFCCC for the 2023 Global Stocktake. https://doi.org/10.51414/sei2023.040

Khor, M. (2010). Preliminary notes on the green economy, in the context of sustainable development. https://sdgs.un.org/sites/default/files/statements/18725southcentre.pdf

McKinsey & Company. (2023, October 18). Global energy perspective 2023. https://www.mckinsey.com/industries/oil-and-gas/our-insights/global-energy-perspective-2023

McKinsey & Company. (2024). Global materials perspective 2024. https://www.mckinsey.com/industries/energy-and-materials/our-insights/global-materials-perspective

Pearce, D. (1989). Blueprint for a green economy. Internet Archive. https://archive.org/details/isbn_1853830666

Robson, D. (2023, August 25). BRICS accounts for almost 45% of global oil reserves after expansion. ROGTEC. https://www.rogtecmagazine.com/brics-accounts-for-almost-45-of-global-oil-reserves-after-expansion/#:~:text=BRICS%20Accounts%20for%20Almost%2045%25%20of%20Global%20Oil%20Reserves%20After%20Expansion,-%E2%80%94%20August%2025%2C%202023&text=The%20BRICS%20group%20(Brazil%2C%20Russia,of%20the%20world's%20oil%20reserves

Stechemesser, A., Koch, N., Mark, E., Dilger, E., Klösel, P., Menicacci, L., Nachtigall, D., Pretis, F., Ritter, N., Schwarz, M., Vossen, H., & Wenzel, A. (2024). Climate policies that achieved major emission reductions: Global evidence from two decades. *Science*, 385(6711), 884–892. https://doi.org/10.1126/science.adl6547

UN Environment Programme. (2024a). Emissions gap report 2024. https://www.unep.org/resources/emissions-gap-report-2024

UN Environment Programme. (2024b). Global resource outlook 2024. https://www.unep.org/resources/Global-Resource-Outlook-2024

United Nations. (1987). Report of the World Commission on environment and development. Our Common Future. https://www.alor.org/Storage/Library/PDF/Our_Common_Future_Brundtland_Report1987.pdf

United Nations. (2015). Paris Agreement. https://unfccc.int/files/essential_background/convention/application/pdf/english_paris_agreement.pdf

United Nations. (2024). Synergy solutions for climate and SDG action: Bridging the ambition gap for the future we want 2024. https://sdgs.un.org/sites/default/files/2024-08/UN%20Synergy%20Solutions%20for%20Climate%20and%20SDG%20Action-4_0.pdf

United Nations. (n.d.-a). For a livable climate: Net-zero commitments must be backed by credible action. https://www.un.org/en/climatechange/net-zero-coalition

United Nations. (n.d.-b). The 17 goals | Sustainable development. https://sdgs.un.org/goals

United Nations Conference on Trade and Development. (2023, March 16). Technology and innovation report 2023. https://unctad.org/tir2023

United Nations Department of Economic and Social Affairs. (n.d.). Harnessing climate and SDGs synergies. https://sdgs.un.org/climate-sdgs-synergies#expert_group

United Nations Economic and Social Council. (2005, May 4). Report on the outcomes of the 5th ministerial conference on environment and development in Asia and the Pacific. https://digitallibrary.un.org/record/552295#record-files-collapse-header

United Nations Framework Convention on Climate Change. Conference of the Parties Serving as the Meeting of the Parties to the Paris Agreement (CMA). (2025). Report of the conference of the parties serving as the meeting of the parties to the Paris Agreement on its sixth session, held in Baku from 11 to 24 November 2024. Addendum. Part two. https://unfccc.int/documents/644937

Verney, P., & Verney, P. (2023, November 7). France outlines new SRI label with fossil fuel exclusions and transition plan requirements. Responsible Investor. https://www.responsible-investor.com/france-outlines-new-sri-label-with-fossil-fuel-exclusions-and-transition-plan-requirements/

World Bank Group. (2023). World development report 2023. https://www.worldbank.org/en/publication/wdr2023

World Bank Group. (2024a, May 21). Global carbon pricing revenues top a record $100 billion. https://www.worldbank.org/en/news/press-release/2024/05/21/global-carbon-pricing-revenues-top-a-record-100-billion

World Bank Group. (2024b). World Bank annual report 2024. https://www.worldbank.org/en/about/annual-report/working-achieve-development-goals

World Economic Forum. (2024). Business on the edge: Building industry resilience to climate hazards. https://www.weforum.org/publications/business-on-the-edge-building-industry-resilience-to-climate-hazards/

6 Models of financing energy transition

Differences and results

Andrea Almawi

Introduction

For over five decades, scientific research and environmental advocacy have underscored the critical need for sustainable energy solutions. Today, there is a stronger global consensus than ever on the urgency of transitioning to renewable energy to combat climate change. In the pursuit of a sustainable future, the significance of financing in attaining the ambitious objectives of energy transition becomes a crucial yet intricate challenge. This issue involves ensuring and harmonizing secured and affordable access to energy (the demand side) through a sustainable and viable provision of energy resources and mechanisms (the supply side) under the constraint of the structural (and radical) transformation of the economic and social models in force for many centuries. Since such a transformation can be regarded as a problem of provision of a global public good, the transition process. In our (mainly) market-led and wealth accumulation/growth-oriented economies, the transition requires specific ways and mechanisms of bringing together the public good provision process and the market mechanisms and dynamics. On the one hand, these mechanisms should not suffer from the pitfalls of rigid centralization, being blind to the flexibility necessary for any process of structural change, which should be supported by the innovative dynamics of the components of society. On the other hand, they should not fall prey to market mechanisms' appetite for speculation and short-term financial efficiency, which may be positive for short-sighted private interests, but are disastrous for the stability and sustainability of economies (and societies) in the longer term. Concerning these constraints, a notable discrepancy exists between global pledges to advance renewable energy initiatives and the practical measures taken to fulfill the required commitments.

This chapter examines the cases of France, Germany, and China, scrutinizing their substantial yet diverse commitments to renewable energy within the context of their specific political, economic, and environmental circumstances. By conducting a comparative analysis of these countries—each at different stages of energy transition and employing various financing mechanisms—a nuanced understanding of the complexities involved in financing renewable energy initiatives is developed in order to put forward the points of convergences and divergences and to draw some possible common roots to handle such a structural change process.

The selection of France, Germany, and China is based on their diverse political systems, economic models, and environmental issues, providing a comprehensive context for studying the challenges of implementing an energy transition. France's substantial nuclear industry, Germany's leadership in technological advancement and commitment to the Energiewende, and China's rapid growth in renewable technology production amid severe pollution challenges exemplify diverse routes to sustainability. The roles of Germany in the European Union, of France in the Paris Agreement, and of China as the largest greenhouse gas (GHG) emitter and a

DOI: 10.4324/9781003663539-7

leader in renewable production underscore the significance of political will, economic priorities, and technological advancements in shaping global energy transitions.

These three economies have emerged as prominent actors in the global energy transition landscape. France is known for its ambitious carbon neutrality target by 2050 and its commitment to increasing the share of renewables in its energy mix. Germany, with its Energiewende (Energy Transition) initiative, has set a precedent in phasing out nuclear energy and coal while significantly expanding its renewable energy capacity. China, as the world's largest emitter of GHGs, has recently pledged to achieve carbon neutrality by 2060 and peak emissions before 2030, reflecting its growing responsibility in the global climate agenda.

This study seeks to investigate the disparities between policy intentions and practical executions by addressing the following inquiry:

To what extent do the financing strategies for the energy transition in France, Germany, and China align with their declared policies and real-world implementation?

The objective is to reveal the inconsistencies between policy declarations and their execution and to suggest alternative financing frameworks that consider the energy transition as a societal benefit within the context of a capitalist accumulation economy. This comparison highlights the distinct strategies and challenges faced by each country, emphasizing their capacity to influence global renewable energy policies and practices.

This chapter is organized into four sections. The first three sections are dedicated to a comprehensive analysis of France, Germany, and China, respectively. For each country, the study examines its specific energy-related and climate-related goals, providing a detailed overview of its strategic objectives in the context of national and international commitments. This is followed by an evaluation of the achievements and challenges, which assesses the progress made toward these goals, highlighting key successes, obstacles, and the dynamics influencing the energy transition of each country. The final sub-section in each country-specific analysis explores the diverse financing models and mechanisms, scrutinizing the various approaches to funding their energy transitions.

The fourth section transitions into a comparative analysis, synthesizing the findings from the previous sections and offering a comprehensive comparative overview of the energy and climate goals of France, Germany, and China. It provides a rigorous analysis of the differences and similarities in their approaches, allowing for a deeper understanding of the diverse pathways these countries are taking toward their energy transitions. Additionally, the comparative overview of financing models assesses the success and sustainability of the various strategies employed, identifying common success factors and shared challenges that can inform future policy and financial frameworks.

Through an analysis of the disparities between declared policies and their practical execution, this study aims to pave the way for innovative solutions that can expedite the global shift to renewable energy. By examining how policy intentions are implemented in France, Germany, and China, this chapter lays the foundation for a deeper understanding of the overall impact of financial mechanisms on the global advancement of renewable energy. The insights gained will be crucial for policymakers, investors, and stakeholders in developing more effective and sustainable financing strategies, ultimately contributing to a more coordinated and accelerated transition to renewable energy worldwide.

France: energy-related and climate-related policies and goals

Since the 2000s, France has implemented an ambitious energy and climate policy aimed at achieving several key objectives. The policy is based on two main pillars: reducing energy consumption and eliminating fossil fuel use to fully decarbonize the energy mix by 2050. This involves the development of low-carbon energy sources, including renewable energy and nuclear power.

Key projects

- SNBC (Stratégie nationale bas-carbone, National Low-Carbon Strategy): Defines the roadmap for reducing GHG emissions, establishing carbon budgets and sectoral targets to drive down emissions across all sectors of the economy (mitigation policy) (Ministry of Ecological Transition, 2020a).
- PNACC (Plan national d'adaptation au changement climatique, National Climate Change Adaptation Plan): defines strategies and actions to prepare France for the impacts of climate change, ensuring resilience of populations, ecosystems, and economic activities under projected warming scenarios (adaptation policy) (Ministry of Ecological Transition, Biodiversity, Forests, Seas and Fisheries, 2025).
- PPE (Programmation pluriannuelle de l'énergie, Multiannual Energy Plan): Guides energy policy for the upcoming decade, setting priorities and actions to achieve the SNBC goals. The PPE aims for 40% of electricity production from renewables by 2030, the closure of coal plants by 2022, and maintaining 50% nuclear power in the energy mix by 2035. The PPE is critical in operationalizing the SNBC's long-term goals into actionable short and medium-term steps (Ministry of Ecological Transition, 2020b).

Key laws

- Energy Transition for Green Growth Act (2015): Focused on reducing energy consumption and ending fossil fuel use to achieve total decarbonization by 2050 (Ministry of Ecological Transition, 2016).
- Energy and Climate Law (2019): Reinforced targets for carbon neutrality and intermediate goals, including updates to carbon budgets and renewable energy targets (French Government, 2019).
- Climate and Resilience Law (2021): Detailed measures to combat climate change and enhance resilience, addressing both mitigation and adaptation strategies (European Commission, 2021).

Climate policy pillars

Adaptation

France implemented its first National Plan for Climate Change Adaptation (PNACC-1) in 2011, covering the period 2011–2015. This plan outlined tangible strategies for adapting to and capitalizing on emerging climate conditions, resulting from intense consultation in 2010. It aimed to make France more resilient to climate change impacts, with goals focused on protecting people and property, reducing inequality in risk exposure, limiting costs, and preserving natural heritage. While PNACC-1 didn't specify numerical goals like emission reduction percentages, it laid the groundwork for comprehensive adaptation measures with more than 200 recommendations across 20 sectors (Ministry of Ecological Transition, 2011).

The 2014 Environmental Conference held in Paris emphasized the necessity of enhancing the national adaptation strategy. Subsequently, the PNACC-1 underwent an external assessment by the Council for Environment and Sustainable Development in June 2015, resulting in the introduction of the second National Adaptation Plan (PNACC-2) in 2018, covering the period 2018–2022. This update aligns France's adaptation policy with the Paris Agreement. The objective of PNACC-2 was to implement necessary actions to adapt the territories of metropolitan France and overseas regions to expected regional climate changes by 2050, considering a projected global temperature increase of +1.5 to 2°C (Ministry of Ecological Transition, 2018).

The transition to PNACC-3, which is set to be published in 2024, is based on the assessments and lessons learned from PNACC-2. The objective is to tackle the growing necessity of climate resilience, in anticipation of a temperature increase of up to +4°C by the year 2100. France has implemented the Reference Warming Trajectory for Climate Adaptation (TRACC) to promote synchronized climate adaptation. TRACC will serve as the fundamental basis for all adaptation endeavors. This guarantees a unified and strong strategy for addressing the effects of climate change while adjusting to new scientific discoveries and policy circumstances. The objective is to secure influential political backing and guarantee the essential public and human resources for the successful implementation of effective adaptation measures (Ministry of Ecological Transition, 2024a, b).

Although PNACC has a primary focus on adaptation, the transition from aiming to limit global temperature increase to 1.5 to 2°C by 2050 in PNACC-2, to now preparing for a potential increase of up to 4°C by 2100 in PNACC-3, suggests that global efforts to reduce GHG emissions, including those by France, have not been successful in sufficiently curbing emissions to prevent more severe climate consequences. This emphasizes the continuous requirement for more robust measures to reduce the impact of climate change, in addition to the actions taken to adjust to its effects.

Mitigation

The Energy Transition for Green Growth Act, also known as the Loi de transition energétique pour la croissance verte, implemented in 2015, followed the adaptive strategies laid out in the PNACC but placed a stronger emphasis on mitigation measures. This act is supported by key strategic frameworks such as the National Low-Carbon Strategy (SNBC) and the Multiannual Energy Plan (PPE) (Ministry of Ecological Transition, 2020a, b, 2022). It established goals to reduce GHG emissions, decrease fossil fuel consumption, and increase renewable energy usage:

GREENHOUSE GAS EMISSIONS

- Original Goal: Reduce GHG emissions by 40% by 2030 compared to 1990 levels, and by 75% by 2050 (reduce by a factor of 4).
- Revised Goal: SNBC-3 sets a more ambitious target to reduce GHG emissions by a factor of 6 by 2050 compared to 1990 levels, aiming for carbon neutrality.

FOSSIL FUEL CONSUMPTION

- Original Goal: Decrease fossil fuel consumption by 30% by 2030 compared to 2012 levels.
- Revised Goal: Increased to a 40% reduction by 2030 under the Energy and Climate Law (2019).

RENEWABLE ENERGY

Increase the share of renewable energy to 32% of total energy consumption by 2030 compared to 2012 levels, and ensure 40% of electricity production comes from renewable sources by 2030.

ENERGY EFFICIENCY

Halve final energy consumption by 2050 compared to 2012 levels, with an intermediate target of a 20% reduction by 2030.

NUCLEAR ENERGY

- Original Goal: Reduce nuclear energy's share in electricity production to 50% by 2025.
- Revised Goal: Extended to 2035 in the Energy and Climate Law (in May 2019). This revision was formalized in the Energy and Climate Law, adopted in November 2019. However, in 2023, the objective to reduce nuclear energy's share to 50% was abandoned. Instead, the focus shifted toward maintaining nuclear power as a major component of the energy mix. In February 2022, France announced plans to build six new nuclear reactors and to consider constructing an additional eight.

CARBON BUDGETS COMPLIANCE

The SNBC sets detailed carbon budgets and legally binding limits on GHG emissions for specific periods, ensuring progressive emission reductions. The first carbon budget (2015–2018) aimed for 442 Mt CO_2e (Metric tons of carbon dioxide equivalent) per year but was not met, with actual emissions averaging 457.6 Mt CO_2e per year. The second carbon budget (2019–2023) targeted 422 Mt CO_2e per year and is likely to be met, aided by temporary reductions during the COVID-19 pandemic. Future budgets set more stringent targets, aiming for 359 Mt CO_2e per year (2024–2028) and 300 Mt CO_2e per year (2029–2033).

These frameworks emphasize energy efficiency, renewable energy, and sectoral decarbonization to meet France's long-term climate goals and international commitments, such as those under the Paris Agreement. Continuous monitoring and structural changes are essential to maintain compliance and achieve the ultimate goal of carbon neutrality by 2050.

The Multiannual Energy Plans (PPE) and the National Low-Carbon Strategy (SNBC) are complementary frameworks that work hand in hand to achieve France's climate and energy goals. While the SNBC sets the long-term vision and overarching goals for reducing GHG emissions and achieving carbon neutrality by 2050, the PPE provides detailed plans and specific targets for the energy sector over shorter periods. Both strategies include goals for increasing renewable energy, improving energy efficiency, and reducing reliance on fossil fuels, but they focus on different aspects and timeframes. The PPE outlines the immediate steps and investments needed in the energy sector to meet the SNBC's broader objectives, ensuring a cohesive approach to France's energy transition and climate commitments.

The alignment between PPE and SNBC is crucial for ensuring that the short-term actions and policies in the energy sector contribute effectively to the long-term climate goals set by the SNBC. This integrated approach allows for adjustments and updates based on progress and new developments, providing a robust and flexible pathway toward sustainability.

The "Loi sur la lutte contre le dérèglement climatique et le renforcement de la résilience face à ses effets" (Climate and Resilience Law), enacted in 2021, aims to significantly reduce GHG emissions and to enhance resilience to climate impacts. It targets a reduction in emissions by 40% by 2030 compared to 1990 levels and achieving carbon neutrality by 2050. This law aligns with the Multiannual Energy Plans (PPE) and the National Low-Carbon Strategy (SNBC), ensuring cohesive efforts toward sustainable energy transition and climate resilience. Key measures include improving energy efficiency, expanding renewable energy, and enhancing infrastructure to withstand extreme weather events. The law also promotes biodiversity preservation and sustainable agricultural practices, reflecting France's comprehensive approach to addressing climate change.

France: current status and discussion of energy-related and climate-related policies and goals

The ambitious goals set by France are crucial for addressing climate change, but achieving them requires overcoming significant hurdles. The progress made so far indicates a positive direction, but the pace and scale of implementation must be accelerated. Key issues include:

- Policy Implementation: Ensuring that policies are effectively translated into action on the ground. This requires strong governance, adequate funding, and continuous monitoring.
- Technological and Economic Challenges: Developing and deploying new technologies, particularly in renewable energy and energy efficiency, while ensuring economic viability and competitiveness.
- Public and Political Will: Maintaining public support and political commitment, especially in light of economic and social challenges such as energy prices and employment.
- Infrastructure and Investment: Upgrading infrastructure to support renewable energy integration and securing investments for large-scale projects.

France: financing and implementation challenges of the energy transition

The French government plays a pivotal role in facilitating the energy transition through a variety of public financing mechanisms, including direct investments, tax incentives, and subsidies. Financial instruments such as feed-in tariffs and tax credits are designed to lower economic barriers to the adoption of renewable energy, thereby increasing its appeal to both consumers and producers. These measures are central to France's strategy of reducing carbon emissions and promoting sustainable energy.

Despite the strong public sector involvement, the financing of France's energy transition also hinges on active private sector participation. The government has increasingly fostered partnerships between private companies and public entities to develop and finance renewable energy projects. This collaboration is crucial for scaling up renewable energy installations across the country and addressing the substantial capital requirements of the transition.

A cornerstone of France's financing strategy is the Programme d'Investissements d'Avenir (PIA), or the Investments for the Future Program, which was launched in 2010 and later expanded. The PIA has allocated billions of euros toward innovative projects that drive infrastructure development, research and development, and the implementation of new technologies, including those related to green and renewable energy. By focusing on projects with long-term societal impacts, the PIA exemplifies the French government's synergistic approach to financing the energy transition, combining public investment with private sector innovation (French Government, 2021).

However, France's energy transition faces practical implementation challenges, particularly when it comes to translating ambitious policy goals into concrete actions. The nation's dependence on nuclear power as a fundamental element of its plan to establish a low-carbon economy is both an advantage and a source of controversy. Nuclear energy's reliability and minimal carbon footprint are advantageous. Still, its prevalence in the energy sector raises worries about the variety of energy sources and the system's ability to incorporate more renewable energies (Sadorsky, 2020).

A key challenge lies in the disconnect between the legislative aspirations outlined in the Law of Energy Transition and Green Growth to decrease carbon emissions and increase the proportion of renewable energy sources and the concrete policy actions implemented to attain those objectives (Ayagapin et al., 2021). This discrepancy indicates systemic obstacles to translating high-level objectives into actionable strategies and specific projects.

The transition to a fully renewable energy system in France is not just a technical challenge but also an institutional one. France's energy system has historically depended on centralized, large-scale production facilities, similar to those used for fossil and nuclear fuels. This centralized model, as critiqued by Sansilvestri et al. (2021), may hinder the development of more flexible and decentralized renewable energy systems, which are necessary for a successful energy transition.

The broader issue of inertia in the energy sector is exemplified by the contrast observed by Fagan (2023) between the swift implementation of nuclear power and the more gradual shift away from coal. Sovacool (2016) has written on the duration of time required to implement new energy regimens. He remarked that the swift integration of nuclear energy into France, facilitated by centralized decision-making, occurred within a mere decade, in contrast to the country's 65-year transition from coal to gas, oil, or electricity. Potentially less effective at fostering a decentralized and diverse renewable energy landscape may be the centralized decision-making processes that enabled the rapid expansion of nuclear energy in France.

In summary, France's energy transition is supported by substantial public and private financing efforts, yet it is confronted by significant implementation challenges. These include aligning policy aspirations with actionable strategies, addressing the institutional inertia within the energy sector, and transitioning from a centralized to a more decentralized energy system capable of integrating diverse renewable energy sources.

France: conclusion

When analyzing these results, it is crucial to acknowledge the complex nature of the energy transition challenge in France. The country's current infrastructure, institutional frameworks, and policy mechanisms are closely connected to its historical energy decisions, especially regarding nuclear power. Transitioning to a diversified and renewable energy system requires overcoming technical, institutional, and societal challenges. Legislative intent and practical measures, such as investing in renewable technologies, implementing regulatory reforms to promote decentralization and innovation, and involving various stakeholders in the energy transition process, are necessary.

Despite progress, France must accelerate its efforts to meet these goals. Between 1990 and 2021, emissions fell by 23%, short of the 40% reduction target by 2030, now revised to a 55% reduction to align with new EU objectives. Trends in energy consumption and the share of renewables in final energy consumption are critical indicators of progress. Ongoing updates to policies and goals reflect France's adaptive approach to achieving its long-term climate and energy targets. Enhanced measures in energy efficiency and renewable energy adoption are essential to ensure that France meets its ambitious climate objectives.

While France has made commendable strides toward its energy and climate goals, significant efforts are needed to meet the ambitious targets. Addressing the identified challenges through robust policy frameworks, technological innovation, and sustained public and political support will be essential for France to achieve its vision of a carbon-neutral and climate-resilient future.

France's energy transition is marked by ambitious goals and significant public and private sector involvement. However, achieving these objectives requires overcoming institutional inertia, ensuring effective policy implementation, and balancing the reliance on nuclear power with the need for renewable energy diversification. Addressing these challenges will be crucial for France to successfully transition to a sustainable and resilient energy future.

Germany: energy-related and climate-related policies and goals

Germany has been a pioneer in the energy transition, known as the Energiewende, which involves a comprehensive restructuring of the energy supply system encompassing electricity, heat, and transportation. The Energiewende aims to reduce CO_2 emissions significantly, phase out nuclear power, increase renewable energy sources, and enhance energy efficiency.

Following the Kyoto Protocol in 1997, Germany committed to reducing its GHG emissions by 21% by 2012 compared to 1990 levels between 2008 and 2012 (Umweltbundesamt, 2013). This commitment has driven a series of legislative actions aimed at promoting renewable energy and reducing the country's carbon footprint. To meet its Kyoto Protocol commitments and drive the Energiewende, Germany implemented several key laws.

Key laws and policies

The Renewable Energy Sources Act (EGG 2000) in Germany, known as the Erneuerbare-Energien-Gesetz, is a series of laws aimed at promoting renewable energy. Initially introduced on April 1, 2000, it replaced the Electricity Feed-In Act (Stromeinspeisungsgesetz or StrEG) of 1991. Its main objectives are to increase the share of renewable energy in Germany's electricity supply, ensure the stability and reliability of the power grid, and reduce GHG emissions. It established fixed feed-in tariffs for different types of renewable energy, ensuring that producers received a guaranteed price for the electricity they generated from renewable sources (International Energy Agency, 2014). The EEG has undergone several revisions since its inception in 2000, aimed at promoting renewable energy and aligning with evolving market and technological landscapes. While early revisions like EEG 2004 and EEG 2009 mainly adjusted feed-in tariffs and introduced degression rates (meaning the tariffs would decrease annually to reflect the falling costs of renewable energy technologies), the most significant changes began with EEG 2012, which introduced a market premium model allowing renewable energy producers to sell directly on the market with a premium to cover the price difference (Federal Ministry for Economic Affairs and Climate Action, 2015). EEG 2014 marked a substantial shift by introducing competitive auctions for large-scale renewable projects to enhance cost-effectiveness with the goal of 40%–45% of electricity consumption coming from renewables by 2025, 55%–60% by 2035, and up to 80% by 2050. The 2017 revision fully transitioned to competitive auctions, setting specific expansion corridors for different technologies to control growth (International Energy Agency, 2016a). The latest significant update, EEG 2021, aligned Germany's targets with the EU Green Deal, setting ambitious goals such as achieving 65% of electricity consumption from renewables by 2030 and establishing annual capacity targets for onshore wind, offshore wind, and solar PV (Direction Générale du Trésor, 2021). These revisions collectively aim to make Germany's renewable energy system more market-oriented and cost-efficient, while significantly boosting the share of renewables in the energy mix.

In addition to the EEG, in 2002, Germany committed to phasing out nuclear power by 2022. Following the Fukushima Daiichi nuclear disaster in 2011, Germany accelerated its nuclear phase-out. This decision reinforced the importance of renewable energy as the cornerstone of Germany's future energy supply. Germany closed its last three nuclear power plants—Isar 2 in Bavaria, Emsland in Lower Saxony, and Neckarwestheim 2 in Baden-Württemberg—on April

15, 2023 (Federal Ministry for the Environment, Nature Conservation, Nuclear Safety and Consumer Protection, 2023). This marked the culmination of a long-term plan to phase out nuclear energy in the country. The closure had been initially planned for December 31, 2022, but was extended due to the energy crisis exacerbated by geopolitical tensions, particularly the war in Ukraine.

In 2007, Germany's Integrated Energy and Climate Programme set early goals for reducing GHG emissions, enhancing energy efficiency, and expanding the use of renewable energy across various sectors. This program aims to cut GHG emissions by 40% by 2020 compared with 1990 levels (Federal Ministry for the Environment, Nature Conservation and Nuclear Safety, 2007). A significant milestone was reached in 2010 with the Energy Concept, which built on this target and set further long-term goals for the coming decades: reducing GHG emissions by 55% by 2030, 70% by 2040, and 80%–95% by 2050 compared to 1990 levels (International Energy Agency, 2017). This policy also aimed to increase the share of renewables in final energy consumption to 60% by 2050 and reduce primary energy consumption by 20% by 2020 and 50% by 2050 compared to 2008 levels.

In March 2019, the government formed a Climate Cabinet to forge a consensus on new emissions reduction measures. Based on the cabinet's proposals, the government adopted the Climate Action Programme 2030 on October 9, 2019 (Federal Government of Germany, 2019). This program includes a phased carbon pricing system for sectors not covered by the EU Emissions Trading System, such as heating and transport. It also provides tax breaks and increased incentives for energy-efficient building renovations, higher subsidies for electric vehicles (EVs), and greater public investment in public transport. Revenues from the carbon pricing system will partly be used to lower costs for households and companies through tax relief and reduced electricity fees. This package represents a significant step toward meeting the 2030 targets.

In 2020, Germany also committed to ending coal-based electricity production by 2038 as part of its broader decarbonization strategy. In 2021, the Climate Action Plan 2050 set even more stringent targets, aiming for net-zero emissions by 2045 and revising the 2030 GHG reduction target to 65% compared to 1990 levels (Federal Ministry for the Environment, Nature Conservation, Nuclear Safety and Consumer Protection, 2016).

Looking ahead, Germany aims to have 80% of its electricity come from renewables by 2030 and achieve near-total reliance on renewable energy sources by 2050 (Federal Government of Germany, 2022).

Germany: current status and discussion of energy-related and climate-related policies and goals

The initial transition to renewable energy was fraught with difficulties in policy implementation and adaptation. Presently, managing the financial and logistical aspects of increasing renewable capacity remains a critical issue. Ensuring the cost-effectiveness of feed-in tariffs and balancing these with market premiums requires careful regulation. The shift toward competitive auctions for renewable projects, while improving cost efficiency, has introduced challenges in maintaining consistent project deployment and managing the rapid expansion pace necessary for grid stability.

This transition is a long-term project that poses challenges at both the national and decentralized levels (Ohlhorst, 2015). Financial citizen participation has been highlighted as crucial for financing the transformation of the energy sector in Germany (Behrendt et al., 2019).

Germany's energy transition has faced criticism and scrutiny, with debates on the efficiency and sustainability of the chosen approach (Gawel et al., 2013). The country's energy transition is considered a case of successful green industrial policy, focusing on renewable energy sources like wind and solar photovoltaic systems (Pegels & Lütkenhorst, 2014). The ownership and organization of the Energiewende at various levels, from villages to regions, have been subjects of study due to the initiative's ambitious nature (Moss et al., 2014).

The regulatory framework in Germany has evolved significantly due to the energy transition, impacting business models in the electricity market (Wagner et al., 2020). The transition involves a shift away from nuclear energy toward renewables, with a strong emphasis on sustainable business models (Edo, 2023). However, there are distributional challenges associated with sustainability policies, including social acceptability and equitable implementation (Gawel et al., 2015). Addressing conflicts of interest and maximizing benefits are crucial for successful local-level implementation of renewable energy projects, such as wind energy (Reitz et al., 2022).

Germany: financing and implementation challenges of the energiewende

Initially, nuclear energy was considered a transitional technology; however, public opposition led to a shift in focus toward renewables (Sonnberger et al., 2021). The financing of Energiewende involves a multifaceted approach, integrating public and private investments along with strategic policies and incentives that have been crucial to its progress:

- Public Financing and Innovation: The German state has played a pivotal role in funding the energy transition. Public financing has driven innovation and provided the necessary support to renewable energy technologies since the 1990s (Mazzucato & Semieniuk, 2017). This support has been crucial in establishing a competitive advantage for German industries in the renewable sector (Storm & Naastepad, 2015).
- Feed-in Tariffs: One of the key policies has been the implementation of feed-in tariffs, which provide long-term investment horizons and have been pivotal in encouraging large-scale investments in renewable energy (Egli & Steffen, 2018). These tariffs ensure that producers of renewable energy receive a fixed price for the electricity they generate, thereby reducing financial risks and encouraging investment.
- International Investments: Germany has also extended its financial support to international renewable energy projects, such as the Ouarzazate concentrated solar power project in Morocco, highlighting its commitment to global energy transformation (Steinbacher, 2015).

Despite the strategic financial frameworks, several challenges impede the smooth implementation of the Energiewende:

- Economic Impacts: The transition to renewable energy technologies impacts the economic performance of regions, such as North Rhine-Westphalia, where traditional energy industries have been predominant (Aniello et al., 2019). Balancing the economic impacts while advancing the energy transition is a significant challenge.
- Public Sentiment and Policy Shifts: The shift from nuclear to renewable energy sources was influenced by public sentiment. This required swift policy adjustments and increased investments in R&D for renewable technologies (Sonnberger et al., 2021).
- Regulatory and Market Adaptation: The dynamic nature of the energy market requires continuous adaptation of regulatory frameworks to accommodate new technologies and financial models (Egli & Steffen, 2018).

Germany's approach to the Energiewende sets a benchmark for the European Union's broader move toward a low-carbon, renewable energy-based economy. The policies and financial strategies that have driven Germany's transition provide a valuable blueprint for other EU countries aiming to achieve similar goals (Bouzarovski & Herrero, 2016). However, the ongoing challenges of balancing economic impacts, public sentiment, and regulatory adaptation highlight the complexity of implementing such an ambitious transition.

Germany: conclusion

Germany has demonstrated notable progress in reducing GHG emissions, achieving a 21% reduction by 2012 and an impressive 46% reduction by 2023 compared to 1990 levels. This significant achievement places Germany's emissions at 1.86% of global emissions, indicating substantial advancement toward the ambitious target of a 55% reduction by 2030. The energy and industry sectors have been pivotal in driving down emissions, showcasing successful decarbonization efforts. However, the building and transport sectors continue to underperform, with emissions remaining stagnant and not meeting set targets.

Renewable energy has seen robust growth, contributing 38.6% to electricity production in 2022 and rising sharply to 55% in 2023. This expansion underscores Germany's commitment to transitioning away from fossil fuels. Additionally, there has been a 5% reduction in per capita energy consumption between 2000 and 2022, complemented by a 37% decrease in the energy intensity of the economy over the same period. These metrics reflect significant strides toward enhancing energy efficiency and reducing overall energy demand.

However, despite these advancements, Germany faces persistent challenges. Achieving higher renewable energy targets necessitates substantial upgrades to grid infrastructure, which is crucial for integrating new renewable inputs. The socio-economic impacts of phasing out coal, particularly in coal-dependent regions, pose significant transition costs and require strategic planning to mitigate adverse effects on local communities. Sector-specific targets, especially for underperforming sectors like transport and buildings, need intensified focus to meet Germany's overarching climate goals. Despite economic stagnation periods that have partially hindered progress, Germany continues to push forward with its climate agenda.

The financing and implementation of Germany's Energiewende involve a strategic mix of public and private investments, supportive policies like feed-in tariffs, and a long-term vision for renewable energy. The German state's proactive role in providing financial support, driving innovation, and fostering a conducive environment for renewable energy development has been crucial. However, the challenges in economic adaptation, public policy shifts, and regulatory frameworks must be continually addressed to ensure the sustained success of the energy transition.

In summary, while Germany's achievements in reducing GHG emissions and expanding renewable energy are commendable, the country must address ongoing challenges to sustain and accelerate its climate progress. This includes overcoming infrastructural, economic, and sector-specific hurdles to fully realize its ambitious climate objectives.

China: energy-related and climate-related policies and goals

China's energy transition is characterized by its significant consumption of fossil fuels while also being the world's leading producer of renewable energy. Since 1978, China has made considerable improvements in energy efficiency and has diversified its energy resources to ensure energy security and address climate change. This journey toward energy transition began earnestly in 2001 for energy security and intensified in 2011 with climate change objectives put in place.

Key public commitments and goals

1 2030 and 2060 Goals: China has committed to peaking its GHG emissions before 2030 and achieving carbon neutrality by 2060 as outlined in the 14th Five-Year Plan (2021–2025) (International Energy Agency, 2021).
2 Coal Plant Construction Abroad: China has pledged to stop building new coal-fired power projects overseas (Centre for Research on Energy and Clean Air, 2023a).
3 Non-Fossil Fuel Mix: The goal is to achieve 80% non-fossil fuels in its energy mix by 2060 (International Energy Agency, 2021).
4 Carbon Intensity Reduction Targets: China set 2005 as its baseline for carbon intensity reduction targets, aiming to reduce CO_2 emissions per unit of GDP by 40%–45% by 2020 from 2005 levels (Carbon Brief, 2023).

Laws and regulations

- Enactment of the Renewable Energy Law in 2006: targeting 15% of energy consumption from renewable sources by 2020 (Ministry of Ecology and Environment of the People's Republic of China, 2006).
- 2009, under the Copenhagen Accord: China reaffirmed to reduce CO_2 intensity by 40%–45% from 2005 levels and achieve 15% of energy from low-carbon sources by 2020 (Finamore, 2010).
- Paris Agreement commitment in 2015: peak carbon emissions by 2030 and increase the share of non-fossil fuels in primary energy consumption to around 20% by 2030 (Center for Climate and Energy Solutions, 2015).
- Revised National Energy Conservation Law in 2016: enhance energy efficiency, with a strategy to incorporate energy conservation into national economic and social planning (International Energy Agency, 2016b).
- First NDC submission under the Paris Agreement: reiterating peak emissions by 2030 and enhanced carbon intensity reduction efforts (Ministry of Ecology and Environment of the People's Republic of China, 2022b).
- New Energy Administration Plan in 2021: increase renewable energy consumption to 1 billion tons of standard coal equivalent by 2025 and raise the share of non-fossil fuels to 20%. Announcement of the goal to achieve carbon neutrality by 2060 (State Council Information Office of the People's Republic of China, 2023).
- Announcement of the updated NDC and Introduction of the 1+N Policy System in 2020: carbon dioxide peaking before 2030, carbon neutrality before 2060, lower carbon dioxide emissions per unit of GDP by over 65% from the 2005 level, increase the share of non-fossil fuels in primary energy consumption to around 25% by 2030, increase installed capacity of wind and solar power to over 1.2 billion kW by 2030 (Ministry of Ecology and Environment of the People's Republic of China, 2022b).
- Publication of the National Strategy on Climate Adaptation in 2022: to enhance climate resilience across various sectors by 2035 (Ministry of Ecology and Environment of the People's Republic of China, 2022b).

- Implementation of carbon emissions trading legislation to promote carbon neutrality and low-carbon development through regulated carbon trading in 2023 (Ministry of Ecology and Environment of the People's Republic of China, 2022a).

Climate policy pillars

The information provided in this section is retrieved from the document of the Ministry of Ecology and Environment of the People's Republic of China (2022a).

New arrangements to combat climate change

China has introduced several new arrangements to enhance its efforts against climate change. These include:

- Improving the Top-level Design for Tackling Climate Change: This involves better coordination and integration of climate policies at the highest levels of government.
- Formulating Mid-term and Long-term Strategies: China is developing comprehensive strategies to address climate change over the coming decades.
- Formulating and Implementing the National Strategy on Climate Change Adaptation: This strategy focuses on preparing the country to deal with the impacts of climate change.
- Incorporating Climate Goals into Five-Year Plans: The Five-Year Plans provide a strategic framework for addressing climate change, with specific targets for reducing carbon intensity, increasing renewable energy usage, and improving energy efficiency.

Mitigating climate change

- Adjusting the Industrial Structure → Shifting toward less carbon-intensive industries.
- Optimizing the Energy Mix → Increasing the share of renewable energy sources such as wind, solar, and hydroelectric power while reducing reliance on coal.
- Promoting Energy Conservation and Efficiency → Implementing measures to improve energy efficiency across various sectors.
- Controlling Non-Carbon Dioxide GHG Emissions → Addressing other GHGs such as methane and nitrous oxide.
- Enhancing the Carbon Sink Capacity of Ecosystems → Increasing forest cover and improving land use practices to absorb more carbon dioxide.
- Increasing Synergy between Reducing Pollution and Carbon Emissions → Combining efforts to reduce air pollution with climate change mitigation.
- Deepening Pilot and Demonstration Programs → Implementing pilot programs to test and demonstrate new technologies and approaches.

Adapting to climate change

- Strengthening Climate Change Monitoring and Early Warning Systems → Improving systems to monitor climate change and provide early warnings of extreme weather events.
- Improving the Capability of Natural Ecosystems → Enhancing the resilience of ecosystems to withstand climate impacts.
- Strengthening the Capability of Economic and Social Systems → Ensuring that economic and social infrastructures can adapt to changing climate conditions.
- Improving the Climate Resilience of Key Vulnerable Areas → Focusing on regions that are particularly vulnerable to climate impacts and implementing measures to protect them.

These pillars reflect China's comprehensive approach to addressing both the causes and effects of climate change through coordinated policy measures, technological advancements, and proactive adaptation strategies.

China: current status and discussion of energy-related and climate-related policies and goals

China's methodical approach, encapsulated in its successive Five-Year Plans and legislative measures, underscores its commitment to reducing carbon emissions and transitioning to a sustainable energy system, supported by substantial investments in renewable energy, energy efficiency, and technological innovation to achieve its long-term climate goals.

China has rapidly expanded its renewable energy capacity, particularly in wind and solar power. By 2023, China had installed as many solar panels as the rest of the world combined in the previous year and increased its wind power capacity by 66% (International Energy Agency, 2023b). It is on track to meet and likely exceed its target of having 1,200 GW of installed wind and solar capacity by 2030 (Global Energy Monitor, 2023).

Additionally, the share of non-fossil fuels in China's primary energy consumption has been increasing. China's target is for non-fossil fuels to account for around 25% of primary energy consumption by 2030, and it is making significant progress toward this goal.

Additionally, the share of non-fossil fuels in China's primary energy consumption has been increasing. China's updated target is to have non-fossil fuels to account for 25% of primary energy consumption by 2030, currently representing an increase of nearly 10% from 2020 levels (International Renewable Energy Agency, 2022).

As of 2021, China's GHG emissions accounted for 31.72% of global emissions, with an increase of 244% since 2000 (International Energy Agency, 2023a). The energy mix in China is gradually improving with a slight decrease in fossil fuel dependence and a modest increase in renewable energy use. In 2021, the energy supply was composed of 18% oil, 8% natural gas, and 61% coal (International Energy Agency, 2023a).

As for the Carbon Intensity Reduction, China pledged to reduce its carbon intensity (CO_2 emissions per unit of GDP) by over 65% from 2005 levels by 2030. Projections indicate that China will achieve a 67% reduction by 2030 (Liu & Shearer, 2022).

However, despite efforts to limit coal consumption, China has continued to approve and build new coal-fired power plants. Between 2020 and 2023, permits for new coal power projects increased fourfold (Centre for Research on Energy and Clean Air, 2023b). This reliance on coal poses a significant challenge to reducing overall emissions and meeting carbon intensity targets.

Additionally, China aimed to reduce energy intensity (energy consumption per unit of GDP) by 13.5% between 2020 and 2025. However, energy intensity fell by only 2% between 2020 and 2023 (Myllyvirta, 2023a). This shortfall indicates that China is not on track to meet its energy intensity reduction target.

Finally, while China aims to peak its CO_2 emissions before 2030, actual emissions increased by 5% in 2021 and are projected to continue rising slightly before peaking around 2025 (Myllyvirta, 2023a). This delay in peaking emissions complicates efforts to achieve the overall emission reductions necessary to meet global climate goals.

China: financing and implementation challenges of energy transition

To finance the energy transition in China, various models and obstacles need to be considered. China's commitment to achieving the "dual carbon" goal (reach its carbon emissions peak before 2030 and become "carbon neutral" before 2060) necessitates energy structure transformation, with financing being a key challenge in this process (Jia et al., 2024). Green finance has emerged as a crucial tool in transitioning toward sustainability in China, supporting the country's efforts in achieving carbon neutrality, although challenges exist in effectively implementing these initiatives (Lin et al., 2022; Hoang & Tuan, 2023; An et al., 2023).

China's energy transition is also influenced by its institutional framework, with a focus on the balance between state and market forces in driving low-carbon energy initiatives (Zhang & Andrews-Speed, 2020). The country's normative power in international financial governance structures, as exemplified by institutions like the AIIB (The Asian Infrastructure Investment Bank), enhances China's influence in promoting sustainable energy practices globally (Peng & Tok, 2016).

Market mechanisms, such as power spot markets, power capacity markets, power futures markets, carbon emission markets, and Tradable Green Certificate markets, have been analyzed to determine their effectiveness in overcoming obstacles in China's energy transition (Pingkuo et al., 2021). Additionally, the role of green finance in transforming China's energy consumption structure has been highlighted, emphasizing the importance of financial support in improving energy consumption patterns (Gu et al., 2023). China's national carbon emissions trading scheme aims to accelerate the energy transition process and achieve carbon neutrality goals (Tian et al., 2022).

Despite these strategic initiatives, the financing of China's energy transition faces several implementation challenges. These include the need to scale up green finance effectively, integrate market mechanisms into a complex and evolving energy landscape, and ensure that institutional frameworks support both domestic and international sustainability objectives. The success of China's energy transition will depend on its ability to address these challenges, leveraging its financial and institutional strengths while overcoming the obstacles inherent in such a massive transformation.

China: conclusion

China has been actively pursuing an energy transition policy to reduce CO_2 emissions and achieve its carbon emission reduction targets by 2030 (Wang et al., 2021). China's energy transition is also influenced by its overseas finance activities in renewable energy projects in countries like Argentina and Brazil, aligning with its energy transition goals (Rubio & Jáuregui, 2022).

Despite these efforts, obstacles persist in China's energy transition, including inefficient energy use hindering sustainable development (Pingkuo et al., 2020). The country's provincial energy efficiency and influencing factors are crucial considerations in addressing these challenges (Pingkuo et al., 2020). Furthermore, the lack of corporate financing poses a significant barrier to economic development in emerging markets like China (Liu et al., 2021). Additionally, China's prioritization of economic growth and energy security has led to continued reliance on fossil fuels, particularly coal. The economic impact of the COVID-19 pandemic and geopolitical factors, such as the war in Ukraine, have also influenced China's energy policies, reinforcing the importance of energy security over rapid decarbonization.

Finally, integrating large-scale renewable energy into the grid poses technical and infrastructure challenges. While renewable capacity has increased, ensuring a consistent and reliable energy supply from these sources remains a complex task.

In conclusion, financing the energy transition in China requires leveraging green finance, implementing effective market mechanisms, and addressing obstacles such as inefficient energy use and corporate financing limitations. By adopting comprehensive strategies and models tailored to China's specific context, the country can advance toward a sustainable and low-carbon energy future. While China has made notable progress in expanding renewable energy and reducing carbon intensity, challenges in reducing coal dependency and achieving significant energy intensity reductions remain. Balancing economic growth with climate commitments continues to be a central challenge for China's climate strategy.

Comparative analysis and discussion

The global shift toward renewable energy is driven by diverse strategies and policies tailored to the unique political, economic, and environmental contexts of individual countries. This section compares the energy transition efforts of France, Germany, and China, focusing on their policies, progress, challenges, financing mechanisms, and the impact of significant events such as the Russian war in Ukraine.

France's energy policy is centered around reducing GHG emissions and increasing the share of renewables in its energy mix. Germany's Energiewende (Energy Transition) initiative aims to overhaul the energy system by phasing out nuclear and coal while boosting renewable energy. China's energy transition is driven by its dual carbon goals of peaking emissions before 2030 and achieving carbon neutrality by 2060.

France has made progress in reducing GHG emissions by 23% from 1990 levels by 2021. However, the pace of change needs acceleration to meet the ambitious 55% reduction target by 2030. The share of renewables in final energy consumption remains modest, with significant improvements needed in energy efficiency and grid integration.

Germany has reduced its GHG emissions by 46% from 1990 levels by 2023. Renewable energy accounted for 55% of electricity production in 2023. However, challenges remain in upgrading grid infrastructure and managing the socio-economic impacts of phasing out coal.

China has rapidly expanded its renewable energy capacity, particularly in wind and solar. Despite this, the reliance on coal persists, with permits for new coal projects continuing. China aims to peak emissions by 2025, but achieving significant energy intensity reductions remains challenging.

France's financing strategy involves public investments, tax incentives, and subsidies. The PIA supports innovative projects in green technologies. Challenges include overcoming institutional inertia and balancing nuclear energy with renewables.

Germany's Energiewende relies on a mix of public and private investments, supported by policies like feed-in tariffs. Challenges include managing the financial and logistical aspects of increasing renewable capacity and ensuring grid stability.

China's financing for the energy transition leverages green finance and market mechanisms like carbon trading. Challenges include addressing inefficient energy use, continued coal dependency, and ensuring consistent and reliable energy supply from renewables.

The Russian war in Ukraine has significantly affected the energy transition strategies of these countries. In France, the war has highlighted the importance of energy security and accelerated efforts to reduce dependence on fossil fuel imports. France's reliance on nuclear power has provided some stability, but there is a renewed push for diversifying energy sources.

The war has underscored Germany's vulnerability due to its reliance on Russian gas. This has expedited Germany's plans to phase out coal and increase renewable energy capacity, despite the challenges of ensuring grid stability and managing the economic impact on coal-dependent regions.

While China's energy policies are less directly impacted by the war, the global energy market's volatility has reinforced the need for energy security and diversification. China continues to expand its renewable energy capacity while balancing its coal dependency.

France, Germany, and China exemplify diverse pathways to achieving energy transition, each with its strengths and challenges. France's balanced approach leverages nuclear and renewables but requires faster implementation. Germany's Energiewende sets a precedent in renewable energy expansion and coal phase-out, though grid stability and socio-economic impacts pose challenges. China's ambitious goals and rapid renewable capacity expansion are offset by its continued coal dependency and energy efficiency issues.

The impact of the Russian war in Ukraine has further influenced these strategies, highlighting the importance of energy security and accelerating renewable energy adoption. Enhanced international cooperation and knowledge exchange can further accelerate progress toward a sustainable and resilient energy future.

Conclusion and perspectives

The comparative analysis of the energy transition strategies in France, Germany, and China reveals both commonalities and distinctive approaches shaped by their unique political, economic, and environmental contexts.

The impact of significant events such as the Russian war in Ukraine has further influenced these strategies. For France and Germany, the conflict has underscored the importance of energy security and expedited renewable energy adoption to reduce dependence on fossil fuel imports. For China, the geopolitical tensions have reinforced the need for energy security, balancing its renewable energy expansion with continued coal dependency.

France needs to further diversify its energy mix by accelerating the integration of renewables alongside nuclear energy. Innovation in energy storage and smart grid technologies will be crucial. Strengthening governance structures and ensuring effective policy implementation through streamlined regulations and incentives will help overcome institutional inertia. Additionally, enhancing public support for renewable energy projects through education and community involvement will be vital for the success of the energy transition.

Upgrading grid infrastructure to handle increased renewable inputs and ensuring a stable energy supply will be critical. Implementing policies to support coal-dependent regions and workers will mitigate the socio-economic impacts of the coal phase-out. Finally, fostering technological advancements in renewable energy and energy efficiency through research and development will sustain the momentum of the Energiewende.

China must find a balance between economic growth and its climate commitments, gradually reducing coal dependency while expanding renewables. Strengthening green finance mechanisms and ensuring their effective implementation will support the energy transition. Finally, engaging in international partnerships and knowledge exchange will help China adopt best practices and innovative solutions for its energy transition.

Enhanced international cooperation and knowledge exchange among countries will be crucial in addressing the global energy transition challenges. Sharing best practices, technological innovations, and financial strategies can accelerate the shift toward a sustainable and resilient energy future. The insights gained from the diverse approaches of France, Germany, and China can inform global efforts to combat climate change and promote renewable energy adoption.

By addressing the identified challenges through robust policy frameworks, technological innovation, and sustained public and political support, France, Germany, and China can continue to lead the way in the global energy transition.

References

An, Q., Lin, C., Li, Q., & Zheng, L. (2023). Research on the impact of green finance development on energy intensity in China. *Frontiers in Earth Science*, 11, 1118939.

Aniello, G., Többen, J., & Kuckshinrichs, W. (2019). The transition to renewable energy technologies—Impact on economic performance of north rhine-westphalia. *Applied Sciences*, 9(18), 3783. https://doi.org/10.3390/app9183783

Ayagapin, L., Praene, J. P., Jaggeshar, D., & Surroop, D. (2021). Prospective life cycle assessment: Effect of electricity decarbonization in building sector. *Energies*, 14(11), 3184.

Behrendt, G., Peter, S., Sterly, S., & Häring, A. (2019). Community financing in the German organic food sector: a key for sustainable food systems? 2019/18. https://doi.org/10.25518/ciriec.wp201918

Bouzarovski, S., & Herrero, S. (2016). The energy divide: integrating energy transitions, regional inequalities and poverty trends in the European Union. *European Urban and Regional Studies*, 24(1), 69–86. https://doi.org/10.1177/0969776415596449

Carbon Brief. (2023). The carbon brief profile: China. Retrieved from https://interactive.carbonbrief.org/the-carbon-brief-profile-china/

Center for Climate and Energy Solutions. (2015). China's contribution to the Paris Climate Agreement. Retrieved from https://www.c2es.org/wp-content/uploads/2015/07/chinas-contribution-paris-climate-agreement.pdf

Centre for Research on Energy and Clean Air. (2023a). 2 years later: China's ban on overseas coal power projects and its global climate impacts. Retrieved July 21, 2024, from https://energyandcleanair.org/publication/2-years-later-chinas-ban-on-overseas-coal-power-projects-and-its-global-climate-impacts/#:~:text=At%20the%202021%20United%20Nations,was%20met%20with%20global%20acclaim

Centre for Research on Energy and Clean Air. (2023b). China risks missing multiple climate commitments as coal power approvals continue. Retrieved July 21, 2024, from https://energyandcleanair.org/publication/china-risks-missing-multiple-climate-commitments-as-coal-power-approvals-continue/

Direction Générale du Trésor. (2021). La réforme des énergies renouvelables en Allemagne (EEG 2021). https://www.tresor.economie.gouv.fr/Articles/8eae961f-c773-45ca-ada0-e15f14bf82e3/files/116731f7-77a5-49b4-acd3-f6d2aa0a5620

Edo, G. (2023). The german energy system: Analysis of past, present, and future developments. *Advanced Energy Conversion Materials*, 4(1),18–28. https://doi.org/10.37256/aecm.4120232207

Egli, F. & Steffen, B. (2018). A dynamic analysis of financing conditions for renewable energy technologies. *Nature Energy*, 3(12), 1084–1092. https://doi.org/10.1038/s41560-018-0277-y

European Commission. (2021). Climate and Resilience Law. Retrieved July 21, 2024, from https://commission.europa.eu/projects/climate-and-resilience-law_en

Fagan, P. (2023). The social justice and human rights benefits of domestic renewable energy. *Advances in Environmental and Engineering Research*, 4(1), 1–29.

Federal Government of Germany. (2019). Climate Action Programme 2030. Retrieved from https://www.bundesregierung.de/breg-en/issues/climate-action

Federal Government of Germany. (2022). Amendment of the Renewables Act. Retrieved from https://www.bundesregierung.de/breg-de/schwerpunkte/klimaschutz/amendment-of-the-renewables-act-2060448

Federal Ministry for Economic Affairs and Climate Action. (2015). 15 years of the EEG: Shaping the energy transition. https://www.bmwk-energiewende.de/EWD/Redaktion/EN/Newsletter/2015/02/Meldung/15-years-of--eeg.html

Federal Ministry for the Environment, Nature Conservation and Nuclear Safety. (2007). Integrated Climate and Energy Programme (IEKP). Climate Change Laws of the World. https://climate-laws.org/documents/integrated-climate-and-energy-programme-iekp_355c?id=integrated-climate-and-energy-programme-iekp_1f17

Federal Ministry for the Environment, Nature Conservation, Nuclear Safety and Consumer Protection (BMUV). (2016). Climate Action Plan 2050. Retrieved from https://www.bmuv.de/en/publication/climate-action-plan-2050-en

Federal Ministry for the Environment, Nature Conservation, Nuclear Safety and Consumer Protection (BMUV). (2023). Germany brings era of nuclear power to an end. https://www.bmuv.de/en/pressrelease/germany-brings-era-of-nuclear-power-to-an-end

Finamore, B. (2010). China records its climate actions by Copenhagen Accord deadline. Natural Resources Defense Council. Retrieved from https://www.nrdc.org/bio/barbara-finamore/china-records-its-climate-actions-copenhagen-accord-deadline

French Government. (2019). Law No. 2019-1147 on Energy and the Climate. Legifrance. Retrieved July 21, 2024, from https://www.legifrance.gouv.fr/jorf/id/JORFTEXT000039355955/

French Government. (2021). Le programme d'investissements d'avenir. Retrieved July 21, 2024, from https://www.info.gouv.fr/actualite/le-programme-d-investissements-d-avenir

Gawel, E., Korte, K., & Tews, K. (2015). Distributional challenges of sustainability policies—The case of the german energy transition. *Sustainability*, 7(12), 16599–16615. https://doi.org/10.3390/su71215834

Gawel, E., Strunz, S., & Lehmann, P. (2013). Germany's energy transition under attack: Is there an inscrutable German sonderweg? *Nature and Culture*, 8(2), 121–133. https://doi.org/10.3167/nc.2013.080201

Global Energy Monitor. (2023). China poised to double wind and solar capacity five years ahead of 2030 target. Retrieved July 21, 2024, from https://globalenergymonitor.org/press-release/china-poised-to-double-wind-and-solar-capacity-five-years-ahead-of-2030-target/

Gu, X., Qin, L., & Zhang, M. (2023). The impact of green finance on the transformation of energy consumption structure: Evidence based on China. *Frontiers in Earth Science*, 10, 1097346.

Hoang, D. C., & Tuan, D. C. (2023). Evaluating the role of green financing, international trade and alternative energies on environmental performance in case of Chinese provinces: Application of quantile regression approach. *International Journal of Energy Economics and Policy*, 13(2), 500–508.

International Energy Agency (IEA). (2014). Renewable Energy Sources Act (Erneuerbare-Energien-Gesetz, EEG). https://www.iea.org/policies/3858-renewable-energy-sources-act-erneuerbare-energien-gesetz-eeg

International Energy Agency (IEA). (2016a). 2014 Amendment of the Renewable Energy Sources Act (EEG 2014). https://www.iea.org/policies/5734-2014-amendment-of-the-renewable-energy-sources-act-eeg-2014

International Energy Agency (IEA). (2016b). National Energy Conservation Law of China (amendments in 2016). Retrieved from https://www.iea.org/policies/7910-national-energy-conservation-law-of-china-amendments-in-2016

International Energy Agency. (2017). *Energy Concept*. IEA Policy Database. https://www.iea.org/policies/106-energy-concept

International Energy Agency (IEA). (2021). An energy sector roadmap to carbon neutrality in China: Executive summary. Retrieved from https://www.iea.org/reports/an-energy-sector-roadmap-to-carbon-neutrality-in-china/executive-summary

International Energy Agency (IEA). (2023a). China. Retrieved from https://www.iea.org/countries/china

International Energy Agency (IEA). (2023b). Renewables 2023: Executive summary. Retrieved July 21, 2024, from https://www.iea.org/reports/renewables-2023/executive-summary

International Renewable Energy Agency. (2022). China's route to carbon neutrality. Retrieved July 21, 2024, from https://www.irena.org/-/media/Files/IRENA/Agency/Publication/2022/Jul/IRENA_China_Carbon_Neutral_2022.pdf?rev=8ab20715805140dcb8ff28f1c064b94d#:~:text=China%20has%20updated%20its%20mid,percentage%20points%20from%202020%20levels

Jia, X., Xu, W., & Wang, K. (2024). Financial openness and energy structure transformation. *Frontiers in Environmental Science*, 11, 1346594.

Liu, Z., Li, W., Hao, C., & Liu, H. (2021). Corporate environmental performance and financing constraints: An empirical study in the Chinese context. *Corporate Social Responsibility and Environmental Management*, 28(2), 616–629.

Lin, Z., Liao, X., & Jia, H. (2022). Could green finance facilitate low-carbon transformation of power generation? Some evidence from China. *International Journal of Climate Change Strategies and Management*, 15(2), 141–158. https://doi.org/10.1108/ijccsm-03-2022-0039

Liu, L., & Shearer, C. (2022). Guest post: Why China is set to significantly overachieve its 2030 climate goals. Carbon Brief. Retrieved July 21, 2024, from https://www.carbonbrief.org/guest-post-why-china-is-set-to-significantly-overachieve-its-2030-climate-goals/

Mazzucato, M., & Semieniuk, G. (2017). Public financing of innovation: new questions. *Oxford Review of Economic Policy*, 33(1), 24–48. https://doi.org/10.1093/oxrep/grw036
Ministry of Ecology and Environment. (2009, December 26). *Renewable Energy Law of the People's Republic of China* (Adopted February 28, 2005; amended December 26, 2009). Retrieved from https://english.mee.gov.cn/Resources/laws/envir_elatedlaws/201705/t20170513_414037.shtml
Ministry of Ecological Transition. (2011). National Climate Change Adaptation Plan (PNACC-1). French Republic. Retrieved July 21, 2024, from https://www.ecologie.gouv.fr/sites/default/files/documents/ONERC_PNACC_1_complet.pdf
Ministry of Ecological Transition. (2016). Energy Transition for Green Growth Act in action: Regions, citizens, business. French Republic. Retrieved July 21, 2024, from https://www.ecologie.gouv.fr/sites/default/files/documents/Energy%20Transition%20for%20Green%20Growth%20Act%20in%20action%20-%20Regions,%20citizens,%20business%20(%2032%20pages%20-%20juillet%202016%20-%20Versions%20anglaise).pdf
Ministry of Ecological Transition. (2018). National Climate Change Adaptation Plan (PNACC-2). French Republic. Retrieved July 21, 2024, from https://www.ecologie.gouv.fr/sites/default/files/documents/2018.12.20_PNACC2.pdf
Ministry of Ecological Transition. (2020a). National Low-Carbon Strategy (SNBC) - Summary. French Republic. Retrieved July 21, 2024, from https://www.ecologie.gouv.fr/sites/default/files/documents/19092_strategie-carbone-EN_oct-20.pdf
Ministry of Ecological Transition. (2020b). Multiannual Energy Plan (PPE) - Executive summary. French Republic. Retrieved July 21, 2024, from https://www.ecologie.gouv.fr/sites/default/files/documents/PPE-Executive%20summary.pdf
Ministry of Ecological Transition. (2022). Loi relative à la transition énergétique pour la croissance verte (TEPCV). French Republic. Retrieved July 21, 2024, from https://www.ecologie.gouv.fr/politiques-publiques/loi-relative-transition-energetique-croissance-verte-tepcv#:~:text=La%20loi%20de%20transition%20%C3%A9nerg%C3%A9tique%20pour%20la%20croissance%20verte%20pr%C3%A9voit,parc%20de%20logements%20%C3%A0%202050
Ministry of Ecological Transition. (2024a). France s'adapte: Christophe Béchu a réuni les élus, citoyens, acteurs économiques et société civile. French Republic. Retrieved July 21, 2024, from https://www.ecologie.gouv.fr/presse/france-sadapte-christophe-bechu-reuni-elus-citoyens-acteurs-economiques-societe-civile
Ministry of Ecological Transition. (2024b). Trajectoire de réchauffement de référence pour l'adaptation au changement climatique (TRACC). French Republic. Retrieved July 21, 2024, from https://www.ecologie.gouv.fr/politiques-publiques/trajectoire-rechauffement-reference-ladaptation-changement-climatique-tracc
Ministry of Ecology and Environment of the People's Republic of China. (2022a). China's policies and actions for addressing climate change. Retrieved July 21, 2024, from https://english.mee.gov.cn/Resources/Reports/reports/202211/P020221110605466439270.pdf
Ministry of Ecology and Environment of the People's Republic of China. (2022b). Progress on the implementation of China's nationally determined contributions. Unofficial translation. Retrieved July 21, 2024, from https://www.mee.gov.cn/ywgz/ydqhbh/qhbhlf/202211/W020221111760730462299.pdf
Ministry of Ecological Transition, Biodiversity, Forests, Seas and Fisheries. (2025). *Plan national d'adaptation au changement climatique (PNACC-3)*. French Republic. Retrieved september 11, 2025, from https://www.adaptation-changement-climatique.gouv.fr/agir/espace-documentaire/presentation-du-plan-national-dadaptation-du-changement-climatique
Moss, T., Becker, S., & Naumann, M. (2014). Whose energy transition is it, anyway? Organisation and ownership of the energiewende in villages, cities and regions. *Local Environment*, 20(12), 1547–1563. https://doi.org/10.1080/13549839.2014.915799
Myllyvirta, L. (2023a). Analysis: Record drop in China's CO_2 emissions needed to meet 2025 target. Carbon Brief. Retrieved July 21, 2024 from https://www.carbonbrief.org/analysis-record-drop-in-chinas-co2-emissions-needed-to-meet-2025-target/
Ohlhorst, D. (2015). Germany's energy transition policy between national targets and decentralized responsibilities. *Journal of Integrative Environmental Sciences*, 12(4), 303–322. https://doi.org/10.1080/1943815x.2015.1125373

Pegels, A., & Lütkenhorst, W. (2014). Is Germany's energy transition a case of successful green industrial policy? Contrasting wind and solar PV. *Energy Policy*, 74, 522–534. https://doi.org/10.1016/j.enpol.2014.06.031

Peng, Z., & Tok, S. (2016). The AIIB and China's normative power in international financial governance structure. *Chinese Political Science Review*, 1(4), 736–753. https://doi.org/10.1007/s41111-016-0042-y

Pingkuo, L., Huan, P., & Zhiwei, W. (2020). Orderly-synergistic development of power generation industry: A China's case study based on evolutionary game model. *Energy*, 211, 118632.

Reitz, S., Goshen, L., & Ohlhorst, D. (2022). Trade-offs in German wind energy expansion: building bridges between different interests, values and priorities. *Energy, Sustainability and Society*, 12(1), 39.

Rubio, T., & Jáuregui, J. (2022). Chinese overseas finance in renewable energy in Argentina and Brazil: Implications for the energy transition. *Journal of Current Chinese Affairs*, 51(1), 137–164. https://doi.org/10.1177/18681026221094852

Sadorsky, P. (2020). Energy related CO_2 emissions before and after the financial crisis. *Sustainability*, 12(9), 3867.

Sansilvestri, R., Cordier, M., & Lescuyer, T. (2021). Winners and losers in energy transition: Study case of wood biomass power-plants implementation in France. *Forests*, 12(9), 1139.

Sonnberger, M., Ruddat, M., Arnold, A., Scheer, D., Poortinga, W., Böhm, G., & Tvinnereim, E. (2021). Climate concerned but anti-nuclear: Exploring (dis)approval of nuclear energy in four European countries. *Energy Research & Social Science*, 75, 102008. https://doi.org/10.1016/j.erss.2021.102008

Sovacool, B. K. (2016). How long will it take? Conceptualizing the temporal dynamics of energy transitions. *Energy Research & Social Science*, 13, 202–215.

State Council Information Office of the People's Republic of China. (2023). By 2025, renewable energy consumption will account for more than 50% of the increase in primary energy consumption. Retrieved from http://www.scio.gov.cn/zfbps/zfbps_2279/202408/t20240829_860523.html

Steinbacher, K. (2015). Drawing lessons when objectives differ? Assessing renewable energy policy transfer from Germany to Morocco. *Politics and Governance*, 3(2), 34–50. https://doi.org/10.17645/pag.v3i2.192

Storm, S., & Naastepad, C. (2015). Crisis and recovery in the german economy: The real lessons. *Structural Change and Economic Dynamics*, 32, 11–24. https://doi.org/10.1016/j.strueco.2015.01.001

Tian, J., Yu, L., Xue, R., Zhuang, S., & Shan, Y. (2022). Global low-carbon energy transition in the post-COVID-19 era. *Applied Energy*, 307, 118205.

Umweltbundesamt. (2013). The German Energiewende: Transforming Germany's energy system. Federal Environment Agency. https://www.umweltbundesamt.de/sites/default/files/medien/378/publikationen/131008_abstract.pdf

Wang, D., Xue, L., Yang, X., Zhang, Z., Wen, X., & Zhao, Y. (2021). China's energy transition policy expectation and its Co_2 emission reduction effect assessment. *Frontiers in Energy Research*, 8, 1–11. https://doi.org/10.3389/fenrg.2020.627096

Wagner, O., Adisorn, T., Tholen, L., & Kiyar, D. (2020). Surviving the energy transition: Development of a proposal for evaluating sustainable business models for incumbents in Germany's electricity market. *Energies*, 13(3), 730. https://doi.org/10.3390/en13030730

Zhang, S., & Andrews-Speed, P. (2020). State versus market in China's low-carbon energy transition: An institutional perspective. *Energy Research & Social Science*, 66, 101503. https://doi.org/10.1016/j.erss.2020.101503

7 Greenium analysis on the supranational twin bond market

Ewa Dziwok

Introduction

Growing environmental concerns and the clear evidence of climate change have intensified the urgency for action (IPCC, 2022). The costs associated with mitigating and adapting to these changes are so substantial that private sector involvement is essential. It is crucial for financial institutions and businesses to align their investments and operations with the United Nations Sustainable Development Goals (SDGs) outlined in the Paris Agreement (United Nations, 2015), and at regional level, with the European Union's goal of achieving net-zero emissions by 2050.

Green bonds play a key role in sustainable financing. They serve a dual purpose: on one hand, the funds raised through their issuance support climate change mitigation efforts, and on the other hand, they offer a traditional investment vehicle with fixed-income returns. Green bonds are essentially fixed-income securities that, in their fundamental structure, closely resemble conventional bonds (Eisinger et al., 2017). However, the proceeds from green bonds are specifically allocated for projects focused on environmental or climate-related initiatives. According to the International Capital Markets Association (ICMA), a green bond is defined as any bond instrument where the proceeds are used exclusively to finance or refinance, in whole or in part, new and/or existing eligible green projects (ICMA, 2018).

The concept of green bonds emerged in the early 21st century as a direct response to the growing awareness of climate change. In 2007, the European Investment Bank (EIB) issued the first green bond, followed by the World Bank in 2008 (EIB, 2022; World Bank, 2019), laying the foundation for the green debt instrument market. While green bonds began as a niche financial product, their growth has been exponential, particularly following the Paris Agreement, supported by various global initiatives (Kanamura, 2020). Despite being labeled "green", there is no universal definition or typology for assessing their level of "greenness". Early on, issuers self-labeled their bonds as "green" and declared their intentions to support projects related to climate change mitigation or adaptation (European Commission et al., 2017). In 2014, the ICMA introduced the Green Bond Principles (GBPs) – a voluntary process that provides the guidance on defining, selecting, and reporting green projects intended for funding (ICMA, 2018). It also encourages issuers to seek external reviews, such as second-party opinion (SPO).

Several organizations, including SPO providers like CICERO, Vigeo, and Sustainalytics, along with third-party evaluators like the Climate Bonds Initiative, Moody's, and S&P Green Evaluation, offer independent verification services to assess compliance with accepted classifications (Ehlers & Packer, 2017; Dorfleitner et al., 2022). To mitigate the risk of "greenwashing" – where issuers falsely claim environmental benefits – many agencies and governments are moving towards standardized classifications (EIB & GFCCSFB, 2017).

DOI: 10.4324/9781003663539-8

Environmental issues have a significant impact on the cost of debt, which in turn affects the rate of return. These cost-reducing factors include environmental, social, and economic components, forming a triad of sustainability elements (Tolliver et al., 2020). Issuers with a strong focus on environmental protection can therefore expect reduced debt spending and improved credit ratings. Regarding green bonds, the main cost driver is growing environmental awareness among investors, which leads to increased demand. Investors show an increased willingness to accept lower returns for holding these bonds, creating an "environmental premium", where they are willing to pay a premium for bonds that align with the SDGs.

This study explores the supranational green bond market to assess the nature of bond greenness in a form of "green bond premium", understood as a separate factor from a concurrently existing liquidity premium in empirical yield spreads (Koziol et al., 2022). We extend the methodological frameworks of earlier studies by creating a conventional and green yield curve representative of the bond segment, rather than matching bonds one by one based on similar coupon and maturity (Zerbib, 2019).

The study poses two key research questions. First, does the green bond premium vary based on maturity terms? This question is addressed by comparing zero-coupon rates estimated from green bonds with those from the most liquid conventional bonds issued by the same entity. Second, is the green bond premium fixed over time? To verify this, we compare bond yields across time using a theoretical zero-coupon yield curve constructed via the Nelson-Siegel-Svensson parametric model.

The data analyzed comes from the European market focusing on bonds issued by the EIB (supranational financial institution with the longest history of issuing Climate Awareness Bonds), including both green-labeled and conventional bonds. Two yield curves – green and conventional – are constructed for the same issuer (EIB), allowing for the extraction of zero-coupon rates with the same format and maturity dates (twin papers). To date, no other study has conducted a time-based greenium analysis using the parametric method to create twin yield curves.

The structure of the study is as follows: the second part reviews the literature on the green premium and greenium related to green bonds. The third part discusses the methodology for constructing the yield curve using the Nelson-Siegel-Svensson model. The fourth section describes the data used in the analysis, followed by part five, which presents the research findings. The final section offers conclusions.

Theoretical aspect of greenium

Research on greenium should be analyzed from different perspectives, with particular emphasis on specific elements related to the characteristics of green bonds (MacAskill et al., 2021). These features include factors such as the type of green bond (sovereign, corporate, municipal), the segment of the green bond market (primary and/or secondary), geographical aspects (issuer country/region), type of industry, issuer ratings, and chosen methodology.

Due to these diverse factors and the relatively limited number of green bond studies, comparing all available results can be challenging. A key issue in this article is the selected methodology for estimating theoretical yields, which, in this study, uses the parametric Nelson-Siegel-Svensson curve estimation model. Hence the adopted estimation methodology is considered crucial.

In previous studies, researchers have employed various methodological approaches to construct synthetic bonds for their analysis. For instance, Agliardi and Agliardi (2019) and Ehlers and Packer (2017) relied on credit spreads data, employing a matching method to analyze the yield curve of green and brown bond pairs. Karpf and Mandel (2018) used yield spreads as a key metric for their analysis. Zerbib (2019) and Wu (2022) selected yields of closest (in terms of maturity) green bonds, and by using an interpolation method, estimated twin bond yield as an average between known data points. Meanwhile, Gianfrate and Peri (2019) applied the score matching technique, while Reboredo (2018) used the copula model.

These diverse methodological approaches reflect the complexity of the subject. Upon reviewing a wide range of sources, it becomes clear that evidence for the existence of greenium is not conclusive. There is no convincing confirmation of its presence, nor of its stability where it does exist. Additionally, there is a significant gap in research concerning the behavior of greenium over time. This underscores the need for a comprehensive study that sheds more light on this aspect of bond markets.

Methodology

There are numerous methods for constructing the yield curve, as extensively described by James and Webber (2000). To achieve a smooth yield curve, two main categories of models are typically considered: parametric models introduced by Nelson and Siegel (1987) and extended by Svensson (1994), as well as cubic splines.

This study focuses on parametric models, which are valued for their simplicity and a minimal number of parameters required for estimation, making them especially useful when data availability is limited. Moreover, the functional form of these models determines three essential attributes – smoothness, flexibility, and stability – expected from a correctly estimated yield curve (Dziwok & Wirth, 2019).

As defined by Nawalkha, Soto, and Beliaeva (2005), the term structure of interest rates describes the relationship between yields for investments of the same credit quality but varying maturities. Typically, a term structure is constructed using a set of liquid and commonly traded assets. However, challenges arise when dealing with non-liquid or emerging market assets, such as green bonds, which may suffer from limited data availability.

Let's consider the price of the zero-coupon bond denoted as P, with a cashflow c at maturity τ and yield to maturity $i(\tau)$ defined as a spot zero-coupon rate. When considering a continuously compound interest, the price is the discounted value of a future cashflow c:

$$P(\tau) = c \cdot e^{-i(\tau)\cdot\tau} \tag{7.1}$$

where: $P(\tau)$ – price of the zero-coupon bond with maturity τ

c – cashflow at time τ

$i(\tau)$ – spot rate

By defining the discount function as:

$$\delta(\tau) = e^{-i(\tau)\cdot\tau} \tag{7.2}$$

for $\delta : \mathfrak{R}_+ \rightarrow (0;1]$, every default-free coupon bond can be represented as a portfolio of zero-coupon bonds with the maturities corresponding to the payment dates. An existence of inter-relation between discount factor $\delta(\tau)$, spot rate $i(\tau)$, and price (in continuous time) could be than illustrated as below:

$$P(\tau) = \delta(\tau) = e^{-i(\tau)\cdot\tau} \tag{7.3}$$

A construction of the term structure begins with gathering a sample of instruments to be used. In the green bond market, which is analyzed here, there is a lack of short-term data, except for several quotations. Therefore, all available quotations were considered with a limited quality check.

Suppose there is a set of k instruments, with market values P_l, $l = 1,2,...,k$ and cashflows $c_{l,j}$ for bond l at time τ_j, $j = 1,2,...,k$. Let $\mathbf{C} = \{c_{l,j}\}_{l=1,..,k,j=1,..,k}$ be the cashflow matrix, typically sparse with many zero entries and $P = \{P_l\}_{l=1,..,k}$ is the price vector. Knowledge of $\mathbf{C}$ and P determines the discount factors:

$$P = \mathbf{C} \cdot \begin{bmatrix} \delta(\tau_1) & \delta(\tau_2) & \cdots & \delta(\tau_3) \end{bmatrix}^T \tag{7.4}$$

To fit the curve, an interpolation method (theoretical function form) must be chosen to obtain discount factors $\bar{\delta}(\tau)$ for all maturities from zero to infinity. McCulloch (1975) used a piecewise polynomial function, but this model had stability issues. The use of a parametric model like Nelson-Siegel-Svensson allows for direct calculation of forward rates, ensuring various shapes for the theoretical term structure.

For further analysis, the Nelson-Siegel-Svensson model with six parameters $\bar{\delta}(\tau) = \bar{\delta}$ $(\tau | \beta_0, \beta_1, \beta_2, \beta_3, v_1, v_2)$ is considered. It allows, through the estimation, for more sophisticated yield curve shapes than an implementation of Nelson-Sigel model, which is characterized by only four parameters.

$$i(\tau) = \beta_0 + (\beta_1 + \beta_2) \frac{1 - e^{-\frac{\tau}{v_1}}}{\frac{\tau}{v_1}} - \beta_2 \cdot e^{-\frac{\tau}{v_1}} + \beta_3 \left(\frac{1 - e^{-\frac{\tau}{v_2}}}{\frac{\tau}{v_2}} - e^{-\frac{\tau}{v_2}} \right) \tag{7.5}$$

where:

$[\beta_0, \beta_1, \beta_2, \beta_3, v_1, v_2]$ – vector of parameters describing the curve:
β_0 – parameter which shows a limit in infinity, $\beta_0 > 0$
β_1 – parameter which shows a limit in infinity, $\beta_0 + \beta_1 \geq 0$
β_2 – parameter which shows a strength of curvature
β_3 – parameter which shows a strength of curvature
v_1 – parameter which shows a place of curvature, $v_1 > 0$
v_2 – parameter which shows a place of curvature, $v_2 > 0$

By joining formulas (7.3) and (7.5), a vector of theoretical prices $\bar{P} = \{\bar{P}_l\}_{l=1,..,k}$ can be expressed as a product of the cashflow matrix $\mathbf{C}$ and the vector of discount factors:

$$\bar{P} = \mathbf{C} \cdot \begin{bmatrix} \bar{\delta}(\tau_1) & \bar{\delta}(\tau_2) & \cdots & \bar{\delta}(\tau_k) \end{bmatrix}^T \tag{7.6}$$

A set of parameters $[\beta_0, \beta_1, \beta_2, \beta_3, v_1, v_2]$ is estimated by minimizing the mean square errors between market prices and theoretical ones (taken from the fitted curve):

$$\frac{\sum_{l=1}^{k} (P_l - \bar{P}_l)^2}{k} \rightarrow \min \tag{7.7a}$$

or between market and theoretical rates:

$$\frac{\sum_{l=1}^{k} (i_l - \bar{i}_l)^2}{k} \rightarrow \min \tag{7.7b}$$

where: $P_l - \overline{P_l}$ – a price error of l-th asset

$i_l - \overline{i_l}$ – a yield error of l-th asset

k – number of bonds

A goodness-of-fit comparison (for prices and yields respectively) is possible by the calculation of errors through time. A low mean value proves the flexibility of the model and shows its ability to fit the data accuracy.

Empirical analysis

The bonds were selected in accordance with the Green Bonds Principles (ICMA GBP). Two sets of bonds from the same issuer were used: one consisting of conventional bonds data and the second of green bonds with similar maturity and issue amounts. This approach aimed to achieve the closest possible comparison between the two types of bonds. The bonds included were either fixed-coupon or zero-coupon papers. All data used were extracted from LSEG Refinitiv Eikon.

To analyze the yield differences between conventional and green bonds, a dataset was created using historical prices of securities that met the following criteria:

- green bonds meeting the GBPs criteria of ICMA,
- issued within the European Union (in Luxembourg here),
- denominated in Euro,
- coupon: fixed (including zero-coupon papers)
- holding Standard and Poor's rating of AAA,
- issued by financial companies (here: EIB).

Additionally, both green and conventional bonds from each company were considered based on the size of the issue. A minimum issue value of EUR 1 billion was set to ensure that liquidity did not cause a price bias. Every effort was made to minimize differences in the characteristics of the green and conventional bond sets.

Selection of green bonds

Given that a sufficient number of bonds is necessary to construct a yield curve, the study's timeframe was determined by issue availability. It was found that in 2019 (the starting point of the analysis), only the EIB had issued securities that allowed for the construction of a yield curve with a maturity of up to 19 years. However, during this period, there were no green bonds with shorter maturities, which could result in potential error when constructing the short end of the yield curve in the initial stage. Although 13 green bonds were selected for analysis, only five already existed at the beginning of the analysis, with others being issued later.

Selection of conventional bonds

Following the selection of green bonds, conventional bonds were chosen to match the size of the green bond issues and to adhere to the previously mentioned criteria. The conventional bond market is significantly more developed, providing a much larger set of securities issued under the assumed criteria. For this study specific conventional bonds were chosen – those that represent Euro Area Reference Notes Programme which started in 1999 to enhance liquidity and diversification of Euro market. This choice not only eliminates the risk of the constructed curve being affected by errors due to selection of data but also ensures homogeneity guaranteed by the issuer by selecting them as benchmark bonds.

Table 7.1 Set of chosen green bonds issued by EIB

	ISIN	*Coupon (in%)*	*Issue date*	*Maturity date*	*Issue amount*	*Maturity in years on:*	
						01-01-2019	*31-12-2023*
1	XS1280834992	0.500	27-08-2015	15-11-2023	2,050,000,000	4.87	–
2	XS1878833695	0.375	13-09-2018	15-05-2026	1,850,000,000	7.37	2.37
3	XS1107718279	1.250	10-09-2014	13-11-2026	2,200,000,000	7.87	2.87
4	XS2419364653	–	09-12-2021	15-11-2027	1,500,000,000	–	3.88
5	XS2587298204	2.750	15-02-2023	28-07-2028	5,000,000,000	–	4.58
6	XS2439543047	0.050	03-02-2022	15-11-2029	2,000,000,000	–	5.88
7	XS2535352962	2.250	21-09-2022	15-03-2030	4,000,000,000	–	6.21
8	XS2314675997	0.010	19-03-2021	15-11-2030	1,000,000,000	–	6.88
9	XS2484093393	1.500	24-05-2022	15-06-2032	5,000,000,000	–	8.46
10	XS1828046570	1.125	29-05-2018	15-11-2032	1,000,000,000	13.88	8.88
11	XS2194790262	0.010	29-06-2020	15-11-2035	2,300,000,000	–	11.88
12	XS1500338618	0.500	05-10-2016	13-11-2037	2,500,000,000	18.88	13.88
13	XS1980857319	1.000	09-04-2019	14-11-2042	1,750,000,000	–	18.88

Source: Own preparation based on Refinitiv Eikon data.

Table 7.2 Set of chosen conventional benchmark ESRN-bonds issued by EIB

	ISIN	*Coupon (in%)*	*Issue date*	*Maturity date*	*Issue amount*	*Maturity in years on:*	
						01-01-2019	*31-12-2023*
1	XS1023039545	2.125	28-01-2014	15-01-2024	3,000,000,000	5.04	0.04
2	XS0290050524	4.125	07-03-2007	15-04-2024	3,000,000,000	5.29	0.29
3	XS1575991358	0.250	08-03-2017	14-10-2024	5,000,000,000	5.79	0.79
4	XS1850111789	0.375	03-07-2018	16-07-2025	4,000,000,000	6.54	1.54
5	XS0427291751	4.500	07-05-2009	15-10-2025	3,500,000,000	6.79	1.79
6	XS1394055872	0.375	12-04-2016	14-04-2026	5,000,000,000	7.29	2.29
7	XS1555331617	0.500	25-01-2017	15-01-2027	5,000,000,000	8.04	3.04
8	XS1791485011	0.875	14-03-2018	14-01-2028	5,000,000,000	9.04	4.04
9	XS2102495673	0.050	16-01-2020	16-01-2030	5,000,000,000	–	6.05
10	XS0505157965	4.000	29-04-2010	15-04-2030	3,000,000,000	11.29	6.29
11	XS1612977717	1.125	16-05-2017	13-04-2033	3,000,000,000	14.29	9.29
12	XS0975634204	3.000	01-10-2013	14-10-2033	3,000,000,000	14.79	9.79
13	XS0219724878	4.000	18-05-2005	15-10-2037	5,000,000,000	18.80	13.80

Source: Own preparation based on Refinitiv Eikon data.

The timeframe for the downloaded data aligns with the scope of green bonds and covers the period from the beginning of 2019 to the end of 2023 for bonds issued by the EIB.

Calculations and results

Following the Nelson-Siegel-Svensson parametric model, zero-yield curves were estimated for both green and conventional bonds over a period of 60 months. The calculations were performed daily starting on the first working day in 2019 until the last working day in 2023 for bonds issued by the EIB in accordance with previously adopted criteria.

For each day in this timeframe, and for both cleaned datasets representing green and conventional bonds, the Nelson-Siegel-Svensson model was used to estimate the yield curves. Then, the green premium was calculated by finding the difference between the estimated yield spread for conventional bonds and that for green bonds, while accounting for liquidity premium spreads, according to the following formula, as a separate factor from the simultaneously prevailing liquidity premium in empirical yield spreads (Koziol et al., 2022):

$$\left(i_{\text{conv}} - i_{\text{green}}\right) = \text{Greenium} + \left(LP_{\text{conv}} - LP_{\text{green}}\right)$$

where i_{conv}, i_{green} are estimated zero-coupon rates for conventional bonds and green bonds respectively, LP_{conv}, LP_{green} are liquidity premium understood as a bid-ask spread for conventional bonds and green bonds, and Greenium is green bond premium.

Difficulties in direct observing a greenium may stem from bond matching problems, this is why we refer to the construction of a market yield curve that enables to eliminate a maturity bias that is naturally involved in pairs consisting on bonds with inequivalent maturity. Nevertheless, a liquidity proxy calculation should be also considered. We follow an idea implemented by Zerbib (2019) and chose bid-ask spread as a widely used measure of the degree of bond's illiquidity.

A greenium analysis for bonds issued by EIB

Since the bonds issued by the EIB are characterized by long maturity, it was possible to construct a yield curve with maturities of up to 20 years (Figure 7.1). Consequently, this enables the analysis of greenium over time for a larger range of maturities.

To analyze greenium over time, maturities of 5, 6, 7, 8, 9, 10, 11, 12, 13, and 14 years were selected. Theoretical yields of conventional bonds were compared with the analogical yields of green bond obtained through the construction of the yield curve using the Nelson-Siegel-Svensson method.

In the initial phase (Figure 7.2), greenium was compared for short and medium maturities (five-, six-, seven-, eight-, nine-year). The results obtained emphasize the importance of careful selection of data for the construction of the yield curve. For the five-year maturity period, the

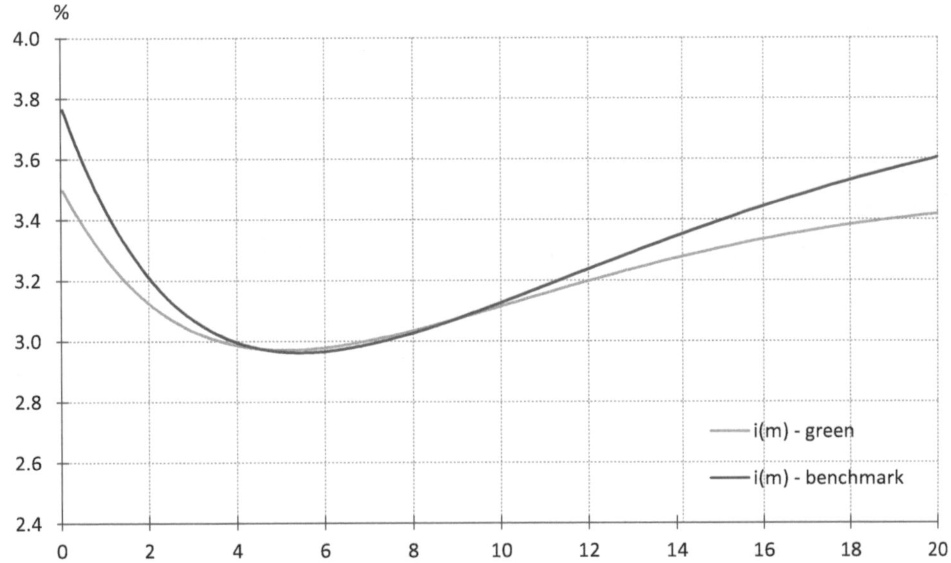

Figure 7.1 Sample yield curves as of December 1, 2023, for green and conventional bonds issued by EIB.

Source: Own calculations.

dataset was limited, resulting in substantial volatility at the short end of the curve. Consequently, results in this segment should be approached with caution. However, for other maturities, gradual changes in greenium values can be observed. Although fluctuating around zero between 2020 and 2022 they turned positive since the end of 2021 and once again to zero since 2023. Despite slightly positive results, the value of greenium was not significantly high. Since the last quarter of 2019, it moved between −0.4% and 0.04% (or −4 to 10 basis points).

Regarding longer maturities (between ten and 14 years), the computed values of greenium is not constant over time and remain either positive or near zero throughout the entire time frame (Figure 7.3). For all maturities, the values closely tracked each other, displaying substantial disparities since 2020. The highest level of greenium for these periods occurred at the beginning of

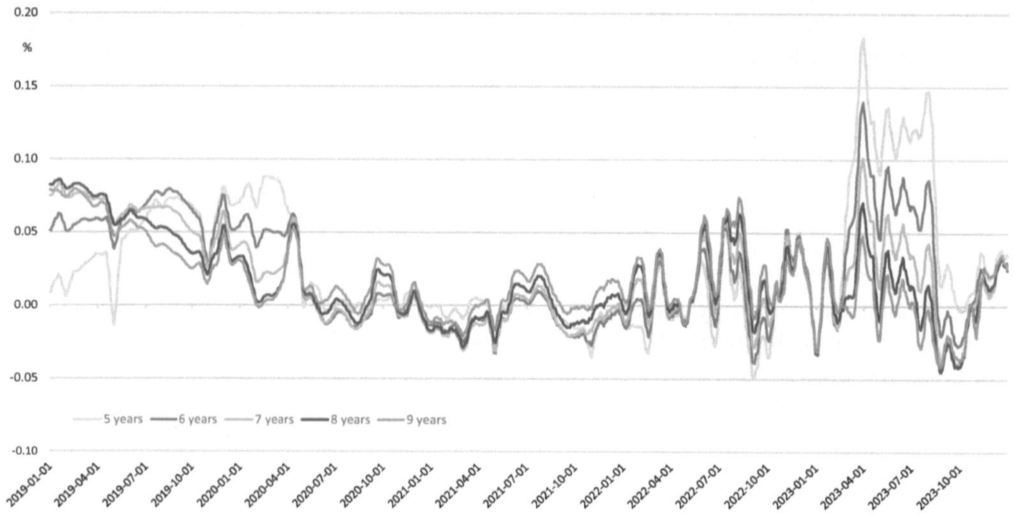

Figure 7.2 Greenium analysis for EIB-issued bonds for maturity five to nine years (2019–2023).
Source: Own calculations.

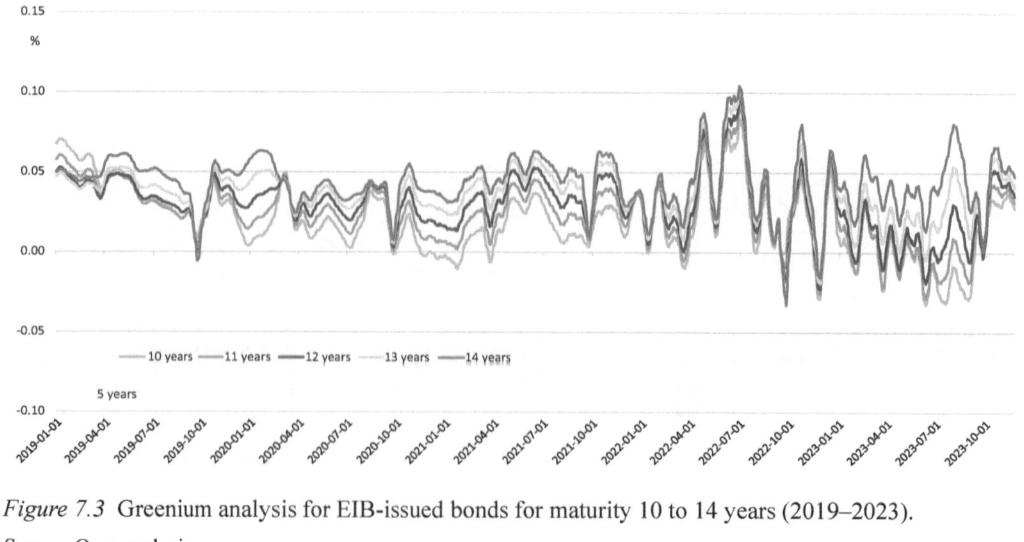

Figure 7.3 Greenium analysis for EIB-issued bonds for maturity 10 to 14 years (2019–2023).
Source: Own analysis.

2022, reaching nearly 0.11% (11 basis points). It should be emphasized that for these maturities, the data set was the largest throughout the entire analysis period.

A descriptive analysis of the greenium for different maturities shows that the distribution is slightly skewed to the left for all ten samples, suggesting the tendency to have a green premium. The shorter the term to maturity, the more outliers on the right tail of the distribution.

Similarly, interdependency between greenium for different maturities shows natural tendency for parallel behavior (boldface in Table 7.3 indicates a significant correlation at 5% level).

Weighted pair-group average Euclidean distances for different greenium maturities shown in a form of a tree diagram confirm a diverse behavior of the green premium for five-year maturity which is a consequence of limited amount of data (Figure 7.4). A separate block consists of short-term greenium maturities (from six to ten years). Additionally, longer maturities (11–14 years) show the greatest similarities.

Table 7.3 Correlation matrix

	5	*6*	*7*	*8*	*9*	*10*	*11*	*12*	*13*	*14*
5	1.000	**0.887**	**0.778**	**0.681**	**0.564**	**0.406**	**0.122**	**−0.143**	**−0.222**	**−0.180**
6	**0.887**	1.000	**0.977**	**0.928**	**0.843**	**0.692**	**0.369**	0.005	**−0.156**	**−0.149**
7	**0.778**	**0.977**	1.000	**0.985**	**0.931**	**0.803**	**0.488**	**0.089**	**−0.117**	**−0.142**
8	**0.681**	**0.928**	**0.985**	1.000	**0.979**	**0.882**	**0.594**	**0.182**	**−0.062**	**−0.122**
9	**0.564**	**0.843**	**0.931**	**0.979**	1.000	**0.952**	**0.724**	**0.324**	0.048	−0.053
10	**0.406**	**0.692**	**0.803**	**0.882**	**0.952**	1.000	**0.892**	**0.566**	**0.285**	**0.147**
11	**0.122**	**0.369**	**0.488**	**0.594**	**0.724**	**0.892**	1.000	**0.871**	**0.654**	**0.498**
12	**−0.143**	0.005	**0.089**	**0.182**	**0.324**	**0.566**	**0.871**	1.000	**0.934**	**0.826**
13	**−0.222**	**−0.156**	**−0.117**	**−0.062**	0.048	**0.285**	**0.654**	**0.934**	**1.000**	**0.968**
14	**−0.180**	**−0.149**	**−0.142**	**−0.122**	−0.053	**0.147**	**0.498**	**0.826**	**0.968**	1.000

Source: Own analysis.

Notes: The table reports correlation coefficient; bolded values are statistically significant at the 5% level.

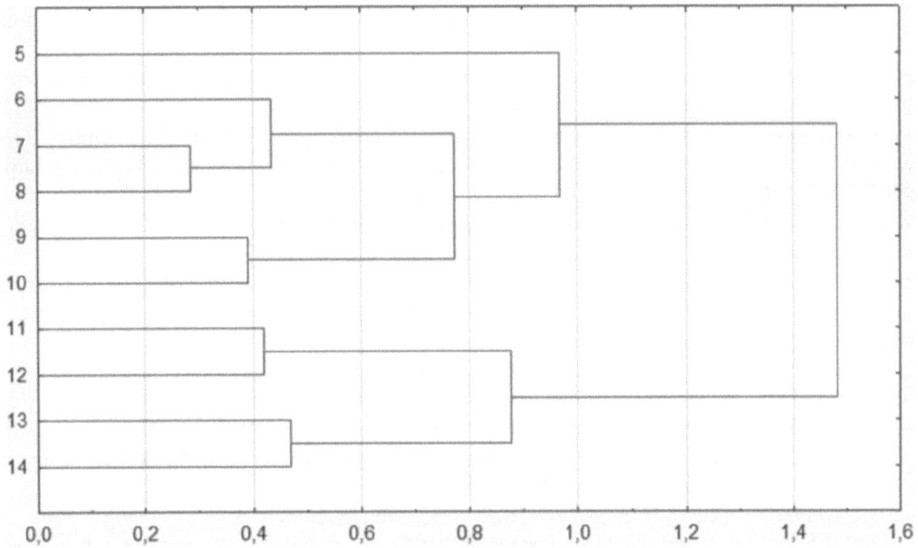

Figure 7.4 Tree diagram for different maturities (vertical axis) of greenium.

Source: Own analysis with the use of Statistica package.

Conclusions

The analysis indicates a positive greenium in the market for bonds issued by the EIB. While the greenium fluctuated around zero in 2020–2021, it began to rise in 2022, reaching nearly 5 basis points that year. An upward trend from 2023 is also evident, particularly for medium-term maturities. For longer maturities (11–14 years), positive greenium values were consistently observed throughout almost the entire analyzed period, possibly driven by increased awareness of the implications of climate change and the importance of sustainable investments.

Moreover, the greenium values for the selected maturities were not constant. This variability may be attributed not only to the volume of available data but also to potential shifts in market participants' behavior, caused by external factors such as the COVID-19 pandemic and Russian aggression against Ukraine. Given the still limited dataset, further analysis is necessary to confirm these initial conclusions.

References

Agliardi, E., & Agliardi, R. (2019). Financing environmentally-sustainable projects with green bonds. *Environment and Development Economics*, *24*(6), 608–623. https://doi.org/10.1017/S1355770X19000020

Dorfleitner, G., Utz, S., & Zhang, R. (2022). The pricing of green bonds: external reviews and the shades of green. *Review of Managerial Science*, *16*(3), 797–834. https://doi.org/10.1007/s11846-021-00458-9

Dziwok, E., & Wirth, M. (2019). Different approaches to the reference yield curve construction—and their application into fund transfer pricing mechanism. In Krzysztof Jajuga, H., Locarek-Junge, L., T. Orlowski, & K. Staehr (Eds.), *Contemporary Trends and Challenges in Finance* (pp. 149–157). Springer. https://doi.org/10.1007/978-3-030-43078-8_12

Ehlers, T., & Packer, F. (2017). Green bond finance and certification. *BIS Quarterly Review*, September. https://www.bis.org/publ/qtrpdf/r_qt1709h.htm

EIB. (2022, July 5). 15 years of EIB green bonds: leading sustainable investment from niche to mainstream. *Media Center*. https://www.eib.org/en/press/all/2022-308-15-years-of-eib-green-bonds-leading-sustainable-investment-from-niche-to-mainstream

EIB, & GFCCSFB. (2017). *The need for a common language in green finance. Towards a standard-neutral taxoomy for the environmental use of proceeds* (Issue November). https://www.eib.org/attachments/press/white-paper-green-finance-common-language-eib-and-green-finance-committee.pdf-finance-committee.pdf

Eisinger, F., Hogg, D., Cochu, A., Georgiev, I., & Walter, K. (2017). *Defining 'green' in the context of green finance*. https://doi.org/10.2779/285586

European Commission, Directorate-General for Environment, Eisinger, F., Hogg, D., Cochu, A., Georgiev, I., & Walter, K. (2017). *Defining "green" in the context of green finance* (Issue October). https://doi.org/10.2779/285586

Gianfrate, G., & Peri, M. (2019). The green advantage: exploring the convenience of issuing green bonds. *Journal of Cleaner Production*, *219*, 127–135. https://doi.org/10.1016/j.jclepro.2019.02.022

ICMA. (2018). *Green bond principles 2018: voluntary process guidelines for issuing green bonds*. https://www.icmagroup.org/assets/documents/Regulatory/Green-Bonds/Green-Bonds-Principles-June-2018-270520.pdf

IPCC. (2022). Climate change 2022: impacts, adaptation, and vulnerability. In Pörtner, H.-O., Roberts, D. C., Tignor, M., Poloczanska, E. S., Mintenbeck, K., Alegría, A., Craig, S., Langsdorf, S., Löschke, S., Möller, V., Okem, A., & Rama, B. (Eds.), *Contribution of Working Group II to the Sixth Assessment Report of the Intergovernmental Panel on Climate Change*. pp. 37–118 .Cambridge University Press. https://doi.org/10.1017/9781009325844

James, J., & Webber, N. (2000). *Interest Rate Modelling*. John Wiley & Sons.

Kanamura, T. (2020). Are green bonds environmentally friendly and good performing assets? *Energy Economics*, *88*, 104767. https://doi.org/10.1016/j.eneco.2020.104767

Karpf, A., & Mandel, A. (2018). The changing value of the 'green' label on the US municipal bond market. *Nature Climate Change*, *8*(2), 161–165. https://doi.org/10.1038/s41558-017-0062-0

Koziol, C., Proelss, J., Roßmann, P., & Schweizer, D. (2022). The price of being green. *Finance Research Letters*, *50*, 103285. https://doi.org/10.1016/j.frl.2022.103285

MacAskill, S., Roca, E., Liu, B., Stewart, R. A., & Sahin, O. (2021). Is there a green premium in the green bond market? Systematic literature review revealing premium determinants. *Journal of Cleaner Production*, *280*, 124491. https://doi.org/10.1016/j.jclepro.2020.124491

McCulloch, J. H. (1975). The tax-adjusted yield curve. *Journal of Finance*, *30*(3), 811–830. https://econpapers.repec.org/RePEc:bla:jfinan:v:30:y:1975:i:3:p:811-30

Nawalkha, S. K., Soto, G. M., & Beliaeva, N. A. (2005). *Interest Rate Risk Modeling*. John Wiley & Sons, Inc.

Nelson, C., & Siegel, A. F. (1987). Parsimonious modeling of yield curves. *The Journal of Business*, *60*(4), 473–489. https://econpapers.repec.org/RePEc:ucp:jnlbus:v:60:y:1987:i:4:p:473-89

Reboredo, J. C. (2018). Green bond and financial markets: co-movement, diversification and price spillover effects. *Energy Economics*, *74*, 38–50. https://doi.org/10.1016/j.eneco.2018.05.030

Svensson, L. E. O. (1994). Estimating and interpreting forward interest rates: Sweden 1992–1994. *IMF Working Papers*, *94*(114), 1. https://doi.org/10.5089/9781451853759.001

Tolliver, C., Keeley, A. R., & Managi, S. (2020). Drivers of green bond market growth: the importance of nationally determined contributions to the Paris Agreement and implications for sustainability. *Journal of Cleaner Production*, *244*, 118643. https://doi.org/10.1016/j.jclepro.2019.118643

United Nations. (2015). Report of the conference of the parties on its twenty-first session, held in Paris from 30 November to 13 December 2015. *Paris Agreement*. https://unfccc.int/resource/docs/2015/cop21/eng/10.pdf

World Bank. (2019, March 18). 10 years of green bonds: creating the blueprint for sustainability across capital markets. *World Bank News*. https://www.worldbank.org/en/news/immersive-story/2019/03/18/10-years-of-green-bonds-creating-the-blueprint-for-sustainability-across-capital-markets

Wu, Y. (2022). Are green bonds priced lower than their conventional peers? *Emerging Markets Review*, *52*, 100909. https://doi.org/10.1016/j.ememar.2022.100909

Zerbib, O. D. (2019). The effect of pro-environmental preferences on bond prices: evidence from green bonds. *Journal of Banking & Finance*, *98*, 39–60. https://doi.org/10.1016/j.jbankfin.2018.10.012

8 Climate risks, parametric insurance, and weather derivatives

Maksym Shylov

As an intermediate link in the food supply chain and providing final food from raw materials, food processors play a very important role in any society. Therefore, financial resilience of the food industry is the key element of the food security. On the other hand, we witness that farming segment is supported by the governments, who provide subsidies and implement various policies (CAP for example), as well as ad hoc measures in the event of natural catastrophes. At the same time, food processors do not receive as much aid compared to farmers; hence, the former should rely on their own and survive in the increasingly volatile, uncertain, complex and ambiguous (VUCA) world.

One of the uncertainties in the food supply chain is the impact of acute and chronic climate-related risks, leading to many negative financial outcomes. In response to this, innovative solutions such as weather derivatives and index (parametric) insurance are offered in insurance and financial markets to not only agricultural and energy segment but also to other industries, including food processing. The essence of these solutions is to provide compensation to a client if a certain weather or statistical parameter triggers, hence indirectly covering losses in the balance sheet, resulted by the adverse weather event. These tools in business practice and scientific literature are deemed to be alternative risk transfer (ART) tools, as standard insurance does not meet fully the growing demands of weather-exposed industries.

The goal of this chapter is to provide a comparative analysis of how alternative weather risk transfer tools differ from standard insurance, present genesis and development of weather derivatives and index (parametric) insurance, show how they are practised in the context of food processing industry and describe the first results of the survey on how food industry in CEE/SEE regions perceive such tools nowadays (companies from Poland and Lithuania have been surveyed).

The scientific literature is focused on the research of these tools mainly in agricultural or energy segments. Some papers stress a lot on the basis of risk as the main drawback of these solutions, which hinders potential customers from investing in index-based contracts, especially in agricultural segment, where the link between weather factors and final realistic yields on a farm is not so strong. Some authors express the point that weather derivatives provide an interesting asset class for speculation and risk diversification for investment funds. At the same time, it is admitted that demand for weather derivatives could increase, if the widely anticipated changes in weather materialise.

However, hardly any scientific research can be identified on how index (parametric) insurance or weather derivatives is applied in the food industry, where certain needs presumably exist. The main evident reference to the application of weather risk transfer tools in food industry can be found in papers concerning beer and cold beverage industry (SwissRe Corporate

DOI: 10.4324/9781003663539-9

Solutions, 2017). Such manufacturers have lower-than-expected earnings as a cool, wet summer triggers lack of demand during the most lucrative sales period of the year. Some papers also mention about food processors as risk integrators (policyholders), making it easier for farmers to gain their first experience with index insurance by transferring part of the risk-transfer benefits of insurance to the farmers.

Despite the fact that many articles refer to the impact of climate-related events on the food processing industry, the financial consequences of such events have hardly been quantified. The author has found only two papers, directly related to the food industry. In one of them, the authors assert that future warming is expected to reduce Chinese food processing firms' profit and industrial output, but the extent to which the reductions depend on the severity of future warming and global climate models. If we use IPCC climate projections, the total profits of China's food processing firms are expected to decrease annually by 12.5% (Xiaoguang et al., 2022). Another paper is addressed to the beer industry. The author refers to the research made by Lloyd Insurance in 1999, based on which a significant relationship was found between beer sales and temperature. The British Meteorological Office has calculated that if temperatures rise with 3°C in the UK, the demand for beer increases with 10% (Hoornaert, 2017).

However, there is no current research on the demand of food processing enterprises for weather risk transfer tools at all. Therefore, this chapter is the first attempt to shed the light on this topic and to quantify the losses, caused by weather, based on surveyed expert opinion of food enterprises. Moreover, the author has extended comparative analysis of standard insurance, parametric insurance and weather derivatives, as well as synthesized the knowledge of various aspects of application of alternative weather risk transfer tools by food processors in the context of food supply chain.

The essence of weather risk transfer tools

Some weather risks can be traditionally transferred via standard indemnity-based insurance (e.g. property damage, cargo, trade disruption, crop or livestock insurances). However, the scope of application of traditional insurance services is quite limited due to the following three main reasons:

- The holder of the insurance policy usually should be the person or entity, who possesses ownership on the insured property. Such a fact especially limits the application of standard insurance to cover contingency business interruption claims, where sometimes actual contingents are not known at all (e.g. losses entailed from cargo delay by river due to low water levels as a result of drought).
- There are some risks, which cannot be traditionally insured (e.g. temperature in property damage insurance).
- Some catastrophic weather events, especially related to agriculture, is difficult to insure on local (national) insurance markets due to high volatility of technical results and need for deep underwriting and serious loss adjustment expertise.

Therefore, ART tools should be used to solve the above-mentioned limitations of conventional indemnity-based insurance. To better understand the essence of alternative weather risk transfer solutions, the comparative analysis of standard indemnity-based insurance, index (parametric) insurance and weather derivatives has been performed. The results of it is summarized in Table 8.1.

Table 8.1 The comparative analysis standard indemnity-based insurance, index (parametric) insurance and weather derivatives

Parameter	*"Standard" indemnity-based insurance*	*Index (parametric) insurance*	*Weather derivatives*
Condition of the insured event	Loss amount exceeding deductible	Triggered parameter of the event	Triggered parameter of the event
Proprietary interest	Connected to the ownership of the asset	Can be estranged from the ownership of the asset	Can be estranged from the ownership of the asset
Loss compensation principle	Link with real physical or financial loss is necessary	Link with real physical or financial loss is still necessary	The holder can gain the profit
Financial service providers	Insurance companies	Insurance companies	Exchanges or financial companies, authorized to issue OTC derivatives
Contractual risk	Protracted debt or insolvency of insurance company	Protracted debt or insolvency of insurance company	Eliminated in case of exchange traded derivatives
Assignment of the indemnity rights	As a rule, not possible	As a rule, not possible	Can be later sold to a third party
Data requirements for risk assessment, monitoring and loss adjustment	Individual (asset specific) data	Data independent from specific asset	Data independent from specific asset
Obligation of the holder to control her risk or loss/right of subrogation	Yes	No	No
Adverse selection	High chance	Low chance	Low chance
Moral hazard	High chance	Low chance	Low chance
Factors, decreasing hedging effectiveness	Deductible and wider list of exclusions	Basis risk and failure of computations	Basis risk and failure of computations
The cumulative nature of the covered risks	Any type of risk, but more specific (idiosyncratic)	Cumulative risk	Cumulative risk
Homogeneity of risk exposure and the necessity of risk pooling	Need for risk pooling of homogeneous risks	Can be only risk transfer due to better access to the international capital	Can be only risk transfer to better access to the international capital
Administration costs	High	Low	Low
Simplicity of the policy wording and dispute resolution	Complex	Simple	Simple (XT, ISDA)
Paperwork	Cumbersome	Less formalities	Less formalities
Speed of pay-out	Slower	Faster	Faster

Source: Author's own work.

The main takeaways from the table are that in contrast to standard indemnity-based insurance, alternative weather risk transfer tools (parametric insurance or weather derivatives):

- are effective, when certain loss-related statistical parameter (e.g. wind speed) triggers, but not when the loss itself should occur as in standard insurance policy;

- trigger for the insured event is based on the data, which is independent from the insured interest (e.g. wind speed data has nothing to deal with features of property that one wants to be protected);
- do not require the need to care for the insured property;
- imply lower adverse risk selection and moral hazard;
- are not so precise, as contain basis risk of underlying weather parameter not to be fully correlated with real loss amount (e.g. real losses caused by strong wind is not of the same amount as insurance indemnity calculated based on formula in parametric insurance policy);
- are applied to hedge against catastrophic risks, as a rule;
- can be designed as tailor made risk transfer tools, which do not necessary require the formation of pool of the homogeneous risks;
- are performed with lower costs, simpler wording, less paper formalities and faster payoffs.

In contrast to insurance, weather derivatives:

- can be bought by any party without the need to prove for ownership interest;
- the link with real physical or financial loss is not necessary;
- are offered by stock exchanges or financial companies, authorized to issue OTC or XT derivatives;
- imply lower contractual risk if traded on an exchange;
- can be later sold to a third party.

Therefore, no requirements to evaluate the risk or occurred loss related to the specific asset on the one hand and lack of financial capacity of local insurance markets to deal with catastrophic risks explain the phenomena of offering alternative weather risk transfer tools.

The genesis and development of alternative weather risk transfer tools

The origin of index (parametric) insurance and weather instruments derives from the development of ART tools. "Alternative Risk Transfer (ART) includes those contracts, structures, and solutions that enable firms either to finance or transfer some of the risks to which they are exposed in a non-traditional way" (Frenkel et al., 2005). Traditional one is deemed to be insurance, but in the 1970s, insurance markets started hardening after series of losses, caused by natural catastrophes, that were reflected in the rise of insurance premiums and shrinking the reinsurance capacities. This forced both insurance companies and corporations to seek financial protection through non-insurance and non-reinsurance manner, respectively. Insurance companies started using new instruments (insurance-linked securities) to attract the "non-reinsurance" capital, such as catastrophe (CAT) bonds, exchange traded catastrophe options, as well as bartered risk exchanges.

However, in its infancy, one of the main barriers for new investors to trading insurance linked securities compared to professional reinsurers was the lack of information and the risk of moral hazard arising from the behaviour of insurers. To solve these problems, the concept of indices embedded in securities was introduced. The basic idea was to use the value of a special index in insurance-linked securities to trigger payouts based on such a document, but not to follow the fortunes of the insurer in terms of actual losses, as it is in the case of a traditional reinsurance contract.

On the other side, corporate end-users, but not only insurers, had the demand in solutions that should have been appropriate and flexible. Some of them, also migrated to the ART market to make use of finite programs, risk retention techniques, captives, and contingent securities instead of the traditional markets (e.g., insurance, financial derivatives). One particular example was the emergence of weather derivatives market. The first parties to issue weather derivatives in 1996 were energy companies, which after the deregulation of energy markets were exposed to weather risk.

In the context of food supply chain, the start of index-based contracts for final customers was firstly evident in the US agricultural insurance system. In his article, Miranda (1991) mentions that the federal crop insurance system does not operate on a sound actuarial basis, revealing problems with standard crop insurance, such as adverse selection, when farmers know more about the risks they face that they may better assess the actual cost of risk than the insurance company. In addition, the author mentions other problems with existing individual crop insurance regarding administrative costs and moral hazard. Such administrative costs are related to record keeping and human resource requirements to verify individual production records and adjust individual crop loss claims, but such moral hazard implies a change in the behaviour of farmers, who purchase crop insurance to ensure the best care for their crops. In order to deal with the above-mentioned problems typical of classic insurance, insurance based on area yield statistics was introduced. Miranda hereby emphasizes that area yield protection is not true insurance, but rather a hedging instrument, since payments to producers are not based on their own yield losses, but on aggregate yield data of all farmers located in a specific area.

The above-mentioned experience of using index agricultural insurance in the US was further imported into the developing countries, in order to facilitate the application of insurance capital, what cannot be done effectively through standard conventional insurance, and create financial resilience for further technological growth in rural areas. Why agriculture was the main area for application of index contracts can be explained by the fact that in such countries most part of population was engaged in agricultural production or related industries; hence, catastrophic agricultural losses would have a much greater impact on GDP than may occur in developed countries (Hess et al., 2005).

Plenty of crop and livestock index insurance pilot projects were implemented in many developing countries at the turn of the 21st century to the benefit of farmers. This implementation was always accompanied by the manifestation of the responsibility of the state as an entity providing certain social security for a population (Johnson, 2013). Moreover, in many cases, the dominant factor in the political sense was the desire of international organizations, such as, for example, the World Bank, to solve the problem of rural poverty in developing parts of the world (mainly in Africa and Asia), with the ultimate goal of creating opportunities for banks to finance this category of farmers for technologies adaptation to climate change (Hess et al., 2005).

The report issued by GIZ (2021) states that insurance programs cover a variety of risks, but drought and flood are the most common, through weather or area yield index. Besides this, similar kinds of index insurance contracts can be written against other natural disasters, including flood, excess rainfall, wind speed from hurricanes, earthquake events using the Richter scale, mortality rates for animals in Mongolia etc.

In contrast to US area yield experience, pilot projects of agricultural index insurance in developing countries were aimed to cover agricultural losses mostly through insurance of the so-called weather index. This is mainly explained by the lack of reliable statistical data on crop yields in these countries and by the dominance of the main threat (drought, flood, etc.) that result from the decision to introduce a specific weather indicator (Skees, 2000).

Despite the excitement and enthusiasm of international institutions and donors, the launch of index insurance pilot projects in developing countries in the 2000s ultimately faced the great problem of low demand and low penetration. Researches find that demand typically is low and faces constraints such as liquidity constraint, lack of trust, lack of interest, and limited salience; on the other hand, demand can be increased through financial literacy education, recent experience with a payout, or certain type of marketing intervention (Lin & Kwon, 2020). In light of this issue, many scientific studies were developed trying to explain farmers' willingness to pay for index insurance, in particular focusing mainly on the issue of basis risk, demand optimization in the design of index products, and methods for calculating the hedging effectiveness for weather risk transfer tools. The latest of these are focused on the use of new data sources (e.g. satellite) and new data processing technologies (e.g. blockchain, neural networks) to increase the efficiency of alternative weather risk transfer tools.

Index-based risk transfer contracts in the context of the food supply chain

Based on the development of risk management theory in the food supply chain and the index-based weather risk transfer solutions described above, this section will synthesize scientific achievements combined with empirical research and business practice.

Johnson (2013) stresses that as the objects of index insurance contracts are environmental variables rather than observed losses, a policyholder is not required to prove ownership of any assets at the time of purchase. Therefore, it means that any elements of the food supply chain who bear the risk caused by environment can be the policyholder. Index insurance can be beneficial for clients who are not agricultural producers: governments, relief agencies, financial service providers, input suppliers, businesses, agricultural processors, food companies, farmers' organizations and producers' associations could all use index insurance.

The use of index solutions in the context of the food processing industry, which is an element of the entire food supply chain, can be considered in several aspects, which are listed below.

Accidental first party loss financing

Index insurance or weather derivatives can be used to compensate for loss in the balance sheet of a food processor or any other stakeholder in the food supply chain, which is defined as a network of organizations that are involved—through upstream linkages to farms and downstream linkages to consumers—in different processes and activities that produce value in the form of food products and food services for consumers (Paloviita & Järvelä, 2015).

If indemnity-based insurance cannot cover the first party direct material damage, business interruption or liability loss fully or partially, index insurance or weather derivative can be used for that. All the more so because there is a need for alternative weather risk transfer tools to cover indirect losses of a food processor in the food supply chain, arising as a result of an event on the premises of a third party (e.g. on farmers' fields), as the possibilities of classic indemnity-based insurance are even more restrictive compared to solutions covering the direct loss of the first party. According to Allianz report (2022), global supply chains are creating more and more complex exposures, with many companies reliant on a small number of key suppliers for materials, parts and services. Such interconnectivity of supply chains results in more contingency business interruption exposures and can have a substantial impact on various industries, sometimes in excess of $1bn or more.

Several researchers have highlighted the role of index insurance and weather derivatives in mitigating the losses mentioned above. The emphasis was placed on the use of such weather risk transfer solutions to cover the losses of food companies caused by a direct decline in sales or a reduction in the volumes of raw material deliveries. For example, Mirasgedis et al. (2014) stressed that the demand for number of products especially in the manufacturing sector is greatly influenced by weather conditions and thus their sales will probably be favourably affected by a future changes in climate. Štulec (2017) conducted empirical analysis of beverage sales in 60 large food stores in Croatia and examined the performance of monthly temperature put options during the summer season. Results showed that weather has a statistically significant effect on beverage sales and that weather derivatives proved to be effective in compensating beverage sales reduction. Vroege et al. (2020) claimed that heat waves affect dairy production. When it is hot and humid, cows produce less milk and of a lower quality, while mortality and animal sales increase and feed production decreases. Insurance solutions to address weather risk in dairy production are not well developed yet, which was explained by these diverse responses and because quantifying weather-related damages is complicated due to the continuous, but seasonally dependent, character of dairy production. Pelka and Mußhoff (2015) analysed how much weather index insurance can reduce risk in a food processor, as the amount of sugar beet raw material available to the company for processing therefore depends on the yield of their sugar beet producing suppliers. The sugar yield of all sugar beet producing companies that deliver their sugar beets reflects the volume risk of the sugar processing company.

Integrating small farming holdings into the food supply chain system

Index insurance projects have often been considered the missing link in facilitating the integration of smallholder farmers into agricultural value chains. By this logic, insurance policies function as a type of collateral, making policyholders more creditworthy and increasing their access to loans from financial institutions. These loans in turn facilitate more production risk-taking such as investing in high-yielding seed varieties, which in its turn necessary to scale up production for integration into domestic, regional or even global commodity circuits (Johnson, 2013). Thus, with index insurance, farmers can take on greater risk by investing more money (and therefore bearing greater risk exposure) in more productive technologies, which in turn results in greater financial resilience for farmers in relation to other elements of the food supply chain. "This approach envisions insurance as a technology to support the chain, which can facilitate or consolidate the incorporation of certain places and populations into otherwise weakly articulated agricultural value chains" (Johnson, 2013).

Aggregating index insurance or weather derivatives

Index insurance or weather derivatives can be sold to anyone in the entire food supply chain. It means that policyholders need not be farmers nor even have to live or work in the region. "The insurance should be attractive to anybody whose income is correlated with the insured event, including agricultural traders and processors, input suppliers, banks, shopkeepers, and laborers" (Skees & Hazell, 2005). In addition to traditional insurance and reinsurance contracts, risk financing can also be accessed by large corporations, insurers and governments through innovative financial products developed in the capital markets (OECD, 2015, p. 58).

> The most promising way forward is to tie the insurance of contracts with aggregators, such as credit providers, input suppliers or purchasers in contract farming situations. While insuring individual farmers or their credit may have only limited potential, insurance can be used by the aggregators or by governments to insure their own weather-related risks.
>
> (Binswanger-Mkhize, 2012)

On the other hand, Hazell et al. (2010) put forward the view that other elements of the food supply chain are more interested in the direct use of index insurance by farmers. This is explained by the fact that receiving compensation from the insurer, the food processor will not solve the problem of farmers' insolvency. The scholar wonders, whether financial service providers (or other actors in the supply chain) would be interested in using index insurance to cover their own lending portfolios against highly covariate events. In principle, such policies would protect them, but would not help their household-level borrowers cope with risk nor would they help repair providers' relationships with clients after the clients have defaulted. The provider would still have the bad loans on its records, and it would be very reluctant to lend to these borrowers again. As a result, financial service providers may prefer that their borrowers use the index insurance as part of their household risk management strategy and thus deal directly with the risk where it occurs. In this case, the final responsibility for repaying the loan remains with the individual borrower, while in times of distress, the payouts from the index insurance would repay the debt and prevent the eventual rescheduling of the loan or default. However, food processor can still serve as a policyholder, as bought capacity; hence, received pay-off can be split in small parts for small farmers as final users. Food companies can release the hurdle for seller's side and encourage more farmers side to buy weather index insurance by smoothing some of its drawbacks.

> The use of aggregators is key to reducing these transaction costs, reaching more clients, and eventually bringing the reach of the products to a meaningful scale. To achieve this, index insurance products could be designed to cover the portfolios of aggregators as well as the household-level risk of individual farmers. Under this strategy, the aggregators that are still facing major systemic risks could mitigate part of the risk with an index insurance policy, while a longer-term effort reaches out to cover individual households with index insurance as part of a wider development and disaster management approach.
>
> (Hazell et al., 2010, p. 25)

Bundling insurance into the main product or service

One way to aggregate farmers' production risk insurance is to bundle insurance into a core product or service. Insurance could also be built into credit and into the purchase price of key inputs like seeds, fertilizers and chemicals (Skees & Hazell, 2005). Contract farming is another form of bundling that has long been used to combine insurance with inputs, extension services, credit and market together with privileged access to a market, especially for industrial crops and high-value agricultural products (GIZ, 2021). The CAP in the EU assumes the allocation of fair value between all elements of the food supply chain. In light of this, food processors, acting as de facto aggregators, may become more involved in investing from their marginality in risk financing tools to incorporate them into their core offering (purchase of raw materials in the case of a food processor).

Some scientific research has been done on the "bundling" of insurance. Combining insurance with credit intends to promote the adoption of new crop technology adversely affected demand for the loan. Bulte et al. (2020) stress that the value of insurance must be very low, if the promise of free insurance does not increase the adoption of modern seeds. By comparing the uptake of improved crop varieties between the treated and control group, the scholars obtained a measure of willingness to pay for formal insurance. The study, done by Kajwang (2022), recommends that weather index insurance should be linked to an existing development program or other market opportunities to provide added value to the client. As a stand-alone product, weather index insurance may be seen as an unnecessary cost and have little demand from farmers who face a variety of other risks in addition to weather risks. The study also recommends partnership between weather index insurance programs and other risk management programs.

Strengthening cooperation between food processors and farmers through weather risk transfer solutions

Many insurers work successfully with intermediaries like banks and agrodealers to provide agricultural insurance. Such intermediaries often have a local presence and set up relationships with farmers, which can be helpful when farmers have little knowledge or trust in insurance. Intermediaries can also bundle insurance with credit and other agricultural inputs and services that make insurance more valuable for farmers (GIZ, 2021; Carter et al., 2016).

Like insurers, financial institutions are searching for opportunities to expand and diversify revenues in uncorrelated areas, by using insurance and ART tools.

> For instance, several large investment and universal banks have been at the forefront of insurance-related capital market issues (e.g., catastrophe bonds, contingent capital structures), and various others have actively sought to transfer capital markets risks to the reinsurance market. Some have also become involved in trading insurance related-derivatives (e.g., weather derivatives).
>
> (Banks, 2008)

Food processors in some cases may also act as financial institutions, e.g. by providing trade credit, especially for the cultivation of plants (raw materials), which requires large investments and increased control over production risk management. Such loans also tie the farmer to the food processor and motivate her to complete the crop and deliver it on time.

Even without the direct link to the loan, index insurance or weather derivative is the good tool to strengthen cooperation between food processors and supplying farmers. For example, "PepsiCo added index insurance to its contract farming package not only to limit farmers' weather risk, but also to establish long-term relationships with farmers and limit the risk in its supply chain" (Hazell et al., 2010). In India, insurance company ICICI Lombard started selling an index insurance product to potato farmers in 2007 as part of a package of services provided through contract farming arrangements with the global agricultural company. Hereby, despite receiving no premium subsidy from donor or government, the insurance uptake has been high (more than 80% in the first two years), largely due to it being integrated with other services. Potato farmers purchased this index insurance to protect themselves against the late blight disease. The parametric trigger is a combination of humidity and temperature index. Insured farmers are financed to cover their upfront costs of producing potatoes and to improve the quantity and quality of production. In turn, PepsiCo offers insurance policy on potatoes sold to insured farmers (Lin & Kwon, 2020).

In addition, Horton (2018) stressed about adversarial context of tort liability claims versus contractual context of index insurance. Parties to a liability claim have a relationship that is fundamentally antagonistic in nature, inhabiting the roles of claimant and defendant and seek to win their case before a judge or jury. This contradiction derives from the legal character of torts. By contrast, insurance is fundamentally contractual in nature. Policyholders sign agreement with insurance providers prior to an event. If a subsequent event triggers, payouts are distributed according to contract terms and conditions. Based on Horton's statement, we can assume a role in moderating the relationship between the food processor and supplying farmers. Some tort or contractual liability claims (remediation) related to the cultivation of specialty crops under a commercial agricultural contract between farmers and a food processor may be transferred to pay off settlements under the index insurance policy or weather derivative.

Reducing basis risk and increasing the hedging effectiveness of index-based products

> Competition for new types of clients could lead to developing policies and marketing aimed at meso-level and/or wholesale clients (e.g., local governments, NGOs, farmer cooperatives, or lending institutions) that are also sensitive to covariate shocks but for which basis risk is less of an issue due to internal aggregation across members, clients, constituents, or borrowers.
>
> (Jensen & Barrett, 2016)

Food processors are very close to farmers, because they ultimately pay farmers money for crop raw materials. Therefore, food processors can potentially have individual yield data, at least as far as farmers' performance is concerned. This creates the potential to reduce basis risk. Basis risk reduction can be done by default, because food processors aggregate positive and negative idiosyncratic (specific) basis risk of individual farmers. In the case of normal distribution and a representative number of individual farmers in the portfolio, the expected basis risk (residual in regression) reaches zero. Moreover, if farmers work closely with a food processor, they can provide key agronomic data to implement more precise yield index model for each more homogeneous cluster of the insureds. One can refer to Pelka and Mußhoff (2015), who claimed that by aggregating the sugar yield time series, the basis risk when using weather index insurance is reduced and the risk reduction potential is increased.

And last, but not least, food processors can more precisely tailor index-based solutions. According to Bucheli, Dalhaus, and Finger (2021), tailoring insurance contracts should not only include the definition of farm-specific tick size and strike level but also the identification of the most risk-reducing underlying drought index. Such tailoring of insurance contracts requires rich farm-specific yield records. Recalibration of insurance contracts at every renewal will reduce potential biases of currently short time series and take into account the ongoing climate change. New data sources (e.g. due to the digitalization of agriculture) and inclusion of data from similar farms can help to improve calibration of index insurance model.

How are weather-related losses and weather risk transfer tools perceived by food enterprises of Central and Eastern Europe

As stated in the previous sections, parametric insurance and weather derivatives imply high level of flexibility for international risk takers to diversify climate-related risks on a global scale. On the other hand, many advantages of such weather risk transfer tools (e.g. independent data, simplicity, lack of proof of ownership) open high opportunities for food enterprises to enforce the financial resilience of their supply chain.

However, in order for any tool to operate effectively and develop in the market on sustainable basis, several preconditions should be fulfilled. At the end of the day, the growth rate of consumption volumes of weather derivatives and parametric insurance is the function of decision of a food enterprise to invest into weather risk transfer tools on the one side and the willingness of a risk capital provide (e.g. insurance company, bank, hedge-fund) to take weather-related risk. The demand side in its turn can be described in Figure 8.1.

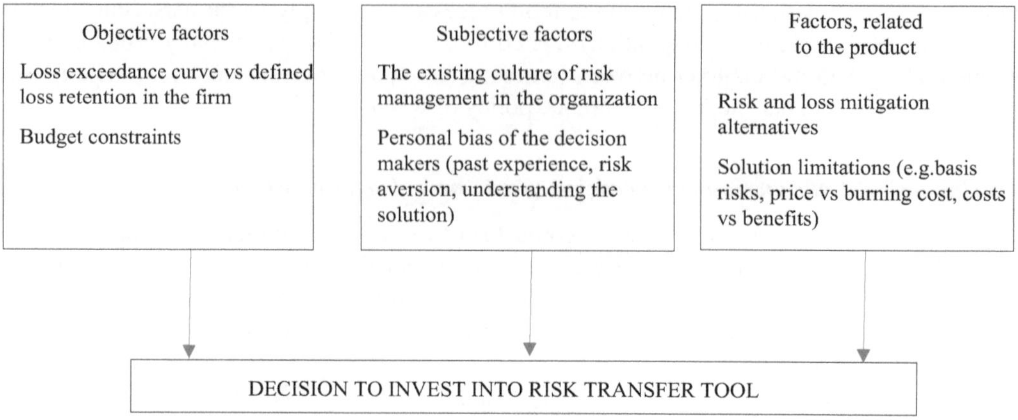

Figure 8.1 Factors, impacting the decision to invest into weather risk transfer tools.

Source: Author's own work.

Based on the presented model of factors, impacting the decisions making to invest into the weather risk transfer tools, the author conducted additional survey research among food enterprises in Poland and Lithuania to identify and quantify the elements presented in the model. In order to do so, ten questions were asked to top managers of food companies:

1 What problems can severe bad weather cause in your company (choose up to three answers)?
2 What causes the severity of such a loss (choose up to three answers)?
3 What protects you from greater losses caused by severe bad weather (choose up to three answers)?
4 Your rough (intuitive) estimation of the maximum loss (in % of your turnover) that the worst weather can bring to your company?
5 Your rough (intuitive) estimation, how often such the worst event could happen?
6 What is the current situation regarding weather derivatives/parametric insurance in your company?
7 What hinders you from investing in weather derivatives / parametric insurance (choose up to three answers)?
8 Turnover of your company?
9 The main products of your company (share of which is >25% in total turnover)?
10 The main countries, where your plants are located (share of which is >25% in total turnover)?

LinkedIn was used as a communication tool. The questionnaire was created on Google Forms platform and the link to the questionnaire was sent over to decision-makers of food enterprises in LinkedIn environment. As a result, the author managed to get answers from 30 companies, 24 located in Poland and six in Lithuania. Most companies (24) were of large size (turnover >40 mln EUR according to EU definition of big enterprise), three of them were medium sized (turnover 10–40 mln EUR) and three were small (turnover <2 mln EUR). The types of economic activities are presented in Figure 8.2.

The full results of the research are presented in Figures 8.3–8.8. The key takeaways are as follows: 90% of respondents see the main consequence of weather in increasing prices of raw materials, as a result of occurrence of acute climate risk (Figure 8.3).

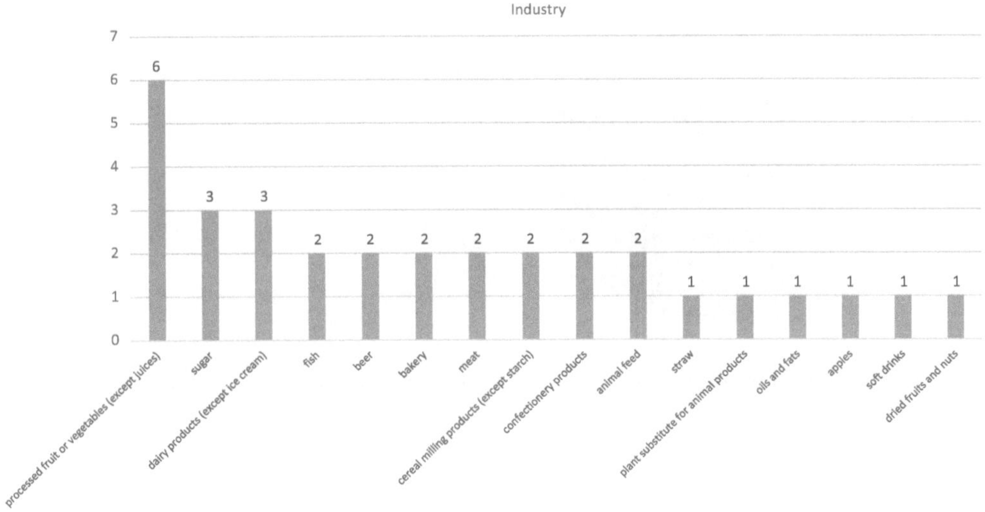

Figure 8.2 The breakdown of economic activities among the respondents from the food industry.
Source: Author's own work.

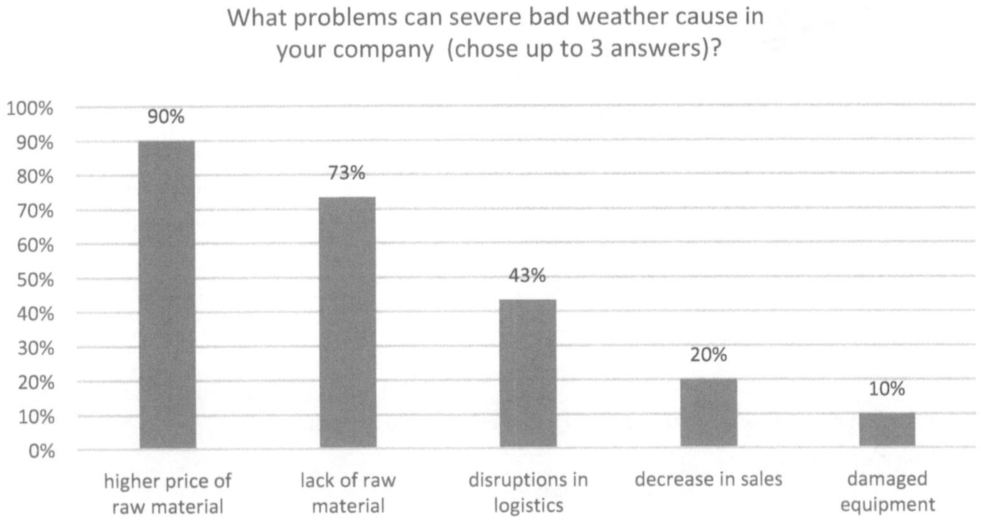

Figure 8.3 Problems that can severe bad weather cause in company.
Source: Author's own work.

Besides higher prices, 73% think that raw material could be the problem as well as 43% consider disruptions in logistics. Only 10% see the consequence of bad weather in damage of their property. Decrease in sales as a problem is also considered by only 1/5 of food companies. Herewith, 37% of respondents see the maximal potential loss caused by weather in amount of up to 10% of revenues. 17% see the loss even higher and only 10% estimated the worst scenario of loss up to 1% of their turnover (Figure 8.4). One can conclude that opinions vary, though more than half of the respondents see the loss at least above 5% of revenues. As for the frequency of

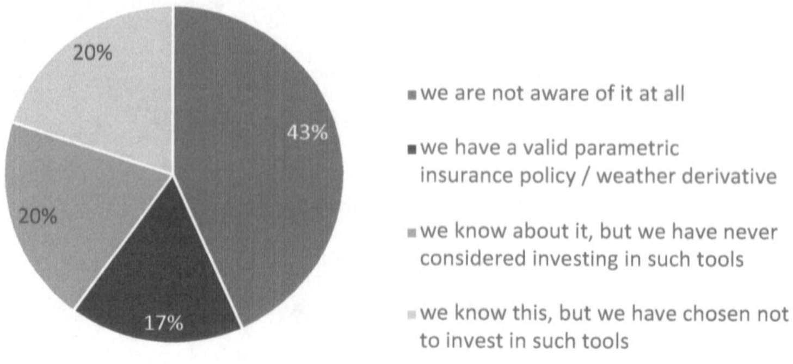

Figure 8.4 Estimation of the maximum loss (in % of your turnover) that the worst weather can bring to a food company.

Source: Author's own work.

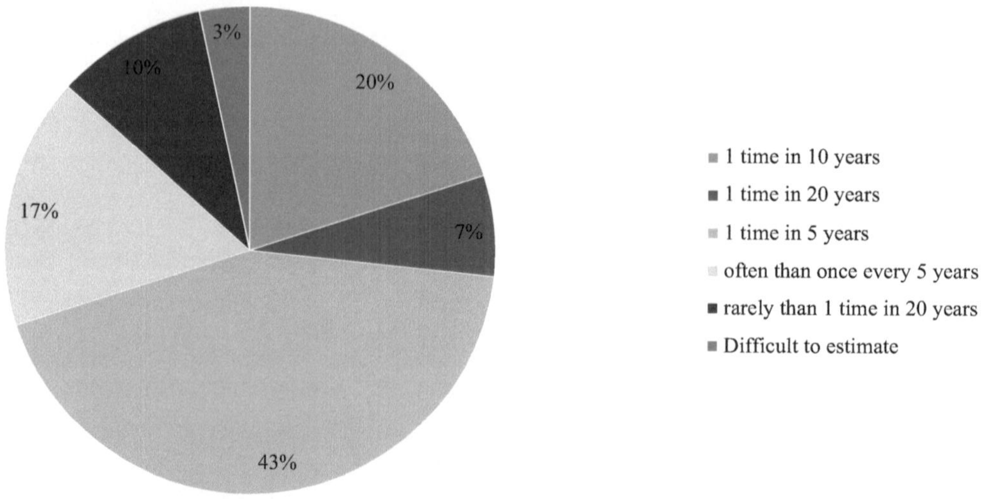

Figure 8.5 Estimation, how often the worst weather event could happen?

Source: Author's own work.

the worst loss scenario caused by adverse weather, the highest share of food companies (43%) predict it once every five years, whereas 17% see it even more often and 20% once every ten years (Figure 8.5). It means that 80% of food enterprises might be exposed to such losses at least once in ten years and 60% at least once in five years.

As seen in Figures 8.4 and 8.5, based on the "expert" opinion obtained from the top management of food enterprises, it can be concluded that the expected frequency of a weather event leading to the worst loss scenario is 5.5 years, whereas expected severity of loss is 7.7% of annual turnover. Therefore, expected "amortized" annual loss is 1.4% of annual revenue. On the other hand, extreme scenarios of annual loss are as follows: the most positive scenario is 0.0125% (frequency 2.5% multiplied by the severity of 0.5%) and the most negative scenario is 8% (frequency 40% multiplied by the severity of 20%).

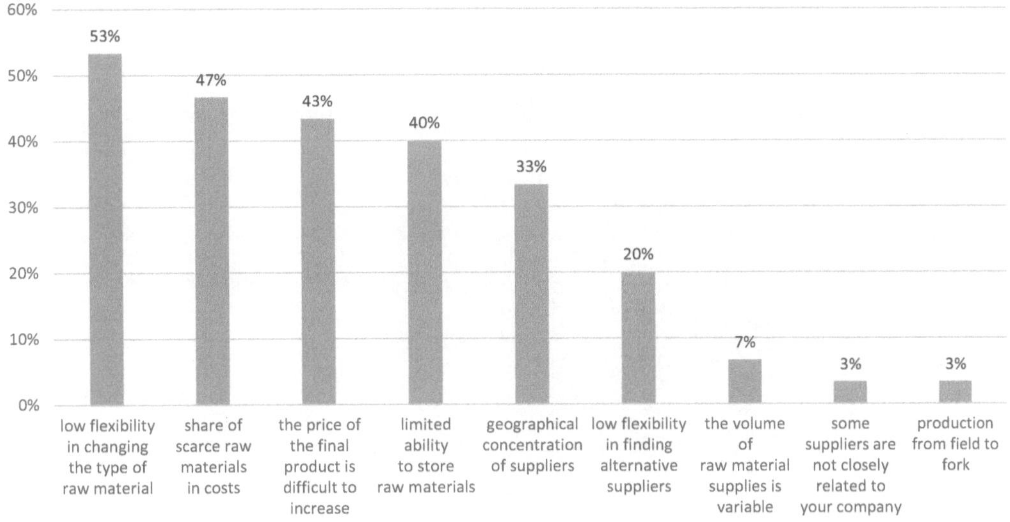

Figure 8.6 Causes of the severity of loss.

Source: Author's own work.

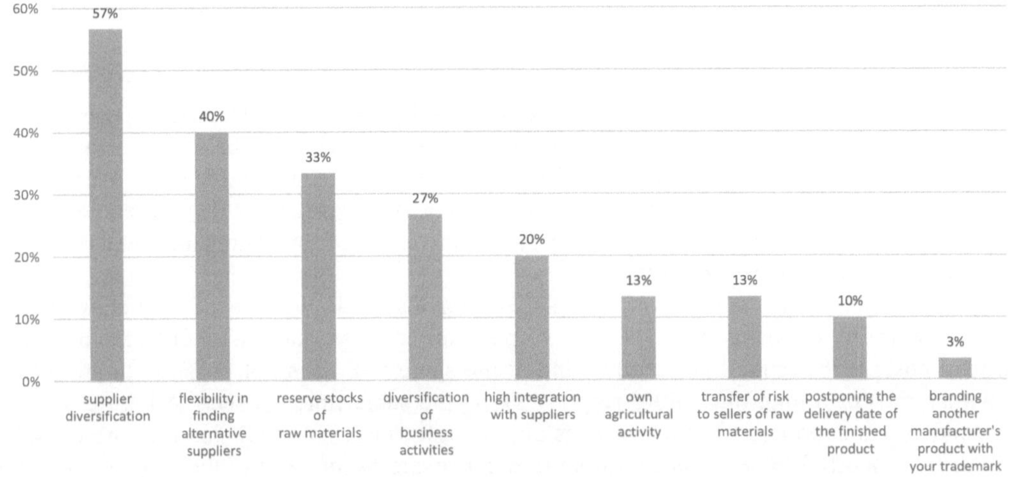

Figure 8.7 Protection measures from greater losses caused by severe bad weather.

Source: Author's own work.

As in enterprise, risk tolerance can be defined as certain level of marginality of sales, the above-mentioned results can be additionally aligned with such an approach. In the context of using a percentage of turnover as a measure for risk tolerance, a common figure typically chosen ranges between 1% and 5% of turnover. Eventually, this range is considered individually, based on the current financial state of a food enterprise by simulating how the worst scenario will impact on liquidity and solvency of a company. On the other hand, we can use dataset of financial indicators of food enterprises obtained from EMIS database. Based on this data taken from Polish and Lithuanian food companies with yearly turnover above 1m EUR for period

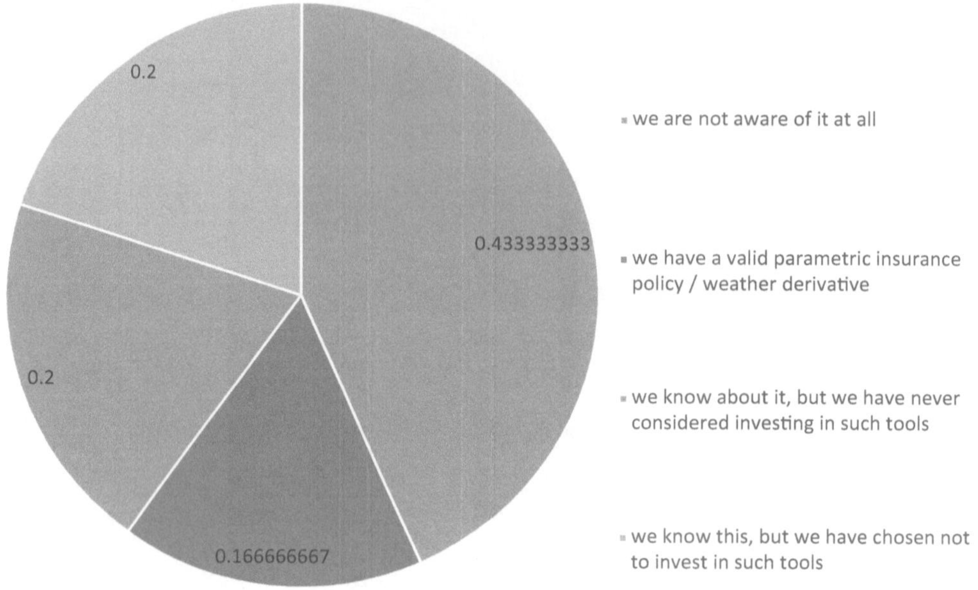

Figure 8.8 Current situation regarding weather derivatives/parametric insurance in the company.
Source: Author's own work.

2013–2021, average net profit margin in food industry is around 4%. Herewith, approximately 50% of observations in EMIS reached marginality of sales of 2.5% and below, whereas 17% of observations showed zero profit or loss. Therefore, the above-mentioned level of average loss can significantly impact on solvency of a food company. If referring to EMIS, if average adverse weather loss scenario (loss of 4% of revenues) occurs, 62.5% of food companies will have zero profit or losses in their P&L reports.

What impacts on the severity of adverse weather losses (Figure 8.6), 53% believe is due to low flexibility to change the type of raw material, and row materials hold very big share in total costs (47% replied positively), and at the same time it is not possible to store such raw material for a long time (40% responses). At the same time, as seen in Figure 8.7, 1/3 responded that suppliers diversification is not enough to mitigate their losses, whereas 43% thinks that incurred losses is not feasible to compensate by increasing the price of the final product. On the other hand, the following loss mitigation strategies are the most often used: suppliers diversification (57%), flexibility in finding alternative suppliers (40%), reserve stocks of raw materials (33%).

Despite high potential exposure to losses caused by acute climate events, only 17% of surveyed companies practice weather derivatives and parametric insurance (Figure 8.8). Taking into account that most surveyed companies are big ones according to EU definition, it is supposed that such a figure among small- and medium-sized enterprises can be lower.

In addition, 20% of respondents decided not to invest in such tools, but 43% was not aware at all (Figure 8.9). As for obstacles in decision making to invest into weather risk transfer tools, 50% responses are related to the lack of information or non-awareness. 23% see that the price of such tools is too high compared to perceived benefits.

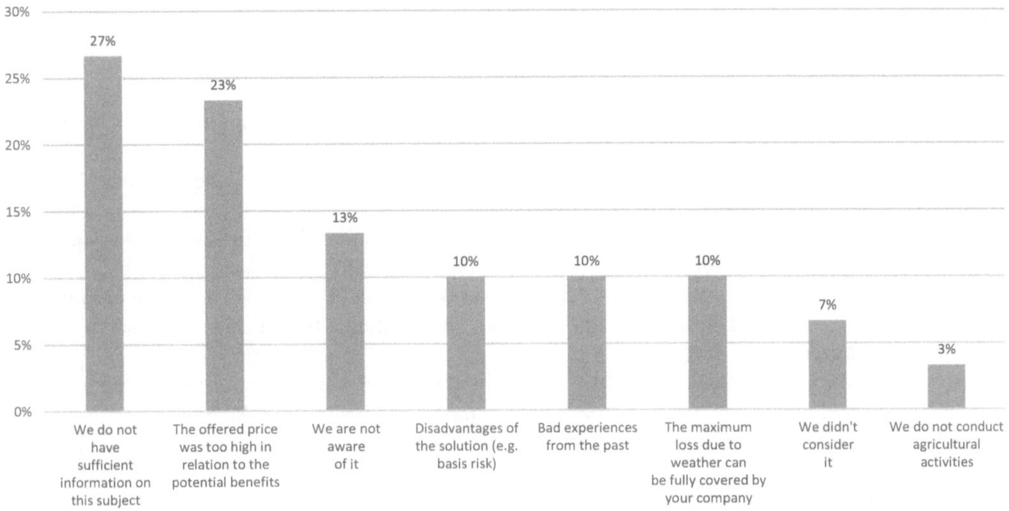

Figure 8.9 Barriers in the investing in weather derivatives/parametric insurance.

Source: Author's own work.

Unfortunately, until now it was not possible for the author to use categorical variables such as type of the main product or country of origin to distinguish differences in loss estimations and preferences regarding usage of weather risk transfer tools. This is the task of the further research by expanding the sampling for survey.

Conclusions

We are living in the era of global climate changes, affecting many aspects of our life including food industry. The growing frequency and severity of losses in food supply chain can change the standard way how risks were handled in the past. It concerns firstly to the fact that efficiency of risk retention and mitigation strategies is decreasing; hence, the need of alternative weather risk transfer tools will be increasing. In this chapter, the author has presented a comparative analysis of standard insurance contracts and index contracts and described the origins and development of theory and practice in the field of alternative weather risk transfer tools. In addition, the first results of surveys among food enterprises were presented, which show that food enterprises perceive large potential losses, caused by adverse weather. This strengthens the hypothesis that the demand from the food industry for index and parametric insurance will grow.

Such tools not only protect a food company's balance sheet but also increase the resilience of the entire food supply chain. This is explained by the fact that alternative weather risk tools can be promoted by food processors, acting like integrators, by attaching insurance to the preposition of sale or purchase, which ultimately increases the risk hedging effectiveness of such solutions and facilitates the strengthening of relationships between elements in the food supply chain process. Further quantitative and qualitative research is needed to better understand food processor needs for weather risk transfer tools, increase the validity of the research results by increasing the sample size and enabling differentiation between different countries and types of economic activities.

References

Allianz (2022). Global claims review 2022. https://www.allianz.com/content/dam/onemarketing/azcom/Allianz_com/AGCS-Global-Claims-Review-2022.pdf

Banks, E. (2008). *Alternative risk transfer: Integrated risk management through insurance, reinsurance, and the capital markets* (Repr). Wiley finance series. Wiley.

Binswanger-Mkhize, H. (2012). *Is there too much hype about index-based agricultural insurance?* Advance online publication.

Bucheli, J., Dalhaus, T., & Finger, R. (2021). The optimal drought index for designing weather index insurance. *European Review of Agricultural Economics*, 48(3), 573–597.

Bulte, E., Cecchi, F., Lensink, R., Marr, A., & van Asseldonk, M. (2020). Does bundling crop insurance with certified seeds crowd-in investments? Experimental evidence from Kenya. *Journal of Economic Behavior & Organization*, 180, 744–757.

Carter, M. R., Cheng, L., & Sarris, A. (2016). Where and how index insurance can boost the adoption of improved agricultural technologies. *Journal of Development Economics*, 118, 59–71.

Frenkel, M., Hommel, U., Rudolf, M., & Dufey, G. (2005). *Risk management: Challenge and opportunity* (2nd rev. and enl. ed.). Springer.

GIZ (2021). *Innovations and emerging trends in agricultural insurance for smallholder farmers – An update* [Press release].

Hazell, P., Anderson, J., Balzer, N., Clemmensen, H., Hess U., & Rispoli, F. (2010). *The potential for scale and sustainability in weather index insurance for agriculture and rural livelihoods*. International Fund for Agricultural Development (IFAD) & World Food Programme (WFP).

Hess, U., Skees, J. R., Stoppa, A., Barnett, B. J., & Nash, J. (2005). *Managing agricultural production risk: Innovations in developing countries*. Agriculture and Rural Development (ARD) Department Report.

Hoornaert, A. (2017). *Hedging weather risk using weather derivatives*. Ghent University.

Horton, J. B. (2018). Parametric insurance as an alternative to liability for compensating climate harms. *Carbon & Climate Law Review*, 12(4), 285–296.

Jensen, N., & Barrett, C. B. (2016). *Agricultural index insurance for development*. Advance online publication.

Johnson, L. (2013). Index insurance and the articulation of risk-bearing subjects. *Environment and Planning*, 45, 663–2681.

Kajwang, B. (2022). Weather based index insurance and its role in agricultural production. *International Journal of Agriculture*, 7(1), 13–25.

Lin, X., & Kwon, W. J. (2020). Application of parametric insurance in principle-compliant and innovative ways. *Risk Management and Insurance Review*, 23(2), 121–150.

Miranda, M. J. (1991). Area-yield crop insurance reconsidered. *American Journal of Agricultural Economics*, 73(2), 233–242.

Mirasgedis, S., Georgopoulou, E., Sarafidis, Y., Papagiannaki, K., & Lalas, D. P. (2014). The impact of climate change on the pattern of demand for bottled water and non-alcoholic beverages. *Business Strategy and the Environment*, 23(4), 272–288.

OECD (2015). *Disaster risk financing: A global survey of practices and challenges*. Organisation for Economic Co-operation and Development. https://doi.org/10.1787/9789264234246-en

Paloviita, A., & Järvelä, M. (2015). *Climate change adaptation and food supply chain management: An overview*. Routledge.

Pelka, N., & Mußhoff, O. (2015). Risk reduction potential of weather index-based insurance in agribusiness – The importance of the aggregation level of yield time series. *German Journal of Agricultural Economics*, 64(2), 76–88.

Skees, J. R. (2000). A role for capital markets in natural disasters: A piece of the food security puzzle. *Food Policy*, 25, 365–378.

Skees, J. R., & Hazell, P. (2005). Insuring against bad weather: Recent thinking. In R. Radhakrishna, S. K. Rao, S. Mahendra Dev, & K. Subbarao (Eds.), *India in a globalising world: Some aspects of macroeconomy, agriculture, and poverty*. Academic Foundation & Centre for Economic and Social Studies (CESS).

Štulec, I. (2017). Effectiveness of weather derivatives as a risk management tool in food retail: The case of Croatia. *International Journal of Financial Studies*, 5(1), 2.

SwissRe Corporate Solutions (2017). Solutions for managing weather risks. https://corporatesolutions.swissre.com/dam/jcr%3A3539e4be-8b21-4a3f-9d9a-138edc589aba/solutions-for-managing-weather-risks.pdf?utm_source=chatgpt.com

Vroege, W., & Finger, R. (2020). Insuring Weather Risks in European Agriculture. *EuroChoices*, 19(2), 54–62.

Xiaoguang, C., Khanna, M., & Yang, L. (2022). The impacts of temperature on Chinese food processing firms. *The Australian Journal of Agricultural and Resource Economics*, 66(2), 256–279.

9 Hybrid capital instruments against risks

Kamil Liberadzki

The quality measure of individual own funds' categories should be the ability to absorb losses incurred by the insurer both in the course of its activity and in the event of bankruptcy. In the first case, the absorption of losses is achieved primarily as a result of non-payment of dividends. In the case of hybrid bonds, the same absorption effect is achieved by cancelling the coupon payment (non-cumulative coupon deferral). Another loss absorption tool is the conversion of hybrid bonds into ordinary shares or partial (or even total) write down of their nominal value. Such their feature is a prerequisite for qualifying eligible own funds to Tier 1. Also in the event of bankruptcy, ordinary shares show the greatest ability to absorb losses, since the claims of shareholders arising from the distribution of the assets of the liquidated company are satisfied only after the claims of all other creditors, including bondholders, have been satisfied. The same applies to subordinated bonds, classified to Tier 2 and Tier 3 category of own funds, which are satisfied only after all other liabilities have been paid back.

The hybrid securities issued by insurers are nicknamed "contingent convertibles" (CoCos), counted towards Tier 1 own funds RT1 (Restricted Tier 1). These securities contain a unique mechanism of going concern loss absorption, i.e. during the normal functioning of the issuer, without the need to initiate restructuring or bankruptcy proceedings. In the event of a trigger event in the form of a breach of the Solvency II capital requirements, the bonds are subject to mandatory conversion into issuer's shares (contingent conversion) or write down of part or full of their nominal value (temporary/partial and full/permanent write down). Moreover, these instruments are deeply subordinated,[1] perpetual (although equipped with a call option), with the possibility to postpone the coupon payment and to reset the coupon.

Research issues and literature review

In the case of CoCo instruments, the key issue is to determine the type of event triggering the entire described loss absorption mechanism and to establish the appropriate levels of regulatory capital of the issuer (regulated entity – bank or insurer), the exceeding of which is treated as a trigger event (Jaworski et al., 2017; de Spiegeleer et al., 2017; Marquet, 2017; Deutsche Bundesbank, 2018; Kowalski, 2018). CoCos appeared first in the banking world in 2014 in the context of the CRR (Capital Requirements Regulation)[2] adoption, which is – from the point of view of shaping the banks' capital requirements in the EU – what the Regulation 2015/35 is for insurance and reinsurance undertakings.[3] According to Article 92 of CRR, credit institutions may use CoCo instruments to fill in Additional Tier 1 (AT1) capital. The equivalent of AT1 CoCos in the world of insurers' capital regulation are RT1 CoCos, which show many similarities to AT1 securities (Liberadzki & Liberadzki, 2016). It can be assumed that RT1 CoCo market started in 2016, when Gjensidige Forsikring issued RT1 denominated in Norwegian kroner as the first European

DOI: 10.4324/9781003663539-10

insurance undertaking. It was followed by RSA and Dutch ASR with the first RT1 issue in euros. Research on RT1 CoCo securities presented in the existing literature is limited (Liberadzki & Liberadzki, 2016; Jaworski et al., 2019). The description of these instruments, as well as insurers' Tier 2 and Tier 3 bonds, presented in this chapter, further complements an important research gap.

The empirical part of analysis refers to the case study of Eurovita. The Italian life insurer was rescued (bailed-out) by consortium of banks and insurers after being taken over under the administration by Italian supervision authority because of capital shortage. This resulted from unrealized losses on bond portfolio being an effect of lapse risk. Unwillingness of Eurovita's main shareholder to inject more capital led the institution on the brink of collapse. The conducted simulation shows clearly, that if the full potential of Tier 2 and Tier 3 subordinated bonds issuance was used by Eurovita amplified by the issuance of RT1, the company would meet the minimum own funds requirement. This is the clear evidence, that using the loss-absorbing potential of hybrid and subordinated capital instruments may prevent the insurance companies from unsolvency. What is more, the amount of the necessary subordinated debt and hybrids would be very limited in relation to total assets, so not becoming so burdensome for the issuer.

Capital structure of undertakings under Solvency II

The Solvency II Directive[4] (hereinafter: "the Directive") imposes an obligation on insurance and reinsurance undertakings to maintain adequate values of eligible basic and ancillary own funds divided into three tiers: Tier 1 (T1), Tier 2 (T2), and Tier 3 (T3). According to Article 93(1) of the Directive, classification "shall depend upon whether they are basic own fund or ancillary own-fund items and the extent to which they possess the following characteristics: (i) permanent availability[5] and (ii) subordination".[6]

Pursuant to Article 82 of Commission Delegated Regulation (EU) 2015/35[7] eligible Tier 1 own funds will have to be equal to at least 50% of the SCR (Solvency Capital Requirements). Shares and reserves must form 80% of T1 own funds, which means that T1 hybrid instruments can fill no more than 20% of T1 own funds. Due to this "restriction", hybrid Tier 1 instruments are referred to as RT1 to distinguish them from Unrestricted Tier 1 items. If the insurer has issued hybrid bonds eligible for T1 in a greater volume, this excess is counted towards ancillary T2 items (Ancillary T2). The remaining 50% of the SCR may consist of eligible T2 and T3 instruments, with subordinated debt eligible as T3 representing no more than 15% of the SCR.

In addition, the Directive applies the concept of Minimal Capital Requirements (MCR), which must be covered up to 80% through ordinary shares and reserves, and the remainder by hybrid T1 instruments and T2 funds. However, it is not possible to cover the MCR using T3 instruments.

The amounts of eligible own funds of insurance and reinsurance undertakings in each category of own funds covering the capital requirements of SCR and MCR are shown in Figure 9.1.

Three categories of own funds shape the parameters of three types of bonds: RT1, T2, and T3, which will be presented in more detail in the following sections.

Loss absorption mechanism under Solvency II

RT1 CoCo instruments (Restricted Tier 1 CoCos)

Contractual loss absorption mechanism

Article 82(3) of Regulation 2015/35 provides that up to 20% of the basic own funds, i.e. Tier 1, might be paid-in subordinated liabilities provided that they have all the features listed in

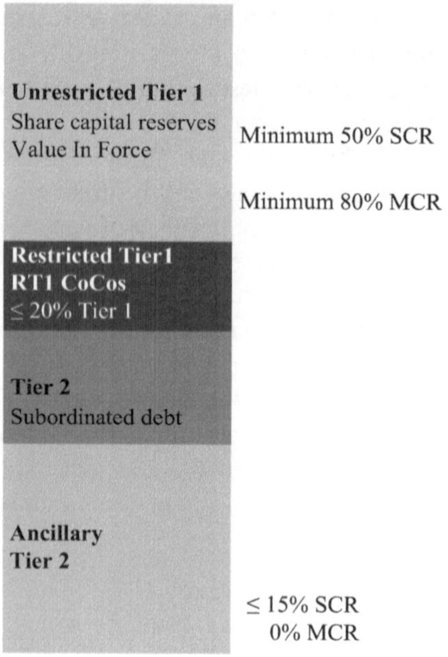

Figure 9.1 Coverage of SCR and MCR with eligible own funds.
Source: Liberadzki and Liberadzki (2019).

Article 71 of Regulation 2015/35. Hybrid instruments that qualify for T1 must be fully available and paid-in, perpetual, subordinated to any liabilities of the issuer and free of any clauses providing incentives for their early redemption (in particular coupon step-up mechanisms). Early redemption may not take place earlier than five years after the issue and only with the prior consent of the supervisor. Such consent is also required for early write down of bonds, which is additionally impossible in the event of a breach of capital requirements by the issuer, as well as in the event that only earlier write down of bonds results in such a breach.

The issuer retains at all times full discretion in suspending payments for an unlimited period of time and on a non-cumulative deferral basis, may use without limits the funds from the suspended payments to satisfy its due liabilities, and the payment itself may be made only from eligible funds for the purpose of dividend payment. Violation of capital requirements by the issuer means mandatory cancellation of the coupon payment. Dividend pusher and dividend stopper mechanisms are also not allowed, so the payment of dividends to shareholders (or lack thereof) does not entail any consequences in terms of coupon payment to holders of RT1 instruments.

Events triggering the activation of the loss absorption mechanism

The nominal amount or principal amount of a basic own-fund item shall cover losses in the event of a trigger constituting a "significant non-compliance with the Solvency Capital Requirement" takes place. The loss-absorbing capacity resulting from the suspension or reduction of payments should not be deemed sufficient to be considered as the main loss absorption mechanism.[8] In the event of a trigger event in the form of a breach of Solvency II capital requirements, the bonds are subject to mandatory conversion into the issuer's shares (contingent conversion) or temporary write down of part or permanent, full write down of their nominal value (temporary/partial and full/permanent write down).

Tier 2 hybrid instruments

Bonds eligible for T2 must be subordinated to the issuer's other liabilities, including – which is particularly important – liabilities resulting from the insurance policies. Another consequence of this condition is the most important difference between T2 instruments and the T1 instruments described earlier: these bonds do not have to be perpetual, it is enough for their maturity to be "sufficient". This criterion is met when the maturity is sufficiently longer than the average maturity of liabilities arising from signed insurance or reinsurance contracts. The provision of Article 93(2) of the Directive applies in this case the concept of "relative duration". Such a factor also distinguishes these instruments from instruments classified as Tier 2 for the purposes of the CRR Regulation. However, the minimum maturity of hybrid bonds shall not be shorter than ten years.[9]

As in the case of T1 instruments, the call option may be exercised at the earliest five years after the bond issue and only after obtaining the appropriate consent of the supervisor. Such consent is also required for the early redemption of bonds, which is impossible in the event of a breach of Solvency II's capital requirements. In other aspects, the requirements for T2 instruments are more liberal: ten years after issue, it is possible to increase the value of the coupon (step-up) by 100 bp, and violation of capital requirements does not result in an automatic conversion or write down of bonds. The requirements related to the payment of the coupon are also clearly more advantageous for investors: the issuer has no longer the absolute discretionary right to cancel the coupon payment, which can only be constructed as a cash-cumulative deferral. Moreover, it is possible to introduce dividend pusher and dividend stopper mechanisms, which increase the attractiveness of the instrument to the investors. In addition, the issuer's breach of the SCR requirement does not cancel the coupon payment, but only delays it. This distinguishes T2 insurers from T2 banks, where it is not possible for the issuer to transfer coupon payments.

As indicated in point 2, T2 can also be covered by excess hybrid bonds eligible for T1. These instruments are then treated as Ancillary Tier 2 own funds.[10]

Tier 3 hybrid instruments

Unlike the CRR Regulation, Solvency II introduces Tier 3 positions that can fill up to 15% of the undertaking's SCR, but T2 and T3 together cannot exceed 50% of the undertaking's SCR (see Figure 9.1). T3's own funds may consist of other financial instruments, i.e. those that do not meet the criteria for classification as T1 or T2.[11] T3 instruments may be subordinated to T2 or equivalent to them. The maturity of such instruments may not be shorter than five years, and early redemption by the issuer is possible only after obtaining the consent of the supervisor. In addition, if the issuer breaches the MCR (and not – as in the case of T2 instruments – SCR), the forced delay in the payment of the coupon should be applied.

The Eurovita case study

The Italian life insurer Eurovita was on the brink of collapse, primarily caused by the rising interest rates. The Italian regulatory and supervisory body (IVASS) appointed a special commissioner to oversee Eurovita, and finally the life insurer was placed under administration by IVASS. Eurovita was rescued by numerous insurance companies and banks (Generali, Intesa Sanpaolo Vita, Poste Vita, UnipolSAI, and Allianz) only after a multi-billion deal has been agreed on (Life Insurance International, 2023).

The problems of Eurovita were caused by significant unrealized losses on portfolio investments, as well as specific weaknesses of this insurer (inadequate risk management, limited capital, and the majority shareholder's reluctance to strengthen the company's capital position as requested by the supervisory authority). The main weaknesses of Eurovita S.p.A. were:

- Exposure to lapse risk due to a high concentration of traditional savings products, which made up about 90% of its portfolio. These products had guaranteed returns that proved to be lower than current market rates, making them less attractive to customers who might prefer switching to more profitable alternatives. This is compounded by the fact that these products have low surrender penalties, reducing the cost of early contract termination for customers.
- The ongoing rise in government bond yields since the end of 2021, which led to a decline in their value within the portfolio. This effect was not offset by the fact that higher interest rates are generally positive for life insurers, as premiums can be invested at higher returns.
- Additionally, the increase in interest rates has heightened lapse risk for Eurovita (and other insurers with similar products). According to IVASS data, the SCR related to lapse risk now constitutes about 90% of insurance risk in life insurance.

Therefore, Eurovita's capitalization decreased "due to an increase in capital requirements as a result of higher exposure to interest rate risk and lapse risk in life insurance" (IVASS). In 2022, Eurovita entered the year with chronically low SCR coverage (136%), below the soft limit tolerance threshold (150%) set by the group's policies. According to the most recent available data, as of June 30, 2022, the minimum capital requirement was already at 117% (see Table 9.1).

Table 9.1 shows that during the six-month period from December 2021 to June 30, 2022, Eurovita was hit in two ways: both by a decrease in Total Own Funds (by €30.54 million) and a simultaneous increase in the SCR requirement by €49.45 million. The drop in own funds was due to the devaluation of the portfolio caused by rising interest rates during the period from December 31, 2021, to June 30, 2022 (see Figure 9.2).

Meanwhile, the simultaneous increase in the SCR requirement is due to the heightened risk of a "mass lapse" (see Figure 9.3).

Here, a critical moment becomes apparent: the rise in interest rates had a one-directional effect, deepening the crisis for the company. The increase in interest rates and the devaluation of the bond portfolio are positively correlated with the "mass lapse", meaning that shrinking own funds are compounded by an increasing SCR requirement. In banking, there is no direct equivalent to this second phenomenon: of course, a drop in the level of own funds below a certain threshold is the primary event that triggers resolution, but this usually occurs with a relatively stable capital requirement (at least in the short to medium term). Meanwhile, in this case, the SCR requirement increased by as much as 10% over six months (see Table 9.1).

Table 9.1 Eurovita capital requirements as of December 31, 2021, and June 30, 2022

Eligible own funds and solvability (EUR million)	*30.06.2022*	*31.12.2021*	*Change*
Tier 1 – Unrestricted	447.92	469.26	−21.34
Tier 1 – Restricted	0	0	0
Tier 2	151.11	167.43	−16.32
Tier 3	13.71	6.59	7.12
Total own funds (OF)	**612.74**	**643.28**	**−30.54**
Solvency capital requirement (SCR)	**520.95**	**471.5**	**49.45**
Ratio OF/SCR	**118%**	**136%**	**−19%**

Source: Borkowska and Tarczyński (2023).

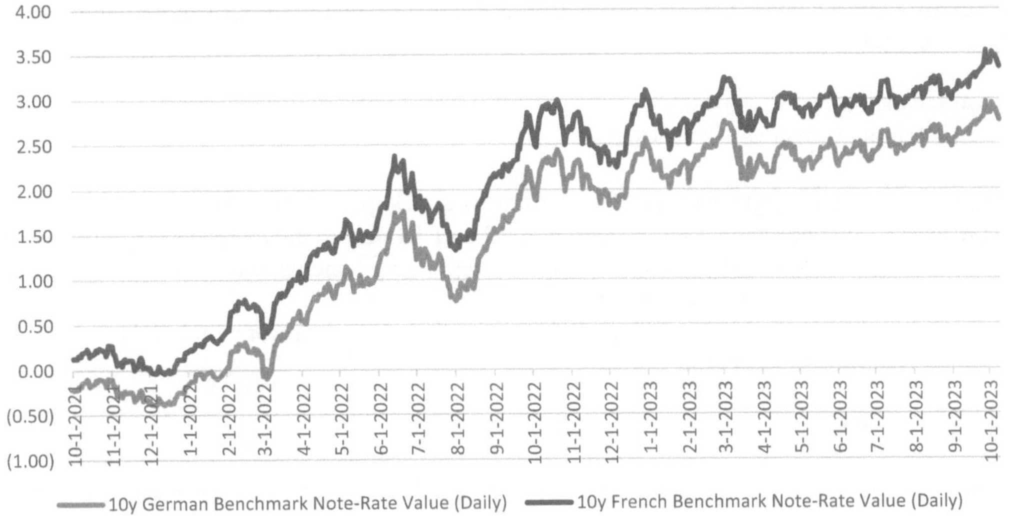

Figure 9.2 Yield of 10-year government bonds of Germany and France from October 9, 2021, to October 9, 2023.

Source: S&P Capital IQ. Yield of 10-year government bonds. Available at https://www.spglobal.com/.

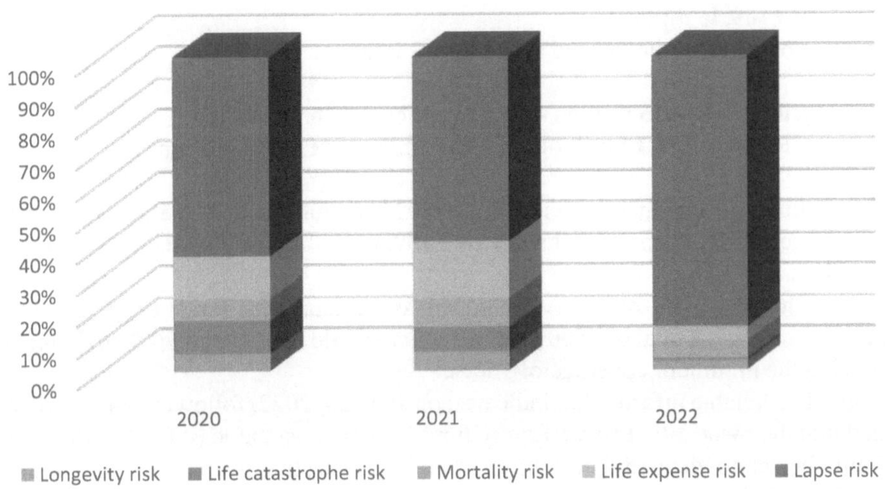

Figure 9.3 Percentage share of types of risks in the capital requirements of Italian life insurance companies.

Source: Borkowska and Tarczyński (2023).

A further equivalent to the rising SCR in banking is a liquidity outflow: both the resolution of Banco Popular in 2017 and the forced sale of Credit Suisse in 2023 show that institutions that continued to meet capital requirements were unable to cope with a situation of deposit outflows.

The static requirement to cover SCR "here and now" leads to a lack of regulatory benefit from holding loss-absorbing Tier 2 (T2) and Tier 3 (T3) instruments beyond the current level of admissibility. This is because Solvency II distinguishes own funds (basic and ancillary) into two categories:

- Available funds to cover SCR
- Eligible funds to cover SCR/MCR.

The problem is that eligible T2 and T3 instruments are capped: 50% of SCR for T2 and 15% of SCR for T3. This means that any issuance of T2 and T3 instruments beyond the limits of 50% and 15% of SCR, respectively, does not provide regulatory benefits at the time of issuance (the instruments remain "available" but "ineligible").

Let's consider this with the example of Eurovita, based on data from Table IV.1:

As of December 31, 2021:

SCR_{2021} = **€471.50** million; $T2_{2021}$ = **€167.43** million.

50% of SCR gives a total space for T2 issuance of **€235.75** million, leaving an unused space for T2 issuance of **€68.32** million.

As of June 30, 2022:

SCR_{1H2022} = **€520.95** million; $T2_{1H2022}$ = **€151.11** million.

50% of SCR gives a total space for T2 issuance of **€260.57** million, leaving an unused space for T2 issuance of **€109.46** million.

In the case of T3 debt, the unused space for T3 issuance was:

$0.15 \times SCR_{2021}$ = **€33.35** million – **€6.59** million = **€26.76** million;
$0.15 \times SCR_{1H2022}$ = **€78.14** million – **€13.71** million = **€64.43** million.

Summing the unused issuance potential in 1H2022, to fully utilize the space for T2 and T3 for the increased SCR, Eurovita fell short by **€109.46** million in T2 + **€64.43** million in T3 = **€173.9** million.

If the amount of €173.9 million were added to the total own funds of €612.74 million in 1H2022, we would get a total of €800 million, which would result in an SCR coverage of 151%, thus ensuring the minimum coverage of 150%.

As publicly available information indicates, on June 28, 2022, following an inspection, Ivass requested that the owner, the Private Equity fund Cinven, inject at least €150 million in capital.

It should be acknowledged that issuing T2 and T3 instruments up to the maximum permissible level would have only delayed, not prevented, Eurovita's descent into insolvency. As clearly shown in Figure 9.1, June 30, 2022, does not in any way mark the end of the cycle of rising government bond yields, which continued the following year. It is enough to say that the ECB's interest rate hike cycle had not yet begun in June 2022. Therefore, as press reports indicate, the required recapitalization amounts demanded by the regulator increased to €200 million, €250 million, and finally to €400 million. Consequently, even the €100 million recapitalization ultimately carried out by Cinven proved insufficient. It should also be noted that Eurovita's share capital was €90.5 million, and together with share premiums, totalled €128.89 million, highlighting the scale of the demand for an additional €300 million in capital.

The cancellation of coupon payments on Tier 2 bonds and their buyback by Cinven

On February 21, 2023, Eurovita suspended coupon payments on €115 million of Tier 2 bonds (ISIN XS2019977557 and XS1325091152). The coupons were 6% and 7%, respectively. Taking an approximate average of 6.5%, this would result in a yield of 6.5% × €115 million = €7.5 million, which was far too little to fill the capital gap.

On September 27, Cinven agreed to buy back Eurovita bonds with a nominal value of €160 million, paying €350 for each €1,000, representing a 65% discount.

Eurovita had credit obligations of over €300 million on its balance sheet to eight banks (including Natwest Group Plc, ING Groep NV, Bank of America Corp., and BNP Paribas SA). This likely explains the banks' willingness to participate in the restructuring process of Eurovita.

Inclusion of Restricted Tier 1 instruments (RT1) (CoCo)

So far, the analysis has focused on Tier 2 and Tier 3 instruments issued by Eurovita (see Table 9.1). If the catalog of possible instruments classified as own funds were expanded to include CoCo bonds that were not issued by Eurovita at all, classified as RT1 (see Table 1, row 2), the eligible RT1 own funds as of December 31, 2021, and June 30, 2022, would be €93.85 million and €89.50 million, respectively.

It can also be assumed that if the SCR remained below 100% after June 30, 2023, or even fell below 75%, such instruments would automatically convert into shares or be redeemed. Regardless, coupon payments would also be canceled, similar to the case with Tier 2 bonds.

Conclusions

If Eurovita had maintained available Tier 2 and Tier 3 liabilities in an additional amount of €173.9 million (in the appropriate proportions), exceeding the permitted €164.92 million in T2 and T3, then by the end of June 2022, they would also have become eligible. Considering Eurovita's total balance sheet of €19 billion, these liabilities would represent just under 1% of the company's balance. If the amount of €173.9 million were added to the total own funds of €612.74 million in 1H2022, we would get a total of €800 million, which would result in an SCR coverage of 151%, thus ensuring the minimum coverage of 150%. If the catalog of possible instruments classified as own funds were expanded to include CoCo bonds that were not issued by Eurovita at all, classified as RT1, the eligible RT1 own funds as of December 31, 2021, and June 30, 2022, would be €93.85 million and €89.50 million, respectively. Issuing debt by the company is simpler, but it must occur in good times, i.e., when the issuer's rating is sufficiently high.

There should be a promotion of a culture of maintaining available (not just eligible) T2 and T3 debt (as well as hybrid instruments classified as RT1), because during the times of Eurovita's distress Cinven did not meet the capital injection requirements, despite having contributed €100 million, which essentially doubled the share capital.

The example of Eurovita shows that additional issuance of T2 and T3 would account for 1% of the company's total balance, which does not seem over-burdensome.

No less important than a static analysis of SCR coverage is the analysis of the dynamics of SCR for individual companies, as well as the examination of the structure and quality of assets and the "stickiness" of policies. Identifying companies with such characteristics, not necessarily the largest in the market (Eurovita was outside the top ten life insurers in Italy), should lead to the aforementioned approach primarily regarding them.

Related to the above, the principle of proportionality must be understood and applied correctly. It cannot be simplistically understood as "smaller entity, smaller requirement." Experience teaches us that turmoil often starts with entities that are not necessarily the largest. This year, global turbulence was triggered by the collapse of the California regional bank SVB, which was carelessly exempted from certain requirements due to its "systemically insignificant" status. As mentioned, Eurovita was a medium-sized entity.

Notes

1 I.e. they are subordinated to all liabilities of the issuer – see section describing the properties of RT1.
2 CRR – Regulation (EU) No. 575/2013 of the European Parliament and of the Council of 26 June 2013 on prudential requirements for credit institutions and investment firms and amending Regulation (EU) No. 648/2012.
3 In principle, individual issues of CoCos by banks have taken place since 2009, but the emergence of a real market for these securities can be said from 2014 after the adoption of the CRR.
4 Directive 2009/138/EC of the European Parliament and of the Council of 25 November 2009 on the taking-up and pursuit of the business of Insurance and Reinsurance (Solvency II) as amended by Directive 2014/51/EU of the European Parliament and of the Council of 16 April 2014.
5 "Continued availability" means that a position is available or can be called upon to pay for in order to fully absorb losses in the event of going concern and liquidation.
6 "Subordination" means that, in the event of liquidation, the total amount of the position may be used to absorb losses and the position is refused to be repaid to the holder until all other obligations, including insurance and reinsurance obligations, are met to policyholders and beneficiaries of insurance and reinsurance contracts.
7 Commission Delegated Regulation (EU) 2015/35 of 10 October 2014 supplementing Directive 2009/138/EC of the European Parliament and of the Council on the taking-up and pursuit of the business of Insurance and Reinsurance.
8 Article 71(o) of Regulation 2015/35.
9 Article 73(4) of Regulation 2015/35.
10 Such ancillary items may also consist of the abovementioned supplementary benefits from members of the mutual society, letters of credit and guarantees, provided that they are loss-absorbing.
11 Article 94(3) of Directive 2009/138/EC.

References

Borkowska, R., & Tarczyński, M. (2023). *Eurovita case study*, presentation for DPSF, May 2023. [PowerPoint slides].

Commission Delegated Regulation (EU) 2015/35 of 10 October 2014 supplementing Directive 2009/138/EC of the European Parliament and of the Council on the taking-up and pursuit of the business of Insurance and Reinsurance. https://eur-lex.europa.eu/eli/reg_del/2015/35/oj/eng

De Spiegeleer, J., Höcht, S., Marquet, I., & Schoutens, W. (2017). CoCo bonds and implied CET1 volatility. *Quantitative Finance*, 17(6), 813–824.

Deutsche Bundesbank (2018). Monatsbericht (Jahrgang), 70(3). https://www.bundesbank.de/resource/blob/723244/b952fee724a73116977222867a27e58f/mL/2018-03-monatsbericht-data.pdf

Directive 2009/138/EC of the European Parliament and of the Council of 25 November 2009 on the taking-up and pursuit of the business of Insurance and Reinsurance (Solvency II) as amended by Directive 2014/51/EU of the European Parliament and of the Council of 16 April 2014. https://eur-lex.europa.eu/legal-content/EN/ALL/?uri=celex%3A32009L0138

Jaworski, P., Kowalski, A., Liberadzki, K., & Liberadzki, M. (2019). *Obligacje typu CoCo i bail-in jako instrumenty rekapitalizacji banków i zwiększenia stabilności finansowej [CoCo and bail-in bonds as instruments for bank recapitalisation and enhancing financial stability]*. National Bank of Poland, Warsaw. https://static.nbp.pl/publikacje/materialy-i-studia/ms335.pdf

Jaworski, P., Liberadzki, K., & Liberadzki, M. (2017). How does issuing contingent convertible bonds improve bank's solvency? A value-at-risk and expected shortfall approach. *Economic Modelling*, 60, 162–168.

Kowalski, A. (2018). Przymusowa restrukturyzacja banku (resolution) w praktyce – przypadki Banco Popular Español, Monte dei Paschi di Siena oraz Banco Popolare di Vicenza i Veneto Banca [Forced restructuring of a bank (resolution) in practice – the cases of Banco Popular Español, Monte dei Paschi di Siena and Banco Popolare di Vicenza and Veneto Banca]. *Monitor Prawniczy [Legal Monitor]*, 22, 1107–1116.

Liberadzki, K., & Liberadzki, M. (2019). *Contingent convertible bonds, corporate hybrid securities and preferred shares. Instruments, regulation, management*. New York and Basingstoke: Palgrave Macmillan.

Liberadzki, M., & Liberadzki, K. (2016). *Konstrukcja, zasady emisji i wycena hybrydowych papierów wartościowych na eurorynku [Construction, issuance rules and valuation of hybrid securities on the Euromarket]*. Warszawa: Oficyna Wolters Kluwer.

Life Insurance International (2023, July 3). *Insurers and banks agree on multi-billion deal to rescue Eurovita*. https://www.lifeinsuranceinternational.com/news/eurovita-multi-billion-rescue-deal/

Marquet, I. (2017). *The risk management of contingent convertible (CoCo) bonds*. [Doctoral dissertation, KU Leuven]. https://kuleuven.limo.libis.be

Regulation (EU) No. 575/2013 of the European Parliament and of the Council of 26 June 2013 on prudential requirements for credit institutions and investment firms (CRR) and amending Regulation (EU) No. 648/2012.

S&P Capital IQ. (2025).Yield of 10-year government bonds. https://www.spglobal.com/

10 Entrepreneurs' financial risk perception under the conditions of geopolitical instability

Lyubov Klapkiv

Introduction

Risk-taking is an important element of a company's growth. In a stable democratic environment that respects an independent judiciary and property rights, with the ability to make certain forecasts, geopolitical relations don't cause a major concern for entrepreneurs. From the perspective of the geopolitical situation, one of the most sensitive groups of entrepreneurs is exporters and importers. Their activity is highly dependent on international relations and trust in the other country.

However, foreign companies trading with contractors from a country with an unstable political regime have no such assurance and thus face a higher risk of losses related to geopolitical situations. This kind of trade relations is burdened with high uncertainty regarding:

- political risk that can materialize through political instabilities, currency inconvertibility, expropriation, and terrorism;
- economic risk – currency exchange rate, depletion of domestic resources, and financial weaknesses;
- legislation risk that can be affected through a payment moratorium;
- physical risk – destruction of goods during the rebellions, disorder, war, terroristic attacks, and high probability of thefts caused by the decrease in security;
- transport/logistic risks – limitation is access to the transport infrastructure and delivery delays.

These issues and other related issues deter most foreign companies from being involved in export or import relations in countries that are in high-risk zones. From the other perspective, instabilities, wars, and conflicts disrupt business processes in the contractor's country, causing deficits in goods/products in the domestic market, which creates a niche for foreign suppliers. In such a situation, companies perceive the potential of the risky trade in different ways: as an opportunity for gains or as a danger causing losses. Due to this, entities' attitudes toward the risky situation can have a frame of *risk-taking* or *risk-avoiding*. As risk is an inherent feature of entrepreneurial activity, companies are pushed to deal with uncertain situations using different management tools and approaches. The problem gets more complicated in the case of high-risk countries, where the lack of information on the environment and prediction limitations disrupt the rational decision-making process.

In such circumstances, along with the rational approach, companies should rely on their intuition, experience, and subjective evaluation. Behavioral economics has already provided a comprehensive study on risk as a factor that influences entrepreneurs' decisions. New

DOI: 10.4324/9781003663539-11

questions have grown with the increase of geopolitical tension in the world, particularly after the Russo-Ukrainian war started in 2022. The scale of this crisis is defined as "the most consequential geopolitical event in the post-Cold War era" (Yan et al., 2022). This kind of geopolitical risk materialized as a systemic country risk with catastrophic features, affecting huge territories. A large number of foreign companies that traded with Ukrainian contractors faced a new "black swan", an extreme event that had never happened before in their history – an interstate war. The complexity of the war-related risks and their multidimensional influence on foreign trade created a research niche that has both theoretical and practical significance.

This chapter contributes to the common knowledge by shedding light on the questions of how companies perceive the financial consequences of geopolitical instability in their export decisions: as a source of loss or as an opportunity for profits. The study's methodology is based on the survey approach that was conducted using the computer-assisted web interview (CAWI) method, as well as literature reviews and descriptive statistics. Current research enriches the state of knowledge on the company's internalization decision-making process under the conditions of geopolitical instability. It has practical value for the public institutions responsible for developing international trade (for instance, insurance credit agencies) in different countries. This research can also contribute to the understanding and improvement of economies that suffer from regional or global uncertainties or conflicts. Further studies on the topic will focus on identifying the weight of different factors that influence the company's subjective perception of geopolitically related risks in internationalization decisions.

The main limitation of the research is the small number of respondents (240), which does not allow us to generalize the findings to the whole population.

Geopolitical instability

The geopolitical situation in the world has become an important factor for the economic development of countries. In particular, international trade relations are closely dependent on geopolitical conditions. Over time, political instability, in a broad sense, was a feature of developing regions like Africa, the Middle East, etc. That has changed after the Russian-Ukrainian war started in 2022, when Western European countries, the United States of America, and some Asian countries became involved as passive parties.

Economists focus their attention on the impact of geopolitical issues on the macro level: economic growth, international trade, labor migration, inflation, etc. Countries' governments and numerous companies are looking for external markets where their goods and products could be exported. At the same time, governments are developing policies that are directed at the protection of the domestic economies from the negative influence of external political decisions. On the micro level, a geopolitical situation matters for the companies that build their production or selling processes around the world.

Along with the opportunity for profit, external markets can be a source of unexpected losses that require deep attention and sensitivity. The exogenous factors faced by entrepreneurs operating in foreign markets are not static, increasing uncertainty in the business conditions. However, in the literature, it is assumed that, regarding internalization, companies make their decisions in a relatively stable environment that has a normal or almost normal distribution of external parameters (Elbanna et al., 2020). Uncertainty cannot be avoided; it is integrated into all individual and corporate activities. Uncertainty is a source of risk. Knight (1921) clarified the distinction between risk and uncertainty: risk has a known or knowable probability distribution, and uncertainty has no possibility of specifying numerical probabilities. The literature presents different ways of risk and uncertainty interpretation, particularly related to companies' business activities. Miller (1992) classified uncertainties in international business as the uncertain general environment, industry risks, and firm-specific variables. General environmental uncertainties include political and government policy instability, as well as macroeconomic, social, and natural uncertainties. Industry uncertainties involve three major classes: input market, product market, and competitive uncertainty. Firm-specific factors are a source of operating, liability, research and development, credit, and behavioral uncertainties.

The last decade showed that companies had to raise their international expansion more and more under the fourfold condition of volatility, uncertainty, complexity, and ambiguity (VUCA). Along with natural disasters and cyber threats, international political tensions have been emerging as a new challenge for entrepreneurs. As mentioned by Comeaux and Kinsella (1994),

> In addition to ordinary business risk, which is faced by every businessman or investor whether investing at home or abroad, investors in developing countries face the political risk that is much greater than that experienced when investing in liberal Western democracies.

For instance, a survey that was conducted by PricewaterhouseCoopers (PwC) of over 1,000 global executives in over 90 countries found that political risk represents the most pressing concern when doing business abroad (PwC, 2020). The "black swans", like the Coronavirus disease (2019–2021) and the Russian-Ukrainian war (since 2022), are well-known sources of VUCA for international economic relations.

According to Caldara and Iacoviello (2022, p. 1197), geopolitical risk can be defined as the threat, realization, and escalation of adverse events associated with wars, terrorism, and any tensions among states and political factors that affect the peaceful course of international relations. The role of geopolitical risks in business activity was studied from different perspectives. Their significant negative effects on international trade were proved by Thakkar and Ayub (2022) in the case of global scale, Kim and Jin (2023) for bilateral trade in Korea, and Singh et al. (2023) underscored the overall detrimental impact of geopolitical risk (GPR) on trade with Latin America, with a disproportionately adverse effect on imports.

Entrepreneurs' risk perception mechanism

Numerous economists discussed the place of risk in the entrepreneurs' activity: Cantillon (2010) stated that the entrepreneur is the economic agent who supports risk emanating from the erratic functioning of the market, Hawley (1907, p. 459) found risk-taking the essential function of the entrepreneur, and Knight (1921, p. 44) emphasized that the main reward in business is leading by unknown risks. Later, the expected utility theory of Von Neumann and Morgenstern (1947) suggested that decision-makers are rational and make a choice under risk, achieving the largest value of an expected "utility" of their decisions (maximizing the profit and minimizing the losses). The key assumption is that the decisions are guided by personal ideas/beliefs about the likelihood of the risks. This thought was developed by modern behavioral theories, where subjective perception of risk and risk attitudes are essential factors of choice between different strategies, particularly in business. As was mentioned by Simon (1990, p. 16), "If we look at the time allocations of economics actors, say, business executives, we find that perhaps the largest fraction of decision-making time is spent in searching for possible courses of action and evaluating them (i.e., estimating their consequences)".

A more realistic view of decision-making under risk can be suggested by the theory of bounded rationality, which was developed by Simon in 1957. He proposed to replace the idea of utility maximization with a more realistic view of economic behavior involving satisfying and adaptation of aspiration levels to success (Simon, 1957). Risk perception analysis departs from the foundations of classical theory, as the comprehensive overview requires the implementation of psychological approaches. Within social science, Kahneman and Tversky (1979) studied a new theory pertaining to risk-taking behavior known as prospect theory. With the implementation of intransitivities in choice behavior, there are departures from classical decision theory (i.e., rationality) in terms of judgments and choices. Prospect theory holds that there are persistent biases driven by behavioral factors that influence individuals' choices under risky conditions for a specific situation or circumstance. It assumes that people are loss-averse when they are more concerned with losses than with gains, and, as a result, a person will assign more significance to avoiding loss than to achieving gain (Kahneman & Tversky, 1979). The field of psychology supports the notion of behavioral decision theory, in which the concepts of bounded rationality, cognitive limitations, and heuristics are the theoretical foundations. Individuals usually make judgments concerning a problem that is not clearly defined, have limited knowledge of possible outcomes and their consequences, and choose a satisfactory outcome.

In the modern literature, there are numerous studies on entrepreneurial risk and decision-making. Ojiako et al. (2014) mentioned that there are two main areas of interest: the first is perceptions that deal with how sensory information is organized, identified, and interpreted to support an understanding of the environment and wider society, whilst the second deals with cognitive attitudes that inform how individuals (entrepreneurs) arrive at decisions. The critically important role of risk perception in entrepreneurial decisions was explained by Simon et al. (2000) through the cognitive biases that influence our perception of events.

Risk perception can be defined as a decision-maker's assessment of the risk inherent in a situation (Sitkin & Pablo, 1992, p. 12). Summarizing the research works in the area of risk perception, Olsen (2011, p. 159) defined its main characteristics:

- Risk is multi-attribute in nature. It involves such elements as feelings of control, dread, and knowledge.
- Risk perceptions are influenced by social and cultural factors such as trust, fairness, and democratic values.
- Risk always contains an emotional or affective dimension.

Risk attitude (propensity) gives an answer about willingness to take risks and stresses consistent patterns of risk-taking or risk aversion that influence how risks are evaluated and what risks are deemed to be accepted (Sitkin & Pablo, 1992, p. 12).

Early proponents of the internalization process model (Johanson & Vahlne, 2006) stressed that a basic feature of firms was "striving to keep risk-taking at a low level". This goes in line with the traditional risk attitude; when having to make a complex decision, rational agents behave as risk-averse individuals intent on minimizing the impact risks might have on their operations (Bunge, 1998). More later study by Wu and Chen (2024) showed that higher perceived geopolitical risk predicts lower future stock returns and reduced free cash flows.

Entrepreneurs' attitudes toward risk remain a key underlying element of what is regarded as entrepreneurial behavior in the international arena, reflected, for instance, in psychological traits such as "risk-taking propensity" (Oviatt & McDougall, 2005, p. 542). To incorporate the psychological aspect into the model of international trade, Liao et al. (2022) adopted the perceived macroeconomic uncertainty as a proxy for macroeconomic uncertainty. Kim (2016) showed that the degree of the negative effect of macroeconomic uncertainty on a firm's exporting decision is lower in risk-averse firms than in risk-taking firms. At the same time, Li and Cheng

(2024) provide evidence that geopolitical risk significantly increases corporate risk-taking at both micro and macro levels in Chinese A-share listed companies.

The goal of research on risk perception is to provide a clearer understanding of the ways in which individuals form judgments about the risks they face (Wilkinson, 2001). Subjective risk perceptions (and assessment) of the level and magnitude of risks associated with international activities are an important antecedent of internationalization propensity, in particular exporting. Despite the centrality of risk in internationalization literature, there has been surprisingly little research into how decision-makers perceive geopolitical risk, particularly in exporting. Studying the measures of geopolitical risk, Bondarenko et al. (2024) underlying perception of geopolitical risk, as reflected in a country's news reporting, based on the Russo-Ukrainian war.

Differences in the scope, speed, and extent of internationalization are likely to be the result of individual differences in how risk is perceived by the decision-maker (Liesch et al., 2011). High international orientation appears to foster lower perceptions of risk in internationalization. There is a set of external and internal factors that are suggested to influence the perception of risk by companies. Ključnikov et al. (2022) studied the export risk perception of tax-related, legislative, and cultural-linguistic factors by small and medium enterprises in selected Visegrad countries. Their results reveal that the perceptions of Czech and Slovak small- and medium-sized enterprises (SMEs) differ regarding legislative and tax-related export barriers. On the other hand, the perceptions of SMEs from various countries do not differ concerning cultural-linguistic export barriers. Simpson and Kujawa (1974) studied the difference in stimuli risk perception between exporters and non-exporters. They found that export stimulus is a significant but not sufficient condition in export decisions.

José Acedo and Florin (2006) suggest that the firm profile, age, size, and scope of national operations act as a reference point and influence decision-makers' perception of risk from international expansion. Authors' results show that individual risk perceptions appear to be the main determinant of internationalization ($\beta = -0.524, p < 0.001$), followed by firm profile ($\beta = 0.253, p < 0.001$) and thirdly by the cognitive characteristics of the entrepreneur ($\beta = 0.166, p < 0.001$). Large companies often have higher financial and legal potential to organize proper export risk management. According to Bonaccorsi (1992, p. 621), decision-makers in small firms should a priori perceive higher risk in international activities due to the lack of appropriate information (market research). At the same time, the author points out that "The effect of company size on risk-aversion is more controversial" (Bonaccorsi, 1992, p. 621). On the other hand, Eroglu (1992) explained that larger firms are less vulnerable to potentially negative outcomes when internationalizing because they have more resources and, therefore, a higher capacity to absorb failure.

Bonaccorsi (1992, p. 620) focused on differences in risk perception and risk-taking propensity between exporters and non-exporters and found that exporters perceived less risk in exporting and maintained a more positive attitude to risk-taking. By dividing companies according to this criterion, it is possible to see whether having experience and, behind it, gathering richer information changes the way companies view geopolitical risk. Positive experience, on the one hand, can be a factor in geopolitical risk tolerance, especially with long-term and stable business operations with foreign counterparties. On the other hand, as a company conducts export business, it also accumulates experience and data and develops business "intuition" toward geopolitical risk. According to Figueira-de-Lemos et al. (2011), it can be expected that international experience decreases perceived risk.

Experiencing the impact of geopolitical events on operations can affect the assessment and perception of risk in the future. As indicated by Sitkin and Pablo (1992, p. 14), one of the determinants of risk behavior is the decision-maker's experience or familiarity with the situation.

Moreover, an important factor in building risk perception is whether the company has experienced positive or negative results. According to Schneider, Kauffman, and Ranieri (2016), a positive experience led to reduced risk-taking in the control set and a negative experience led to increased risk-taking. Lack of experience with export activities can have a twofold effect: companies may not be sensitive to risks related to geopolitics because it has not been affected by them, or they may overestimate risks related to geopolitics (overestimate). Emphasizing the role of experience, March and Shapira (1987) mentioned that when decision-makers are more experienced, they may begin to focus selectively on the evidence of their past ability to overcome obstacles and, therefore, may be willing to undertake risks that less experienced individuals would avoid.

Bauer (2005, p. 5) suggested a criterion of the differentiation between risk-neutral and risk-averse companies: if the decision-maker (e.g. firm) values the uncertain outcomes by their expected values, then it is considered as risk-neutral; if the uncertain outcomes are valued less than their expected value, then it is said the firm is risk-averse. The risk-averse firm takes the uncertainty as a harmful thing and associates additional "costs" with uncertainty. On the other hand, a risk-seeking firm prefers uncertain outcomes to their expected value. Such a firm considers uncertainty as a beneficial feature of the environment.

Based on the literature review, the main research question was formulated: if companies perceive geopolitical instability in trade relations as a potential source of financial losses that limit their risk-taking abilities?

Empirical study

A survey is broadly used as a tool for studying risk perception among companies. Ojiako et al. (2014) studied the key elements of risk perception among SMEs and implemented the survey, which was divided into two parts: a general questionnaire survey and a probability scenario experiment. Our survey was carried out using the CAWI survey technique on a group of respondents, $n = 240$. Their selection was based on a database of Polish SMEs. The selection of the sample was random, and the basis was a group of entities from the whole country, entering the 22 codes that include different export-oriented activities (Figure 10.1). The choice of these industries was determined by the need to reach respondents with the greatest export potential. As can be seen from Figure 10.1, these are companies in the metal and electromechanical industry. According to the Central Statistical Office, the largest share of the total export structure in 2023 was occupied by machinery, equipment, and transportation equipment – 38.2%, food and beverages – about 14%, metallurgical products – about 9.72%, and chemicals and related products – 9.1%.

The survey took into account the characteristics that may affect the attitude (either risk-taking or risk-avoiding) and the way companies perceive risk.

The company's own characteristics: size and the length of time the company has been in business (number of years)

A longer period of operation also allows a company to build a business relationship with a foreign counterparty and gather experience. As can be seen from Table 10.1, among the surveyed companies, there is a preponderance of players who have not been in the market for very long, with more than half operating for no more than five years. The smallest share among the respondents is occupied by companies operating in the market for more than 20 years. In terms of the number of employees, small companies employing up to 50 people prevail with a 57% share among the respondents. A problem that arose during the survey was the lack of response

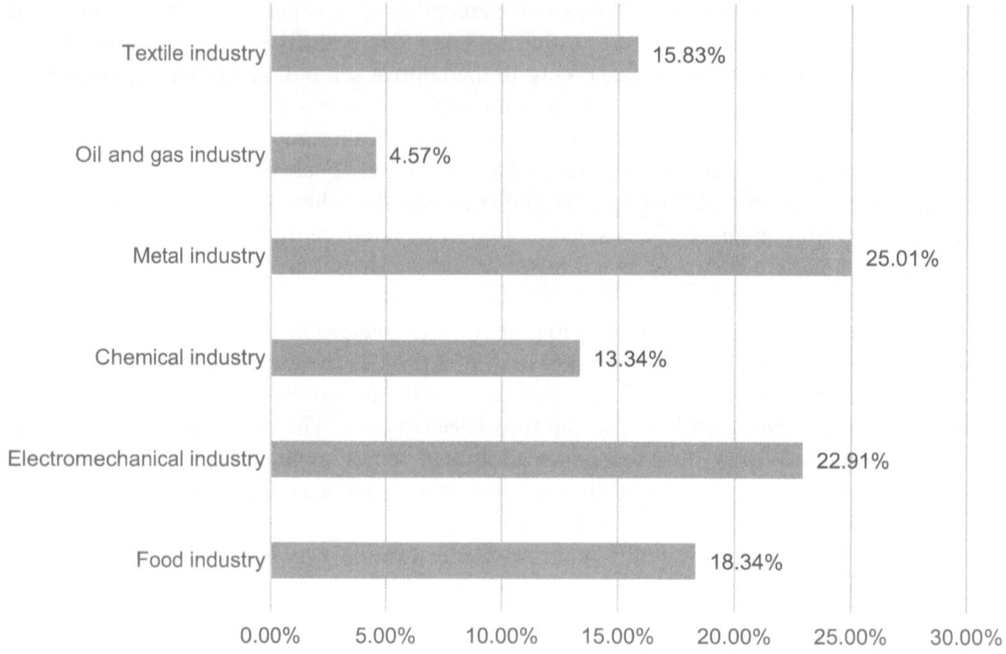

Figure 10.1 Structure of respondents by business sector.

Source: Author's own work based on the survey.

from large companies to the invitation to participate in the survey. On the one hand, this may be related to the difficulty of calling up a person in the company who is responsible for building an export strategy. Quite often, the opinion in this regard is directly within the competence of company management. In micro-, small-, and medium-sized companies, where organizational structures are much simpler and smaller, reaching the company's key people is easier.

Company experience in export activities

From the data in Table 10.1, it can be seen that the share of those with experience was significantly higher, almost 81%. An important feature when evaluating respondent companies was experience in export activities to high-risk countries. This is a group with a share of 70%, which we refer to as potential *risk-takers*; 19% of respondents had never conducted such activity (potential *risk avoiders*). The total number of respondents with experience in business in a high-risk country is 89%, which provides an opportunity for a more realistic view of the "experts'" perception of risk.

Verification of the correctness of the understanding of geopolitical instability through the risk

To determine the correctness of the understanding of geopolitical risk, the interviewed entrepreneurs were asked to select characteristics of geopolitical risk. Five features of geopolitical risk were listed, and one type was incorrect – "high level of government debt". This was to verify the respondents' knowledge of the risk and assess the representativeness of their opinions. As can be

Table 10.1 Sample structure of respondents

Feature		*Share, %*
Number of years of operation of the company (x2), years	Up 5	58
	From 6 to 10	21
	From 11 to 15	7
	From 16 to 20	9
	More than 20	5
Number of people employed by the company (x3), workers	1–9	36
	10–49	57
	50–249	7
Having experience in exporting goods	Yes	81
	No	19
Having experience in exporting goods to countries with higher geopolitical risks	Yes, currently exporting	70
	Yes, it had been exported in the past	19
	No	11

Source: Author's own work based on the survey.

Table 10.2 Geopolitical risk features as assessed by respondents

Category of respondent	*Features of geopolitical risk*					
	Coup	*Hostilities*	*Expropriation of assets by the government*	*High levels of government debt*	*Prohibition of exchange and transfer of currency out of the country*	*Physical damage to cargo*
Exporters, %	94.0	98.2	89.9	17.3	74.4	81.5
Non-exporters, %	73.1	69.2	73.0	3.8	65.9	76.3
Former exporters, %	78.2	89.1	78.2	28.3	73.2	71.7

Source: Author's own work based on the survey.

seen from Table 10.2, 17.3% of companies that are currently engaged in export activities made a mistake in indicating the characteristics of geopolitical risk; from the group of companies not engaged in export activities – 3.8% from the group of former exporters – 28.3%. The results show that the majority of respondents have a correct understanding of the concept/concept of geopolitical risk.

Risk attitudes and probability scenarios

Important are the results of responses to the question about the decision to enter into a contract with a counterparty from a risky country, which has already expressed readiness to purchase goods. Overall, 93.75% of respondents are ready to take risks; this is the group we refer to as risk-takers. The rest of the respondents who do not decide to undertake such business activity (6.25%) represent features of risk avoiders. The share of entrepreneurs with the characteristics of risk-takers is similar to the share of enterprises that have had experience in exporting to high-risk countries and those that are currently engaged in such activities. It can be inferred that

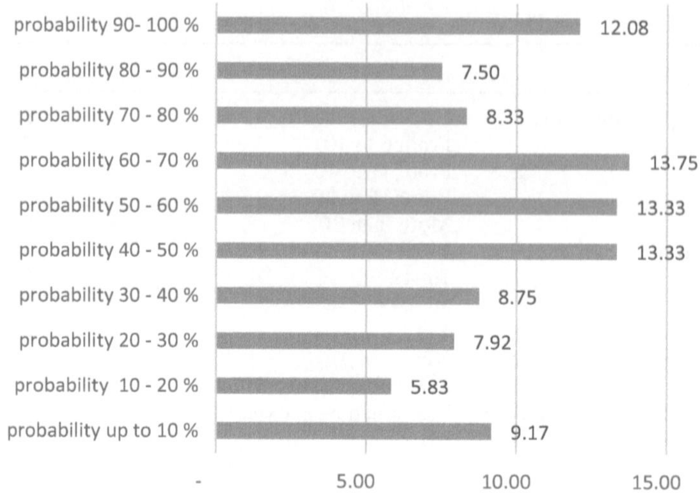

Figure 10.2 Rating the probability of suffering losses when trading with a contractor from a high-risk country.

Source: Author's own work based on the survey.

respondents do not perceive potential geopolitical risks as a significant barrier to export expansion, or the risk premium is sufficient to cross these barriers.

In order to evoke respondents' risk sensitivity related to the probability of obtaining losses when executing a contract with a contractor from a high-risk country (Figure 10.2), probability scenarios were implemented. This approach was suggested by Kunreuther, Novemsky, and Kahneman (2001). Respondents were asked to choose a probability from a 0%–100% scale. Overall, 40% of respondents rated such risk of losses in the 41%–70% range. The distribution of responses revealed two "tails", where about 10% of companies showed extremely optimistic (loss with probability up to 10%) and extremely pessimistic (probability above 91%) scenarios for the financial outcome of a trade with a counterparty from a high-risk country. This is an interesting result given that 91% of respondents nevertheless choose to trade, i.e., they have a very high tolerance for potential risk.

Respondents were also asked to rate the likelihood of profit in trading with a contractor with higher risk (Figure 10.3). This question was designed to reveal whether geopolitical risk is viewed solely as a source of loss. The result shows that the majority of respondents also highly rate the possibility of profits. Moreover, 52% of them rate the probability above 61%.

Conclusions

During the last decades, geopolitical risks have received higher attention in the business environment as an obstacle to export expansion. Increasing pressure on domestic markets pushed entrepreneurs to the gaining of external markets. Developing countries are perceived as a source of opportunities for trade. Business relations with contractors from other countries are very often burdened with high risks related to their geopolitical situation. The main sources of exporters' financial losses are political, economic, legislative, physical, and transport/logistic risks.

For the purpose of understanding the entrepreneur's behavior toward geopolitical risk and answering the question of whether geopolitical risks are a crucial obstacle to export expansion,

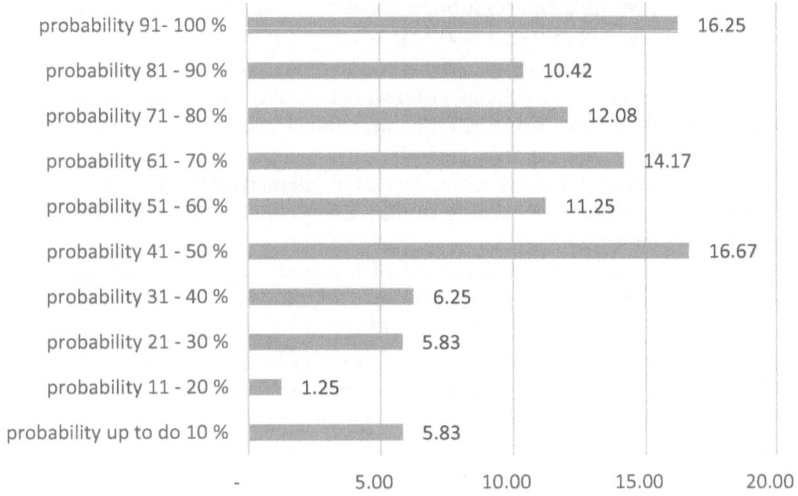

Figure 10.3 Rating the probability of profit in trading with a contractor from a high-risk country.

Source: Author's own work based on the survey.

a survey study was conducted. Based on 240 responses that were received from Polish entrepreneurs, we can assume that:

1 The share of entrepreneurs who are marked as risk-takers is similar to the share of those who have had experience in exporting to high-risk countries and those who are currently engaged in such activities. It can be inferred that respondents do not perceive potential geopolitical risks as a significant barrier to export expansion, or the risk premium is sufficient to cross these barriers. Overall, 93.75% of respondents are willing to take risks if they find a contractor.

2 Respondents rated the probability of obtaining losses when executing a contract with a counterparty from a high-risk country: 40% of respondents rated such risk of losses in the 41%–70% range. The distribution of responses revealed two "tails", where about 10% of companies showed extremely optimistic (loss with probability up to 10%) and extremely pessimistic (probability above 91%) scenarios for the financial outcome of a trade with a counterparty from a high-risk country. This is an interesting result given that 91% of respondents nevertheless choose to trade, i.e., they have a very high tolerance for potential risk. At the same time, the majority of respondents also highly rate the possibility of profits. Moreover, 52% of them rate the probability above 61%.

References

Bauer, M. (2005). *Theory of the Firm under Uncertainty: Financing, Attitude to Risk and Output Behavior*. Working paper Uk FSV nr 71. https://doi.org/10.2139/ssrn.981326

Bonaccorsi, A. (1992). On the relationship between firm size and export intensity. *Journal of International Business Studies*, *23*(4), 605–635.

Bondarenko, Y., Lewis, V., Rottner, M., & Schüler, Y. (2024). Geopolitical risk perceptions. *Journal of International Economics*, *152*, 103005. https://doi.org/10.1016/j.jinteco.2024.104005

Bunge, M. (1998). *Philosophy of Science. From Explanation to Justification*. Routledge.

Caldara, D., & Iacoviello, M. (2022). Measuring geopolitical risk. *American Economic Review*, *112*(4), 1194–1225. https://doi.org/10.1257/aer.20191823

Cantillon, R. (2010). *An Essay on Economic Theory*. Ludwig von Mises Institute.

Comeaux, P., & Kinsella, S. (1994). Reducing political risk in developing countries: Bilateral investment treaties, stabilization clauses, and MIGA & OPIC investment insurance. *New York Law School Journal of Institutional and Comparative Law*, *15*(1), 1–48.

Elbanna, S., Hsieh, L., & Child, J. (2020). Contextualizing internationalization decision-making research in SMEs: Towards an integration of existing studies. *European Management Review*, *17*(2), 573–591. https://doi.org/10.1111/emre.12395

Eroglu, S. (1992). The internationalization process of franchise systems: A conceptual model. *International Marketing Review*, *9*(5), 19–30. https://doi.org/10.1108/02651339210020277

Figueira-de-Lemos, F., Johanson, J., & Vahlne, J.-E. (2011). Risk management in the internationalization process of the firm: A note on the Uppsala model. *Journal of World Business*, *46*(2), 143–153.

Hawley, F.B. (1907). *Enterprise and the Productive Process*. G.P. Puynam's Sons.

Johanson, J., & Vahlne, J.-E. (2006). Commitment and opportunity development in the internationalization process: A note on the Uppsala internationalization process model. *Management International Review*, *46*(2), 165–178. https://doi.org/10.1007/s11575-006-0043-4

José Acedo, F., & Florin, J. (2006). An entrepreneurial cognition perspective on the internationalization of SMEs. *Journal of International Entrepreneurship*, *4*(1), 49–67. https://doi.org/10.1007/s10843-006-0482-9

Kahneman, D., & Tversky, A. (1979). Prospect theory: An analysis of decision under risk. *Econometrica*, *47*(2), 263–292. https://doi.org/10.2307/1914185

Kim, H.-S. (2016). Differential impact of uncertainty on exporting decision in risk-averse and risk-taking firms: Evidence from Korean firms. *Seoul Journal of Economics*, *29*(3), 379–409.

Kim, C.Y., & Jin, H. (2024). Does geopolitical risk affect bilateral trade? Evidence from South Korea. *Journal of the Asia Pacific Economy*, *29*(4), 1834–1853. https://doi.org/10.1080/13547860.2023.2204693

Ključnikov, A., Civelek, M., Klimeš, C., & Farana, R. (2022). Export risk perceptions of SMEs in selected Visegrad countries. *Equilibrium. Quarterly Journal of Economics and Economic Policy*, *17*(1), 173–190. https://doi.org/10.24136/eq.2022.007

Knight, F.H. (1921). *Risk, Uncertainty and Profit*. Houghton Mifflin Company.

Kunreuther, H., Novemsky, N., & Kahneman, D. (2001). Making low probabilities useful. *Journal of Risk and Uncertainty*, *23*(2), 103–120.

Li, L., & Cheng, X. (2024). Do geopolitical risks increase corporate risk-taking?—Based on the perspective of diversification expansion. *Corporate Governance: An International Review*, *32*(3), 428–448.

Liao, J., Luo, L., Xu, X., & Wang, A. (2022). Perceived macroeconomic uncertainty and export: Evidence from cross-country data. *Economic Research-Ekonomska Istraživanja*, *35*(1), 213–229. https://doi.org/10.1080/1331677X.2021.1890176

Liesch, P., Welch, L., & Buckley, P. (2011). Risk and uncertainty in internationalisation and international entrepreneurship studies: Review and conceptual development. *Management International Review*, *51*(6), 851–873. https://doi.org/10.1007/s11575-011-0107-y

March, J., & Shapira, Z. (1987). Managerial perspectives on risk and risk-taking. *Management Science*, *33*(11), 1404–1418.

Miller, K.D.A. (1992). Framework for integrated risk management in international business. *Journal of International Business Studies*, *23*(2), 311–331.

Ojiako, U., Chipulu, M., Marshall, A., & Baboolall, P. (2014). Thematic elements underlying risk perception amongst small and medium enterprise owner-managers. *Acta Commercii*, *14*(1), 1–9.

Olsen, R.A. (2011). Financial risk perceptions: A behavioral perspective. In R. Yazdipour (Ed.), *Advances in Entrepreneurial Finance. With applications from Behavioral Finance and Economics*. Springer, 45–67. https://doi.org/10.1007/978-1-4419-7527-0

Oviatt, B.M., & McDougall, P.P. (2005). Defining international entrepreneurship and modeling the speed of internationalization. *Entrepreneurship: Theory & Practice*, *9*, 537–553. https://doi.org/10.1111/j.1540-6520.2005.00097.x

PwC (2020). 23rd annual global CEO survey - navigating the rising tide of uncertainty. Available at: https://www.pwc.no/no/publikasjoner/ceo-survey-2020/pwc_23rd_annual_global_ceo_survey_2020.pdf (accessed 30.11.2024).

Schneider, S., Kauffman, S., & Ranieri, A. (2016). The effects of surrounding positive and negative experiences on risk. *Judgment and Decision Making*, *11*(5), 424–440. https://doi.org/10.1017/S1930297500004538

Singh, V., Correa da Cunha, H., & Mangal, S. (2023). Do geopolitical risks impact trade patterns in Latin America? *Defence and Peace Economics*, *35*(8), 1102–1119. https://doi.org/10.1080/10242694.2023.2299072

Simon, H.A. (1957). *Models of Man*. John Wiley & Sons.

Simon, H.A. (1990). Bounded rationality. In J. Eatwell, M. Milgate, & P. Newman (Eds.), *Utility and Probability*. 15–18. The New Palgrave. Palgrave Macmillan. https://doi.org/10.1007/978-1-349-20568-4_5

Simon, M., Houghton, S.M., & Aquino, K. (2000). Cognitive biases, risk perception, and venture formation: How individuals decide to start companies. *Journal of Business Venturing*, *15*(2), 113–134.

Simpson, C., & Kujawa, D. (1974). The export decision process: An empirical inquiry. *Journal of International Business Studies*, *5*(1), 107–117.

Sitkin, S., & Pablo, A. (1992). Reconceptualizing the determinants of risk behavior. *The Academy of Management Review*, *17*(1), 9–38. https://doi.org/10.2307/258646

Thakkar, N., & Ayub, K. A. (2022). Geopolitical risk and globalization. *Journal of Applied Business and Economics*, *24*(3), 140–150. https://articlearchives.co/index.php/JABE/article/view/2569

von Neumann, J., & Morgenstern, O. (1947). *Theory of Games and Economic Behavior.* Princeton University Press, 2nd edn, 1947; 3rd edn, 1953.

Wilkinson, I. (2001). Social theories of risk perception: At once indispensable and insufficient. *Current Sociology*, *49*(1), 1–22. https://doi.org/10.1177/0011392101049001002

Wu, X., & Chen, J. (2024). Do management's geopolitical risk perceptions affect stock returns? Evidence from China's A-Share stocks. Available at SSRN: https://doi.org/10.2139/ssrn.5051300

Yan, S., Yao, X., & Ma, B. (2022). Chinese transnational corporations in the Ukraine crisis: Risk perception and mitigation. *Transnational Corporations Review*, *14*(4), 371–381. https://doi.org/10.1080/19186444.2022.2144082

11 Challenges in financing microenterprises in an unstable economic landscape

Ilona Skibińska-Fabrowska

Introduction

Microenterprises as a specific type of enterprises

In most modern economies, both developed and developing countries, microenterprises are an essential element in the structure of economic entities (EU, 2021). In 2021, in the European Union countries, microenterprises accounted for nearly 93% of all enterprises, employing about 30% of all employees. The average employment, including working owners, oscillated around 1.6 people and has decreased in recent years, indicating the popularization of self-employment as a form of running a business. Microenterprises accounted for over 19% of the added value generated in the European Union economy, with a slightly over 17% share in the revenues of enterprises. Similar data for Poland indicate a 96% share of microenterprises in the population of economic entities, with employment at the level of 38% of all employees (on average 1.7 in a microenterprise), an 18.7% share in added value, and a 23% share in revenues.

The criteria for classifying an enterprise as a micro-enterprise are not clear. The regulatory solutions are dominated by a quantitative approach based on accounting values (value of assets, value of revenues) and the level of employment.

However, qualitative features better reflect the specificity of micro-enterprises. They point to the most important feature that distinguishes them from other business entities, which is the unique position and role of the owner (Ibidunni et al., 2018; Bates, 1995; Sajilan et al., 2015). Not only is he the initiator and founder of the company, but also

- directly and independently manages the company. The management style is usually based on close, even family-like relationships with employees, far from any formalization;
- makes all decisions independently, bearing responsibility and consequences, including financial ones. This does not mean that he does not use formal or, more often, informal counseling, but it is his voice that is decisive;
- develops and implements the company's strategy, although it usually has a short horizon and concerns current operational activities;
- often, business decisions are based on his knowledge and intuition.

In addition, micro-enterprises' specificity is manifested in asymmetrical relations with the environment, which strongly affects them. The business's small size and the owner's strong position allow it to respond flexibly to changes in the economic situation while limiting the opportunities to gain the benefits of scale-up. Micro-enterprises often operate in market niches, on local

DOI: 10.4324/9781003663539-12

markets, which allows the offer to be tailored to an individual customer's requirements. In the smallest entities, the role of human capital, primarily the owner and employees, is powerfully revealed. In addition to the high-tech start-up segment, it is most often the knowledge and skills of employees that are the source of success in a micro-enterprise (McGuirk et al., 2015; Berge et al., 2015).

The specificity of micro-enterprises is also noticeable in their financial activity. Anyway:

- in the subsequent phases of the company's development, the sources of financing used change, but equity is not replaced by borrowed capital but by surpluses generated in the company;
- external sources of financing in the form of bank loans are used to a small extent, and leasing is a much more popular way of financing investments;
- due to the small size and scale of operations, the demand for financing operating and investing activities is relatively low;
- trade credit is used to finance current operations, but the degree of its use depends on the knowledge, experience, and competence of the owners.

These specific conditions affect the selection of sources of financing operating and investment activities by micro-enterprises and simultaneously constitute a source of restrictions and barriers in using certain financial services and products.

Sources of financing for business activities and factors determining their choice

The condition for the functioning of a company at every stage of its development is access to sources of financing (Abdulsaleh & Worthington, 2013). At the stage of establishing an enterprise, the funds contributed by the owners become not only the leaven and foundation of the economic side of the enterprise, allowing to finance the purchase of the necessary means of production, but often have a constitutive meaning for the economic entity.[1] During the life of the enterprise, cash allows for maintaining current liquidity, supplementing periodic shortages (financing operational activity) and providing the possibility of making investments (financing development activity). In microenterprises, the funds contributed by the owner at each stage of the company's operation are closely linked to the savings of his household. This relationship is so close, and the flows of funds so frequent and informal, that it is extremely difficult to study their scale. The same applies to funds from the surplus generated by a micro-enterprise. Due to the simplified accounting rules applied in small entities, the surplus from operations is not transformed into profit, which is divided between retained profit in the enterprise and payments to owners,[2] and flows directly into the financing of the activities (Dehejia & Gupta, 2022).

In addition to equity and generated surplus, the primary source of financing for enterprises is repayable debt instruments (Abbasi et al., 2017). These include bank and nonbank credits and loans. Bank loans are the fundamental way enterprises can obtain funds to finance investment and current activities. The variety of loans offered by banks allows them to be tailored to the needs and capabilities of the enterprise. However, formalized requirements, rigid procedures, and relatively high costs limit enterprises' use of this source of financing. In recent years, the development of the credit guarantee system has helped to reduce the problem that the obligation to present collateral posed for some enterprises, improving bank loans' attractiveness. However, it should be remembered that it is the lender, not the client, who decides on the final shape of the loan agreement and the resulting requirements for the borrower (Prilmeier, 2017). Regarding loans granted by non-bank financial institutions and non-financial entities, the agreement can be shaped more flexibly by both parties to the contract. Also, the formal requirements regarding assessing the ability to repay the loan in the future are flexible, but this is usually reflected in the higher costs of such a loan (Chernenko et al., 2022).

Among other sources of financing, leasing should be mentioned, as it is particularly popular in Poland among smaller enterprises. It is dedicated to the purchase of fixed assets, i.e., financing investment activities. In the case of this instrument, despite the standardization of contracts and procedures, the flexibility of shaping the contract is more significant from the entrepreneur's point of view than in the case of loans, and the costs are slightly lower (Moritz et al., 2016; Bartik et al., 2020).

Public aid is an essential source of financing for activities, both in the operational and investment dimension. This broad category includes programs implementing specific development (investment) goals and ongoing enterprise support. An example of the first group is funds from the European Union budget, which go directly to entrepreneurs in individual countries. The second group includes de minimis aid launched in crises, an example of programs launched during the COVID-19 pandemic (Beizitere et al., 2020; Kochaniak et al., 2023).

Trade credit is a financial instrument inextricably linked to enterprises' current operational activity. It involves deferring payment and accepting its execution at an agreed time after the delivery date of the goods or services. For suppliers, it is a mechanism that allows for increasing the scale of operations, while for recipients, it is a financial instrument that allows for reducing the capital gap and managing current liquidity (Bhattacharya & Londhe, 2014; García-Teruel & Martínez-Solano, 2010).

The large variety of sources of financing for enterprises encourages consideration of what factors influence decisions on the choice of a specific solution. Generally, these determinants can be divided into macroeconomic and microeconomic ones (Titman & Wessels, 1988; Daskalakis et al., 2017; Czerwonka & Jaworski, 2021).

Macroeconomic factors similarly affect all enterprises operating in a specific (domestic) market. These are regulatory solutions, especially tax solutions, a business licensing system, and regulations that shape the freedom of undertaking business activities. From the economic perspective, the most important ones include the general state of the economic situation, the level of inflation, the level of unemployment, the level of development and structure of the financial market, and the level of interest rates.

Micro factors are specific to each company. In particular, they are (Szomko, 2020):

- the sector and industry in which the company operates, and above all, the degree of technological advancement and innovation;
- size of the enterprise measured by the amount of annual revenues, the value of the balance sheet total, the amount of employment;
- value and structure of fixed assets of the enterprise, its modernity, and share of intangible assets;
- market position;
- phase of the company's life cycle, period of operation on the market,
- organizational structure, its level of complexity.

Behavioral factors on the part of financial directors/decision-makers are also pointed out, including financial awareness, experience, risk appetite, and resistance to heuristics.

Barriers to accessing external sources of financing

Despite the variety of mechanisms and products available on the financial market that enable obtaining external financing, the possibilities of the smallest business entities are limited in this respect (Bongini et al., 2021). Microenterprises, both in their current operations and in financing investments, primarily use the generated operating surplus (internal source of financing) and bank loans (external source) (Civelek et al., 2019; Martinez Cillero et al., 2019; Romano et al., 2001). Therefore, in practice, the sources of financing for operations could be better diversified and similar in all enterprises.

Additionally, microenterprises need help accessing external sources of financing. This state of affairs is the high level of information asymmetry between the enterprise and the entity providing capital, which is challenging to eliminate in the smallest entities. Simplified accounting principles, close connection between the finances of the enterprise and the finances of the owner's household, and small scale of operations are the main reasons, difficult to overcome, for limited access to information about the activities of microenterprises. The potential costs of obtaining information (monitoring the situation of the enterprise) are so high that financial institutions (banks) are reluctant to finance their activities (Hoang et al., 2018). They perceive microenterprises as risky borrowers, which makes them set higher requirements for the value and quality of the presented security. Additionally, lending institutions compensate for the higher level of risk with a higher credit margin, which makes a loan for microenterprises more expensive than for other economic entities.

Belás et al. (2016) point to additional difficulties that microenterprises may encounter when seeking bank financing. These include:

- an underdeveloped domestic financial market that does not provide access to a wide range of financial products and services;
- excessive regulation;
- lack of transparency in the enterprise environment, especially in regulatory aspects;
- lack of adequate security satisfactory for lenders on the part of enterprises.

Ferrando and Mulier's research (Ferrando&Mulier, 2015) was devoted to the analysis of access to finance in the context of demographic characteristics and financial indicators of enterprises. The conclusions of the study indicate the following regularities:

- the factor that limits access to external finance is the low level of profitability of the business;
- the low level of working capital and the high level of leverage explain the actual limitations in access to finance to a lesser extent;
- the age of the company, but not its size, is essential in explaining both perceived and real financial constraints;
- enterprises with a high level of short-term maturity are more likely to perceive access to finance as limited.

Data and methods

The study was conducted in August 2023 on 265 Polish companies employing at most nine people. The study assumed that this is sufficient to classify the surveyed company into the micro category without analyzing the size of the balance sheet total and the scale of revenues. The

Table 11.1 Descriptive statistics – research sample

Descriptions		*(%)*
Samples (N)		*265 (100%)*
Gender	Female	127 (47.9%)
	Male	138 (52.1%)
Age	Below 25 years	2 (0.8%)
	25–34 years	47 (17.7%)
	35–44 years	71 (26.8%)
	45–54 years	63 (23.8%)
	55 and above	82 (30.9%)
Average age (years)		**59.05**
Median age (years)		**60.0**
Education	Primary	2 (0.8%)
	Vocation (basic level)	12 (4.53%)
	Secondary (general)	58 (21.9%)
	Secondary vocation	24 (9.1%)
	High degree	169 (63.9%)
Business experience	Up to 1 year	16 (6.0%)
	1–3 years	40 (15.1%)
	3–5 years	46 (17.4%)
	5–10 years	43 (16.2%)
	Above 10 years	120 (45.3%)
Average business experience (years)		**11.09**
Median business experience (years)		**12.5**
Annual revenue	Up to 25k EUR	122 (46.0%)
	25k–100k	116 (43.8%)
	100k–250k	16 (6.0%)
	250k–500k	8 (3.0%)
	Above 500k	3 (1.1%)
Average annual revenue		**63.49k**
Median average annual revenue		**62.5k**
	Services	199 (75.1%)
	Manufacturing	23 (8.7%)
	Commerce	43 (16.2%)

Sources: Author's own research.

study was conducted using the computer-assisted web interview method based on an original questionnaire. Table 11.1 presents the statistics of the research sample.

Figure 11.1 presents the demographic structure of the respondents – business owners.

Figure 11.2 presents the characteristics of the enterprises covered by the study.

Figures 11.3 and 11.4 present the sources of financing for the activities in the surveyed enterprises.

The presented data show that the primary financing source for the surveyed enterprises, regardless of whether the financing concerns current operations or investment activities, is current revenues in the form of operating surplus (over 70% for operating activities and 60% for investment activities). The second most important source is the savings of the household of the enterprise owner (approximately 10% for both types of activities). In the case of operating activities, trade credit is also of significant importance. On the other hand, leasing is primarily used to finance enterprise investments. Bank loans and public aid are other sources of investment financing. To sum up, it can be stated that when selecting sources of financing,

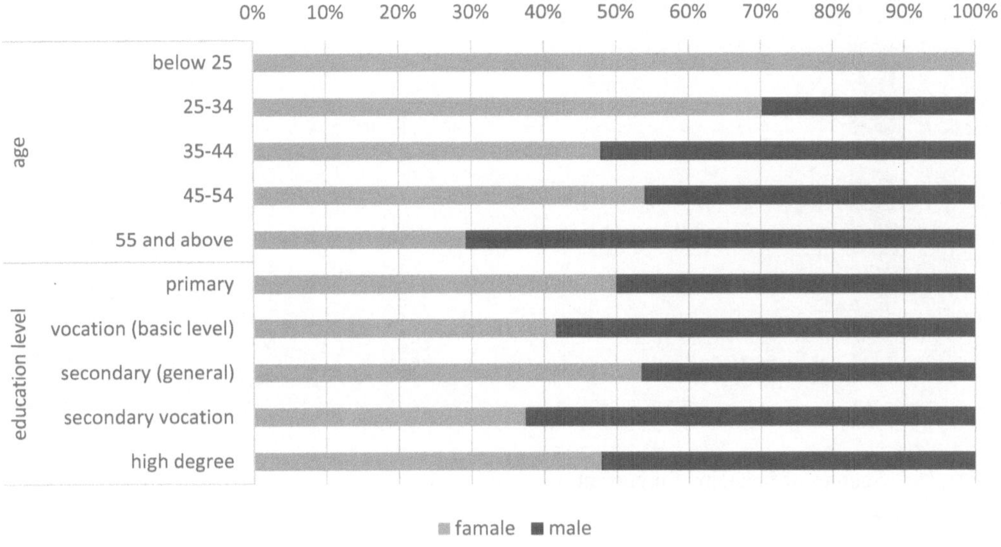

Figure 11.1 Demographic structure of respondents.

Sources: Author's own research.

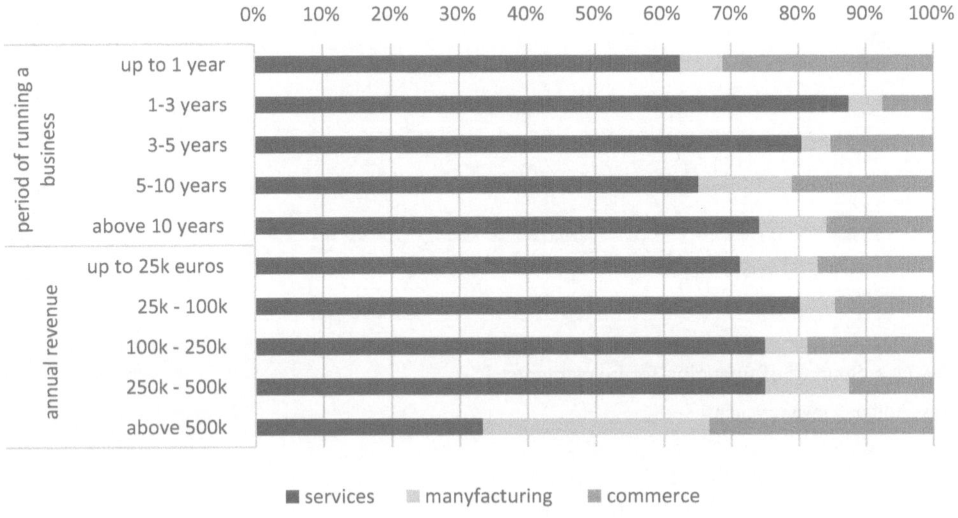

Figure 11.2 Characteristics of enterprises by type of activity, age, and size.

Sources: Author's own research.

entrepreneurs choose the simplest ones from the formal side, which do not require going through complicated, formalized procedures. However, this does not mean that they are the cheapest for them.

The conducted study was preparatory and preliminary in relation to the planned in-depth analysis using multifactor regression models. Given the above, statistical methods of descriptive analysis and graphic methods of presenting results were used.

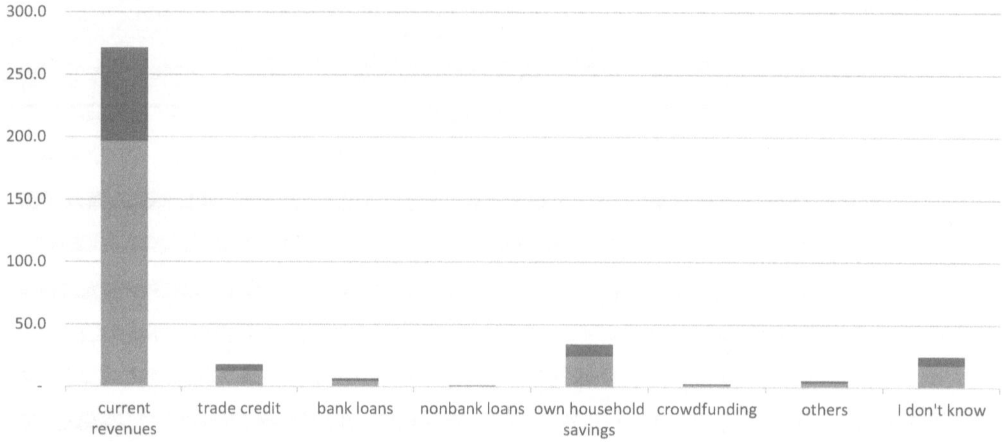

Figure 11.3 Sources of financing for current operations.

Sources: Author's own research.

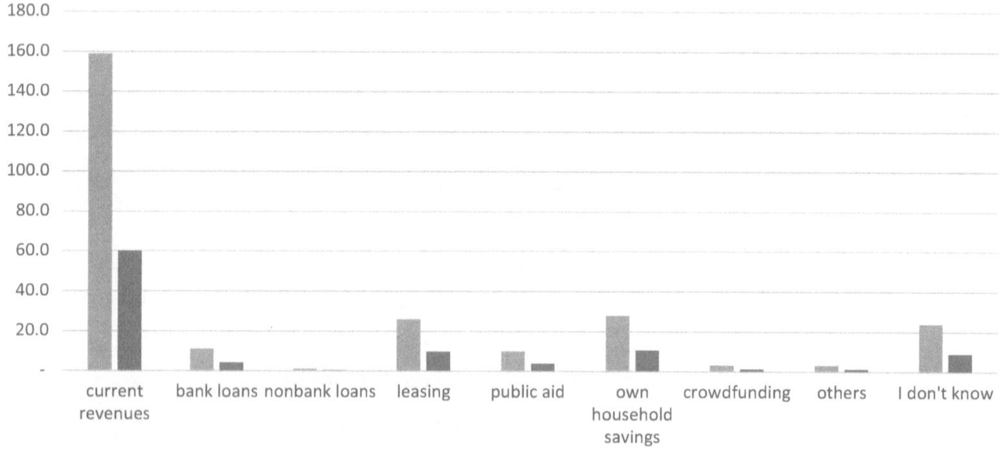

Figure 11.4 Sources of financing for investments.

Sources: Author's own research.

In the next stage of the study, respondents' answers regarding the factors they considered when choosing sources of financing were analyzed. Entrepreneurs were asked to rank the following determinants from the most important to the least important:

- the amount of costs related to the chosen method of financing,
- ease of obtaining financing,
- knowledge of financing sources – "I choose those I have already used",
- advice from other people.

Figures 11.5 and 11.6 present the share of the most important and least important determinants of financing sources in respondents' answers.

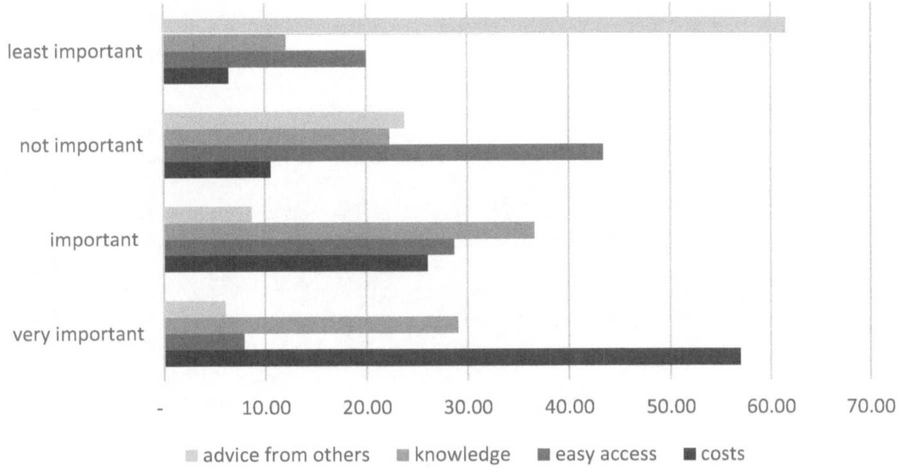

Figure 11.5 Determinants of the choice of financing sources important for entrepreneurs (%).

Sources: Author's own research.

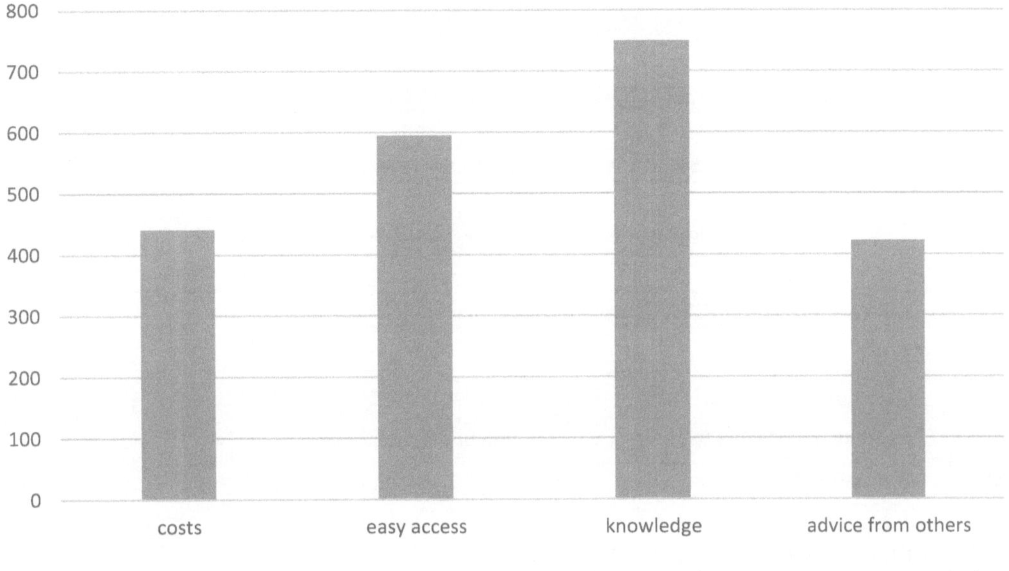

Figure 11.6 Determinants of the choice of financing sources important for entrepreneurs – general view.

Sources: Author's own research.

Analyzing the perception of entrepreneurs of financial barriers to enterprise development, six possible answers were indicated by asking respondents to rank them from the most important to the least important in their opinion. The proposed possible answers are

- lack of sufficient funds,
- high financing costs,

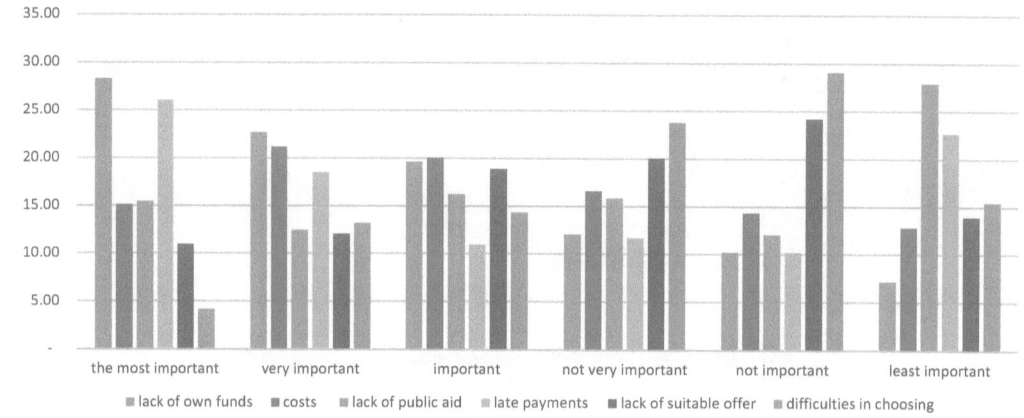

Figure 11.7 Financial barriers to enterprise development (%).
Sources: Author's own research.

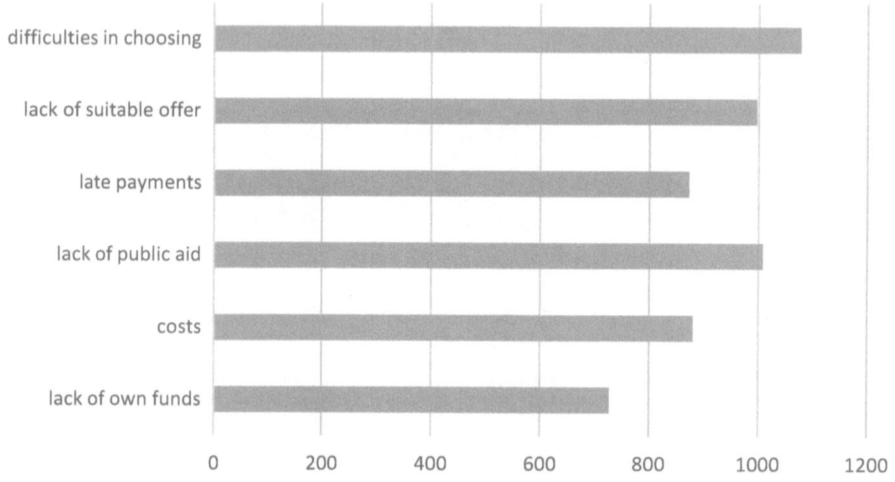

Figure 11.8 Financial barriers to enterprise development – general view.
Sources: Author's own research.

- lack of financial assistance from the government,
- late payments from recipients,
- lack of financial products tailored to the needs of microenterprises, and
- difficulties in choosing the right source of financing.

Figures 11.7 and 11.8 present the respondents' answers.

Results

The study covered two issues – determinants of the choice of sources of financing for microenterprise owners and barriers to access to sources of financing (financial barriers) in the growth of microenterprises. These issues were analyzed based on respondents' declarations, not actual statistical data. The starting point was the analysis of actual sources of financing for the activity in its two aspects – financing of current and investment activities. For both types of activity, the primary source of financing in microenterprises is current revenues from the company's operations. The owner's household savings funds also play a significant role. This indicates the relatively minor importance of external financing. In investment activities, the primary source of financing is leasing (top-rated among microenterprises but also in the entire MSE sector) and, to a lesser extent, bank credit. In operating activities, entrepreneurs support themselves with trade credit.

In the study of factors determining the choice of financing sources, respondents most often indicated knowledge of financing sources as the most crucial factor in their selection. The respondents were the least likely to follow the advice of others in their choices (without specifying whether they were professionals or family and friends). The ease of obtaining funding did not significantly influence their decisions for entrepreneurs. The same applies to financing costs, although in this case, the number of respondents for whom this is the most important factor is high. The summary of responses shown in Chart 6 indicates that knowledge of financing sources and ease of access are the most important, with costs being less important and consulting being of little importance. Among the most important financial barriers to enterprise development, respondents indicated primarily the lack of sufficient own funds, seeing them as the primary source of financing for operations. Another factor hindering development is late payments from contractors. High financing costs were assessed as a more minor barrier than the lack of government support.

However, it should be noted that the lack of government support was often indicated among the most important barriers to enterprise development. The attempt to summarize the answers received, presented in Chart 8, indicates gaps in the knowledge of entrepreneurs, who themselves assess that the difficulties they encounter in choosing the right source of financing are a significant barrier to business development. The lack of support from the government and the mismatch of the financial product offered to the needs and expectations of microenterprises are rated equally highly. Again, entrepreneurs' relatively low importance to financing costs is worth noting. It should be noted that the conducted study is preliminary and will be a starting point for further analyses; nevertheless, at this stage, it can be stated that the results of research by other authors on the determinants of the choice of financing sources by microenterprises, cited in the introduction, correspond to the results obtained. Due to the specificity of entities, including the method of financing, non-cost factors, such as experience and knowledge of financial products, play a more critical role than cost. The situation is similar in the case of development barriers, among which costs are essential but not the most important in the opinion of entrepreneurs.

Conclusion

Microenterprises are an important segment of modern economies. Often, they not only fill market niches that could be less attractive to large entities, create jobs, and meet demand flexibly, but they also are a starting point for developing enterprises operating on a larger scale. On the other hand, the operation's specificity, the owner's crucial role, and their small size restrict access to financing. These restrictions inhibit the development of microenterprises and thus slow down economic development. Therefore, in modern corporate finance, issues related to the finances of the smallest business entities are the subject of research, and their importance is increasing. The image of financing the activities of microenterprises that emerge from the presented research needs to be completed and has the character of a description of only a fragment of reality in its selected aspects.

Nevertheless, it gives an insight into the sources of financing for enterprises, which, according to the predictions and earlier studies by other authors, are internal and not external. The factors determining the choice of financing sources indicated by entrepreneurs and the barriers limiting their use concern primarily non-cost factors; therefore, they are realistically easier to change. Financing costs are not without significance for entrepreneurs, but their weight is lower than that of other factors. Microenterprises need help accessing external sources of financing. However, using only funds generated in the enterprise will not provide a sufficient financing scale and will inhibit further development possibilities. From this point of view, further research on barriers limiting access to external capital for the smallest business entities is not only purposeful but also necessary.

Notes

1 Especially in the case of capital companies, in which the company's establishment depends on the contribution of capital by the owners.
2 Payments to owners in joint-stock companies are in the form of dividends and retained earnings increase capital.

References

Abbasi, W. A., Wang, Z., & Abbasi, D. A. (2017). Potential sources of financing for small and medium enterprises (SMEs) and role of government in supporting SMEs. *Journal of Small Business and Entrepreneurship Development*, *5*(2), 39–47. https://doi.org/10.15640/jsbed.v5n2a4

Abdulsaleh, A. M., & Worthington, A. C. (2013). Small and medium-sized enterprises financing: A review of the literature. *International Journal of Business and Management*, *8*(14), 36. https://doi.org/10.5539/ijbm.v8n14p36

Bartik, A., Cullen, Z., Glaeser, E. L., Luca, M., Stanton, C., & Sunderam, A. (2020). The targeting and impact of paycheck protection program loans to small businesses. *NBER Working Paper* (w27623). https://doi.org/10.2139/ssrn.3676759

Bates, T. (1995). Self-employment entry across industry groups. *Journal of Business Venturing*, *10*, 143–156. https://doi.org/10.1016/0883-9026(94)00018-p

Beizitere, I., Brence, I., & Sloka, B. (2020). Public financing support options to micro-enterprises for innovation. *European Integration Studies*, (14), 172–184. https://doi.org/10.5755/j01.eis.1.14.26569

Belás, J., Vojtovič, S., & Ključnikov, A. (2016). Microenterprises and significant risk factors in loan process. *Economics and Sociology*, *9*(1), 43–59. https://doi.org/10.14254/2071-789x.2016/9-1/3

Berge, L. I. O., Bjorvatn, K., & Tungodden, B. (2015). Human and financial capital for microenterprise development: Evidence from a field and lab experiment. *Management Science*, *61*(4), 707–722. https://doi.org/10.2139/ssrn.1750026

Bhattacharya, S., & Londhe, B. R. (2014). Micro entrepreneurship: Sources of finance & related constraints. *Procedia Economics and Finance*, *11*, 775–783. https://doi.org/10.1016/s2212-5671(14)00241-x

Bongini, P., Ferrando, A., Rossi, E., & Rossolini, M. (2021). SME access to market-based finance across Eurozone countries. *Small Business Economics*, *56*, 1667–1697. https://doi.org/10.1007/s11187-019-00285-z

Chernenko, S., Erel, I., & Prilmeier, R. (2022). Why do firms borrow directly from non-banks? *The Review of Financial Studies*, *35*(11), 4902–4947. https://doi.org/10.3386/w26458

Civelek, M., Ključnikov, A., Krištofík, P., & Rozsa, Z. (2019). Barriers in financing microenterprises from the perspective of Czech and Slovak microentrepreneurs. *Journal of Business Economics and Management*, *20*(2), 244–267. https://doi.org/10.3846/jbem.2019.8114

Czerwonka, L., & Jaworski, J. (2021). Capital structure determinants of small and medium-sized enterprises: Evidence from Central and Eastern Europe. *Journal of Small Business and Enterprise Development*, *28*(2), 277–297. https://doi.org/10.1108/jsbed-09-2020-0326

Daskalakis, N., Balios, D., & Dalla, V. (2017). The behaviour of SMEs' capital structure determinants in different macroeconomic states. *Journal of Corporate Finance*, *46*, 248–260. https://doi.org/10.1016/j.jcorpfin.2017.07.005

Dehejia, R., & Gupta, N. (2022). Financial development and micro-entrepreneurship. *Journal of Financial and Quantitative Analysis*, *57*(5), 1834–1861. https://doi.org/10.1017/s0022109021000569

EU (2021). Small and medium-sized enterprises. Thematic notes on the European Union. https://www.europarl.europa.eu/factsheets/en/sheet/63/small-medium%20enterprises

Ferrando, A., & Mulier, K. (2015). Firms' financing constraints: Do perceptions match the actual situation? *The Economic and Social Review*, *46*(1, Spring), 87–117. https://doi.org/10.2139/ssrn.2305940

García-Teruel, P. J., & Martínez-Solano, P. (2010). Determinants of trade credit: A comparative study of European SMEs. *International Small Business Journal*, *28*(3), 215–233. https://doi.org/10.1177/0266242609360603

Hoang, T. H. V., Nguyen, C. H., & Huynh, V. D. B. (2018). Do crises impact capital structure? A study of French micro-enterprises. *Small Business Economics*, *50*(1), 181–196. https://doi.org/10.1007/s11187-017-9899-x

Ibidunni, A. S., Ibidunni, O. M., Olokundun, A. M., Oke, O. A, Ayeni, A. W., Falola, H. O., Salau, O. P., & Borishade, T. T. (2018). Examining the moderating effect of entrepreneurs' demographic characteristics on strategic entrepreneurial orientations and competitiveness of SMEs. *Journal of Entrepreneurship Education*, *21*(2), 1–8.

Kochaniak, K., Ulman, P., & Zajkowski, R. (2023). Effectiveness of COVID-19 state aid for microenterprises in Poland. *International Review of Economics & Finance*, *86*, 483–497. https://doi.org/10.1016/j.iref.2023.03.038

Martinez Cillero, M., Lawless, M., & O'Toole, C. (2019). *The determinants of SME capital structure across the lifecycle* (No. 614). ESRI Working Paper.

McGuirk, H., Lenihan, H., & Hart, M. (2015). Measuring the impact of innovative human capital on small firms' propensity to innovate. *Research Policy*, *44*(4), 965–976. https://doi.org/10.1016/j.respol.2014.11.008

Moritz, A., Block, J. H., & Heinz, A. (2016). Financing patterns of European SMEs–An empirical taxonomy. *Venture Capital*, *18*(2), 115–148. https://doi.org/10.2139/ssrn.2693564

Prilmeier, R. (2017). Why do loans contain covenants? Evidence from lending relationships. *Journal of Financial Economics*, *123*(3), 558–579. https://doi.org/10.2139/ssrn.2023791

Romano, C. A., Tanewski, G. A., & Smyrnios, K. X. (2001). Capital structure decision making: A model for family business. *Journal of Business Venturing*, *16*(3), 285–310. https://doi.org/10.1016/s0883-9026(99)00053-1

Sajilan, S., Hadi, N. U., & Tehseen, S. (2015). Impact of entrepreneur's demographic characteristics and personal characteristics on firm's performance under the mediating role of entrepreneur orientation. *Review of Integrative Business and Economics Research*, *4*(2), 36.

Szomko, N. (2020). Factors associated with the capital structure of Polish companies in the long and short term. *Gospodarka Narodowa* nr 1. https://doi.org/10.33119/gn/116717

Titman, S., & Wessels, R. (1988). The determinants of capital structure choice. *The Journal of Finance*, *43*(1), 1–19. https://doi.org/10.2307/2328319

12 Financialisation and the role of the insurance market in the economy

Marietta Janowicz-Lomott and Krzysztof Łyskawa

Introduction

In the theory of finance, the concept of the financial system in a market economy is understood as the mechanism of co-creation of purchasing power by non-financial business entities and the flow of cash streams (cash flows) between them, consisting of financial instruments, markets and institutions (organisations), as well as the principles on which they operate (Pietrzak et al., 2004). The financial system is, in a way, the bloodstream of the economy, providing it with the possibility of settlements, financing, and risk hedging. Financial institutions, which are one of the four elements of the financial system, are entities providing services related to concluding transactions in financial instruments. They are financial intermediaries between deficit and surplus entities. Financial institutions should play the role of an intermediary and a trustee; their mission is to serve customers, meet their needs, execute their orders, and help in solving problems (Taft, 2012). However, over the past few decades, financial institutions (mainly through financial innovation) have generated an economy-wide process of financialisation. As a result, the share of the real sphere and innovative activities of entrepreneurs has visibly decreased in favour of the increased importance of the financial sector and speculative activities (Ülgen, 2019). Financialisation reflects a broad set of changes in the relationship between the real sector of the economy and its financial sector, as a result of which the participants of the financial scene and the motives of their activities gain more importance than before (Stockhammer, 2004).

The concept of financialisation better reflects the processes taking place in the global economy in the last half-century than the idea of globalisation and even identifies the contemporary stage of capitalism, defined as financial capitalism, rentier capitalism, stock market capitalism, casino capitalism, or 'coupon clipping' capitalism (Froud et al., 2002). Broadly, financialisation means the increasing role of financial motives, financial markets, financial actors, and financial institutions in the operation of the domestic and international economies (Epstein, 2006). Tobin (1984) defines it as a state in which more and more resources are invested in into activities that generate high private rewards disproportionate to their social productivity. Investments are therefore directed to activities that can generate high private profits, but these profits are usually disproportionate to the social utility of the activity.

Financialisation can be perceived as an imperfection of the modern market system, and at the same time, and perhaps above all, as a deviation in both the theoretical perception of the basic function and key goals of the functioning of the financial sector in relation to the real needs and expectations of the real economy sector (Shaikh, 2016). As noted by Michalski (2017):

> When financial institutions ceased to act as an intermediary acting in favour of the client and began to act as principals of their own interests, we are dealing with a departure from the

DOI: 10.4324/9781003663539-13

> fiduciary principle. The same applies to the principle of servitude and responsibility, and thus ethical considerations. Already in the period preceding the crisis, financial institutions began to believe that the principles of responsibility and servitude based on such features as purposefulness, humility, foresight, integrity in action cannot be accepted as the main guidelines for action. The goal of these institutions, like many other entities operating in the economic sphere, has become their own profit. The interest of the client and economic growth, which were the main guidelines of activity in the current paradigm, receded into the background, egoism dominated responsibility.

Financialisation innately is not a phenomenon that takes the same form in individual economies. Differences in the scale and scope of the analysed occurrence phenomena occur both in the group of developed countries and within developing countries. In the first place, this phenomenon has evolved in the developed countries (especially in the United States), while financialisation in the economies of developing countries is a derivative of this and it is indicated that it is of a subordinate nature.

The turn of the 1970s and 1980s of the last century is generally considered to be the beginning of the period of economic financialisation, but there are grounds to conclude that financialisation was most strongly and fully revealed at the beginning of the 21st century in the US economy.

Considerations on the scale of financialisation became an inspiration to make an attempt to identify anomalies in the insurance market (in the activities of insurance companies in Poland). Insurance is classified as a purely financial phenomenon, and the insurance sector, understood as a set of insurance markets and institutions, is an element of the financial system (Magee et al., 2019). In this aspect, it will be important to try to answer the question whether you can still talk about the insurance company as an entity that helps its clients deal with the effects of risk realisation or whether insurers have a different goal – strong presence on the market assets and investor status. As a consequence, there is a need to develop new solutions in terms of control the insurance sector (Trichet, 2005) and to search for measures of systemic risk (Clemente & Cornaro, 2022).

Against this background, an additional question arises. After all, have not the aspects of profit and enjoying the benefits of financial activities become the main goal? Or, however, as Dembinski (2009) writes: 'The feeling that financialisation is close to exhausting its possibilities and that a new transformation is on the horizon, is beginning to disseminate, even if it still eludes a comprehensive diagnosis'.

Differently than it has been implemented so far in the literature (analysis mainly of the financial aspects of the functioning of insurance companies [Cummins & Weiss, 2014]), an aspect of changing the approach to their tasks, the authors want to assess through the prism of those areas with which the client is faced:

- insurance products have they really become so complicated or unclear or maybe they are created by insurance companies only to 'muddy the issue' that the purpose of the action is a profit of the financial institution,
- insurance distribution, i.e. a method of selling insurance aimed at the highest profit, leaving the value of the product for the consumer in the background; Since financial institutions, and especially insurance companies, most often use financial intermediaries (called financial advisors[1]) to reach clients, they will become the main area of this analysis.
- activities of insurance companies, with an indication of the main areas generating the profitability of the insurer.

Insurance product – is it still for the client?

At the beginning of these considerations, it is worth recalling the definition of a product. A product is a tangible or intangible good or service that provides a certain value to the customer/client. An insurance product is a set of benefits provided to the insured/beneficiary by the insurance company. The subject of exchange on the insurance market is therefore the sum of benefits resulting from the utility value of the insurance product (its ability to meet needs) perceived by specific target groups in exchange for a specific price (exchange value) (Zelizer, 2017).

In each understanding of the product, its value for the customer/client (or the benefits that the latter obtains) is emphasised. However, are the consumers and their benefits really the centre of interest of insurance companies today? One can risk a statement that insurance companies are a bit more conservative in this respect than other financial institutions. The insurance market did not record such spectacularly fraudulent instruments as CDOs or CDSs (Jarrow, 2011) or the 'scandals' of the Polish market, i.e. currency options (Liberadzki, 2015) or loans denominated in the Swiss franc (Manko, 2021). Still, it also has its weaknesses.

However, it is worth looking at the products offered by insurance companies and the individual types of risk generated in this area. Life insurance is a full variety of solutions that meet the different needs of the insured in two areas (protection against the financial consequences of events in the life of the insured or savings), but with different intensity of approach to the implementation of individual functions (see Table 12.1). Their diversity is the result of competition between individual insurance companies, as well as the effect of the development of a given insurance market. Naturally, the largest number of new solutions in the field of life insurance can be found on the American and British markets.

One of the key 'weaknesses' of the insurance market is unit-linked insurance.[2] These insurances appeared in the 1970s of the last century. By definition, they combine a protective element – in the event of the insured's death, with an investment element (where the risk of investing is borne by the policyholder). The construction combining both of these elements (assuming the long-term duration of such a contract) usually did not raise any objections. Over time, however, in many countries, this insurance has become almost exclusively an investment, losing its protective nature. The payment of the benefit in the event of death has become apparent (return of contributions paid, sometimes increased by several hundred euro for contributions of several dozen thousand euro). Life insurance with unit-linked (investment) insurance, although commonly included in the area of life insurance, features its sharp distinctiveness. Their essence is closer to banking and investment products than classic insurance products. They are distinguished by both different sources of risk and different underwriting techniques, similar in nature to the examination of financial capacity of the policyholder to pay the premium in the future (with regular premium) and the ability to cover undepreciated initial costs during the term of the insurance contract, as well as the awareness of policyholders of down investment risk. Therefore, considering the use of liquidation fees in life insurance with an insurance capital fund, one should refer to the axiological justification for their use. Many areas can be referred to here, but the most important are the issues of proper conduct of insurance activities and the issues of fairness of charging such a fee. On the part of clients, there is a greater awareness of the purchased services and, as a result, the requirement of a high value of the sales service itself, but also, later, the appropriate effectiveness of funds. As a consequence, it becomes necessary to customise the products to the client's needs in great detail.

The controversial nature of such insurance contracts has begun to be clearly negatively construed by the courts. For example, in Poland, for the first time, the judgment of the Court of Appeal in Warsaw of May 24, 2019 (V ACa 451/18), invalidated the contract, according to which only 1% of the 'premium' has been allocated (to insurance protection), and its 99% has

Table 12.1 Types of life insurance by purpose of implementation

Type of risk in products	*Type of insureds' needs*		
	Life/health protection	*Protection combined with capital accumulation*	*Saving*
Product	Term insurance Group life insurance Disability insurance Decrepitude insurance Serious illnesses Disability insurance with a death benefit Disability insurance with a higher annuity (depending on the state of health)	Life insurance Universal life insurance Life and endowment insurance Variable (variant-related) life insurance (with unit-linked insurance) Disability insurance – with a regular premium	Deferred fixed and variable annuities Unit-linked insurance – investment insurance Life insurance with guaranteed interest Defined benefit retirement plans
Main risk for the insurance company	Mortality Morbidity Longevity Accident rate Client's cancellations/laps	Mortality Morbidity Longevity Accident Customer dropouts/ laps rate of return on investment Stock market	Return on investment rate Stock market Client's cancellations/ laps
The main source of income	Risk estimation (underwriting) Investment results	Risk estimation (underwriting) Investment results	Investment results Commission result

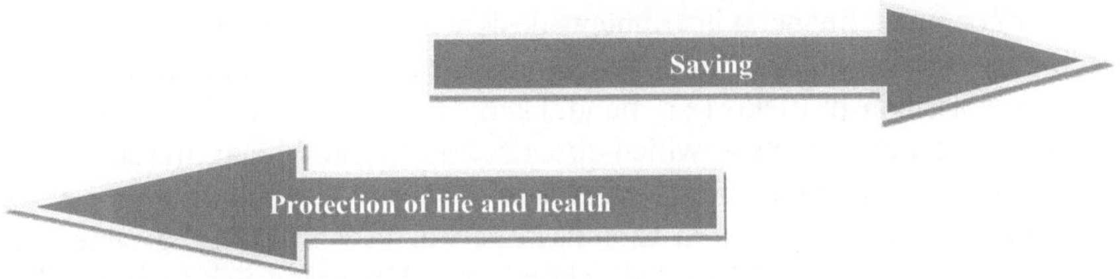

Source: Sigma (2012). Understanding profitability in life insurance, Sigma No. 1/2012. S. 21, SwissRe, p. 21.

been invested in stocks or bonds. The court expressed the view that 'the essence of the insurance contract is the risk-bearing by the insurer'. In life insurance with unit-linked insurance, irrespective of their investment nature, an insurance element must be included, and regardless of its size, it should correspond in its essence to the insurance contract, and therefore the insurer bears the insurance risk related to the payment of the benefit. For this to be the case, the insurance benefit cannot cover only the amounts paid by the insured for the investment purpose, less administrative fees (Słowik, 2019).

It is also worth paying attention to the interpretation doubts that have arisen on this subject in the context of Italian or Spanish jurisprudence. The doubts of the Italian jurisprudence have concerned the classification of unit link insurance contracts and the determination of whether the contract is an insurance contract or a financial product to which the provisions governing these instruments apply. Investment insurance contracts, according to the Italian jurisprudence, are included in the list of financial products and are governed by the Italian Financial Services Act.[3] The Spanish Supreme Court in March 2015 annulled a life insurance contract linked to a capital fund because it could not be considered a life insurance contract. The court pointed out that, regardless of the more or less sophisticated name, any life insurance contract concluded solely for investment purposes carried a significant risk of being declared invalid. The reason for such a decision of the Supreme Court was, above all, the lack of calculation of the insurance risk expressed by the omission of the 'actuarial' method in the calculation of the premium and the insurance benefit (Daszewski, 2019).

In addition to doubts regarding the interpretation of such contracts, in Poland, unit-linked insurance also contained prohibited contractual provisions with regard to liquidation fees in the event of early termination of the contract. The illegal nature of these provisions was indicated in its decisions by the Office of Competition and Consumer Protection (UOKiK), which ruled these provisions several times as illegal contractual provisions (entered in the register of abusive clauses). After interventions of the office, insurance companies have signed settlement contracts. In this respect, the legislator also intervened by placing in the Act on Insurance and Reinsurance Activity (Art. 26.1) a provision on the limit of withdrawal costs (4%, possibly increased by the cost of insurance cover if it has not been settled earlier) on the first anniversary of the policy (within 60 days from receipt of the annual contract information for the first time).

It is worth emphasising that upon issues with unit-linked contracts, insurance companies still offer them, but they do not resemble contracts from a few years ago – they have returned to their traditional form. However, it seems that this has not been the result of self-regulation of the market, but rather the actions of courts and consumer protection institutions (the Financial Ombudsman and the Office of Competition and Consumer Protection [UOKiK]).

Alongside unit-linked insurance, it is also worth pointing out other protection and savings products that are quite popular on the insurance market and bring doubtful benefits to the consumer of the insurance service. This could be referred to as 'wrapped' structured products, which are very complex financial instruments designed, issued, and offered to investors to meet their specific investment requirements. Structured products are most often created by combining the features of classic instruments (e.g. bonds) and derivatives (usually options). They give the opportunity to invest in markets to which direct access for individual investors is difficult (e.g. commodity derivatives market, foreign stock markets), and, depending on their structure, they also guarantee protection the paid-in capital, in part or in whole. At the same time, these are products that are difficult to sell (illiquid), characterised by credit risk (a form of an unsecured contract with the issuer), and the lack of regulations, including in terms of valuation, detailed description, public information, and market supervision. First of all, however, these are very complicated instruments, created by a specialist entity using financial engineering techniques, usually high-risk ones (Janowicz-Lomott & Ostrowska-Dankiewicz, 2011).

The considerations indicate only life insurance products, but this does not mean that insurance (or only a part of it) cannot be found in other insurance areas that could serve as a confirmation of anomalies within this area on the insurance market; however, they are not as clear and common as the presented products.

Insurance intermediation and the problems of the insurance market

In the developed insurance markets, 70%–80% of premium allocated comes from sales through insurance intermediaries. It is worth emphasising that the real flowering of financial intermediation (not only insurance) took place in the 1970s, and since then the evolution of views on the reasons for the existence of financial intermediaries in the economy can be identified. And the theories explaining the role of intermediaries on the financial market are worth reaching for in order to analyse the purposes of intermediaries.

The new institutional economics explains the purpose and legitimacy of financial intermediaries through the theory of transaction costs and information asymmetry. It can therefore be assumed that the functioning of financial intermediaries is the result of the imperfection of the financial market. In the literature, transaction costs are presented as the sum of the costs of concluding the transaction: collecting information, preparing the transaction itself, and then monitoring it and possibly executing it (Williamson, 1985). On the other hand, asymmetry of information, which is related to the lack of an equal access to information by the parties to a financial transaction – the insurance company knows more about itself and the insurance product than the policyholder, who often relies on its own, not very in-depth knowledge and on information provided by the insurance company. Information asymmetry can lead to negative effects both before the transaction (negative selection) and after the transaction (moral hazard). Financial intermediaries, as professionals with knowledge and appropriate tools and empowered by law, can minimise both negative selection and moral hazard (analysis of client's needs, risk management advice, as well as knowledge of the situation of the insured introduces many additional conditions to the contract, including additional exclusions) (Barembruch, 2007). The use of modern technologies and the increasingly easier access to information by the parties to the transaction have reduced transaction costs and the negative effects of information asymmetry (Greenbaum et al., 2019, pp. 56–58). Risk aversion is also important in understanding financial innovation, deposit insurance, and a host of other issues. This is particularly important in the context of building technologically advanced solutions that implement the sharing economy (Rego & Carvalho, 2020, pp. 27–30).

Among the modern (modified) theories of financial intermediation, alternative to the theory of transaction costs and information asymmetry, two are worth pointing out:

- Allen and Santomero (1997), who propose a concept of explaining the reasons for the existence of financial intermediation based on risk trading and participation costs. By participation costs they understand the costs of learning how to use the financial market effectively, as well as participating in it on a daily basis. Consumers often do not have the knowledge and experience to manage their capital on their own and use professionals – financial intermediaries – for this purpose.
- Scholtens and Wensveen (2003), in which the issues of customisation are key, i.e. adapting the financial product to the needs of the client and creating value for the latter, financial innovation, and risk management.

The theory confirms the extremely important role of insurance intermediaries for the functioning of the insurance market. At the same time, the literature on the subject emphasises that although the existence of financial intermediaries would not make sense if the client had perfect information at the same time, their operation is not devoid of moral hazard (Table 12.2).

As indicated in the source literature, the way in which intermediaries are remunerated by financial institutions, and not clients they 'advise', is the main reason for their unethical behaviour, especially since they are usually remunerated in the piecework form, charging commissions on the financial instrument sold (Pawłowicz, 2017).

It is moral hazard that seems to be the main reason for misselling, i.e. offering consumers financial services that do not meet their needs. Most definitions of misselling emphasise the unethical behaviour of sellers, consisting in misleading clients. Most often, the unauthorised sale of financial services occurs as a result of the lack of reliable information about the products

Table 12.2 Causes and effects of moral hazard in the activities of financial intermediaries

Causes	*Consequences*
Information asymmetry	Reducing market transparency Rejecting potentially good clients Concluding a contract characterised by excessively high transaction costs Limited opportunities to negotiate due to the lack of information and the need to accept the imposed contractual conditions
Legal regulations and supervision; lack of direct supervision over the activities of financial advisers	Leaky internal prudential regulations of financial institutions Avoidance of responsibility for unethical behaviour, feeling of impunity of the intermediary Protection of financial intermediaries against the consequences of their mistakes increases the phenomenon of moral hazard Liberal rules of granting loans and insurance Inability to secure the client's interests due to a weaker economic position in relation to the financial intermediary Forcing the consumer to enter into bundled transactions
Remuneration system – commission (piecework)	Sales under the pressure of the result Loss of some clients as a result of aggressive sales interest in sales, not due to the client relations, rewarding the quantitative rather than the qualitative aspect of sales Superficial analysis of a financial situation of the client resulting from, among others, with a desire to earn money quickly Competitive position of financial intermediaries using more aggressive sales is strengthening competition in sales forces behaviour characterised by moral hazard

Source: Barembruch (2007).

sold. The lack of clarity and transparency in the preparation of certain financial contracts makes it impossible for the average buyer to assess the actual risk and possible benefits of the purchase. It also excludes the possibility of assessing the usefulness of these products.

The term misselling itself has its origin in Great Britain. An important factor in noticing the problem has been the sale (or rather adding) of unit-linked insurance contracts, in particular to mortgage loans. The borrower has been obliged to repay only the interest, while the loan principal itself has had to be repaid from the funds invested in the policy. Certainly, the consumer has been obliged to regularly pay a premium for investment and insurance coverage. According to the statistics kept by the British regulator in 2000, 6 million households had about 11 million policies which secured the repayment of mortgage loans. The main cause of the problems was the market situation, which meant that the value of funds invested in the policy at the end of the contract was less than the amount of the loan principal remaining to be paid; as a result, borrowers were unable to repay mortgage loans when the obligation to pay the mortgage loan was already due. The problem identified by the Ombudsman (Polish Financial Ombudsman Service) has been primarily the lack of information that the contracts concluded has not had a guarantee of return on investment, which could have resulted in a decrease in the value of the invested funds.

Unfair practices have also affected other European countries, such as the Netherlands, Italy, Ireland, Portugal, Hungary and France. The main subject of misselling there has been bundling – making the granting of a mortgage loan dependent on the obligation to have a second product, which has not taken into account the needs of the consumer.

In Poland, misselling is commonly seen as the reason for resigning from unit-linked insurance – both in banks and through other intermediaries, these contracts have been sold as a short-term product presented as an attractive alternative to a bank deposit to people with doubtful ability to participate in a savings program in the long term. Therefore, it has been in investment life insurance that the need to adjust the product to the needs of the client has been first introduced (in the detailed recommendations of the Polish Financial Supervision Authority, Recommendations for insurance companies regarding product adequacy testing[4]). However, these recommendations were introduced on March 22, 2016, i.e. several years after the intensive sale of these contracts, but also before the Act on Insurance Distribution, which requires the analysis and assessment of client's needs.

The problem of misselling can also be seen in the latest activities on the agricultural insurance market, in the insurance of crops against the effects of drought in Poland. Drought has been a common phenomenon in Poland for several years; at the same time the number of crop insurance contracts against the effects of drought is small 14.7 thousand in 2008 up to 85 units in 2014. In 2018, the Act on crop insurance introduced a deductible, which allowed for the use of contracts to reduce compensation by 20%/25%/30% of the sum insured, significantly reducing the liability of the insurer. However, insurance companies went further in 'shaping their security'. In order to obtain a coverage in the field of drought insurance, it has been necessary to report a given crop against all risks covered by the Act. In many cases, these are completely unnecessary scopes of protection, because the damage caused by them is so small that they will not result in compensation payments (e.g. torrential rain in maize).

Tying was also clearly observed in the bancassurance channel. The model role of a bank in insurance distribution is to act as a policyholder on someone else's account (in the case of collective contracts) or as an intermediary. The analysis of the bancassurance channel in Poland indicated a number of irregularities,[5] including combining the functions of the policyholder and insurance intermediary by banks, limiting the freedom to choose an insurance company, disproportionate amount of commission, but also often offering products that contain the highest commissions.[6] The reaction to these errors has been, first of all, self-regulatory actions initiated by the Polish Bank Association and the Polish Insurance Association, and then Recommendation of the Polish Financial Supervision Authority. The Recommendation organises the principles of bancassurance operation (including the rules of sale, the role of the bank and the bank authorities, customer relations, or the bancassurance control system), but above all, in the light of the recommendation, insurance under a group contract offered by the Bank as the policyholder cannot be a source of income for the Bank, and the target model should be a bank offering individual insurance contracts, acting transparently as an insurance agent.

It is therefore easy to observe that the theoretical objectives of financial intermediation should reinforce the ethical activities of financial institutions. In practice, however, a number of distortions can also be found in this area, confirming the principle that 'greed triumphs over servitude'.

The concept of enterprise value and the activity of insurance companies

Since the late 1980s, the theory of Value Based Management (VBM) focused on creating value for shareholders (Shareholders Value) has been gaining more and more popularity in the United States. It dominated the science of managing capital companies. It has focused on measuring the value of the entity for shareholders, capital allocation based on the risk-adjusted rate of return on capital, and remuneration systems related to the increase in the value of the company for shareholders (Pawłowicz, 2017). As a result of competitive forces, there has also been a change in the management of capital companies in Europe – from the concept of creating value for stakeholders[7] to shareholders value. VBM has also dominated the management of financial institutions previously considered public trust institutions.

As a result of thinking about shareholder value, both financial institutions and products and services they offer have become very complicated and complex. The importance of global corporations, including financial ones, is systematically growing.[8] As a result, financial institutions maintain increasingly weak relations with their clients and at the same time become very profitable. The efficiency of financial institutions before the crisis on the American market reached sky-high proportions (measured, for example, by the rate of return on equity) – in the case of banks, the efficiency of equity even exceeded ROE for companies included in the FORTUNE 500 list. It should be emphasised, however, that such good financial results of the banking sector before the crisis are mainly due to the increase in mergers and acquisitions (M&A), securitisation, securities trading, or the sale of derivatives, rather than strictly banking activity (Steindel, 2011). The decline directly related to the financial crisis in 2007 and, above all, 2008 was halted in 2009,[9] and since that year we have been observing a slow improvement in the profitability of financial institutions in the United States (Figure 12.1).

In Europe, in many countries during the crisis, the return on equity involved in the insurance sector also fell significantly, and in some countries, it was even clearly negative, e.g. in life insurance in Belgium, Italy, Portugal, and non-life insurance in Belgium, Italy, Portugal, and Slovakia (Table 12.3). However, it quickly began to show an upward trend. It can be noticed, however, that in individual cases over the period under review, we are dealing with a negative ROE. The year 2011 was special for life insurance, when the ROE was clearly negative in the countries of Greece, Italy, Ireland, and Portugal.[10]

It can therefore be said that so far we have only dealt with a short-term slowdown in the trend of generating high profits by financial institutions and a slow return to pressure on achieving high profitability by the same institutions. It seems, however, that the earlier actions of financial

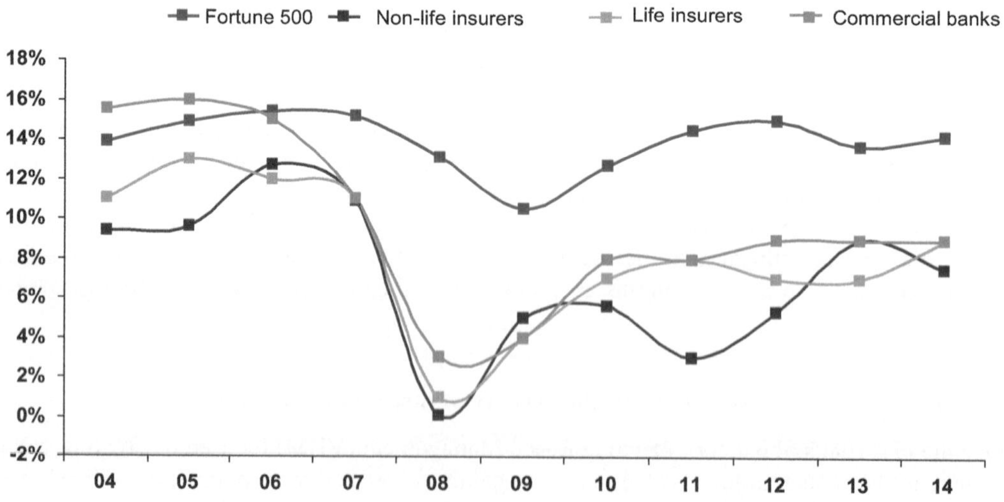

Figure 12.1 Return on equity ratio – financial sector versus FORTUNE 500 companies in 2004–2014.

Source: Hartwig, R. P. (2016). Overview & outlook for the P/C, insurance industry: trends, challenges, disruptors & opportunities. www.iii.org.

Table 12.3 Return on equity (ROE) of insurance companies in the selected European countries in 2008–2019

a. Life insurance

Country	*2008*	*2009*	*2010*	*2011*	*2012*	*2013*	*2014*	*2015*	*2016*	*2017*	*2018*	*2019*
Belgium	−29.3	10.9	5.9	3.4	10.6	8	7.3	1.3	2.8	8.5	5.5	6.9
Czech Republic	6.8	–	–	14	9.9	11.3	19.4	19.4	–	–	25.2	29.6
Denmark	–	–	–	3	9.6	3.2	9.5	3.6	7.6	6	−4.8	7.1
Finland	–	–	21.2	−2.7	21.8	13.5	5.5	6.5	9.3	26	28.5	21.7
France	16.7	8	6.4	2.5	5.5	5.3	5.5	6.4	–			
Greece	–	–	7	−6	−14.5	7.1	0.3	6.4	–			
Spain	–	–	–	–	24.6	13.9	17.3	10.7	–	11.4	13.3	10.1
The Netherlands	–	9.9	–	–	–	2.6	−10.9	11.8	–	–	9.5	–
Ireland	−0.9	−7.3	−6.1	−8.2	10.5	14.5	23.5	17.1	–			
Island	–	–	25.3	21.4	18.2	18.8	–	24.4	–	35.5	25.5	41.3
Luxemburg	3.8	6.6	7.5	3.7	7.3	8.9	10.1	8.3	7.3	9.5	6.8	11.0
Germany	7.6	9.8	9.8	9.7	9.6	6.1	5.1	3.2	2.2	3.7	5.4	4.8
Norway	–	–	–	–	10.9	7	7	13.4	7.4		8.7	7.5
Poland	22.6	31.8	27.2	22.5	21.6	20.4	23	24.1	18.2	19	8.9	9.6
Portugal	−8.4	13.2	16.2	−7.8	17.6	30.6	7.5	10.7	1.7	7.4	4.1	2.4
Slovakia	6.5	0.1	7.7	6.1	−3.8	9.4	10.3	10	–			
Switzerland	–	14.6	13.1	20.7	8	10.5	8.2		6.8	8.8	8.9	9.4
Hungary	–	–	−13	−0.8	−8.1	6.6	6.8	7.9	11.7	15.2	11.5	8.4
Great Britain	–	–	–	7	3.2	12.9	8	14.2	14.2			
Italy	−17.3	6.4	−2.6	−16.5	25.1	9.9	12	12	8.7	10.1	−0.1	14.8
Median	5.15	9.8	7.7	3.55	10.2	9.4	8.1	10.7	7.5	10.1	8.9	9.5

(*Continued*)

Table 12.3 (Continued)

b. Non-life insurance

Kraj	*2008*	*2009*	*2010*	*2011*	*2012*	*2013*	*2014*	*2015*	*2016*	*2017*	*2018*	*2019*
Belgium	−8.1	5.4	8.5	5.7	6.2	3.8	7.1	7.3	−9.6	14	8.5	3.3
Czech Republic	0.9	–	–	−8.4	−2.7	−7.8	–	–	9.2	2.9	14.4	11.9
Denmark	–	–	19.3	6.7	15	11.5	17.1	10.7	16.3	17	10.5	17.2
Estonia	–	–	14.6	13.8	16.7	4.8	10.6	12.9	–	13.5	15.8	19.1
Finland	–	–	17.6	10.2	24.7	27.5	25.6	19.7	19.3	20.1	7.7	15.6
France	17.8	10.5	7	7.1	3.6	7.4	8	8.5	–	–		
Greece	–	–	12.5	10.1	18.8	18.4	21.2	18	–	–		
Spain	–	–	–	–	11.2	11.3	11.2	10.7	–	10.3	11.2	12.5
The Netherlands	–	–				7.8	6.4	5.4		1.4	3.7	
Ireland	6.1	18.5	8.7	10	14.6	9.2	18.1	0.6	10.4	9.4		
Island	–	–	9.7	12.3	20.4	10.4	9	10.4		14.5	9.9	20.5
Luxemburg	10.6	11.1	14.2	22.7	23.2	8.5	11.5	7.1	9.8	8.5	5.8	1.4
Latvia	–	–	–	–	–	6.7	6.3	−1.2	–	11.7	11.5	17.2
Germany	3.9	4.5	3.8	3.8	3.9	4.3	3.9	4.1	4.1	4.8	4.3	3.9
Norway	–	–			36.1	16.1	28.1	20.1	19.5	20.3	7.9	18.9
Poland	14.7	9.3	18.8	18	16.8	29.1	17.5	12.3	8.9	14.7	10.7	12
Portugal	−0.9	3.9	2	3	−0.1	0.5	−22.1	4.9	−2.2	4.2	8.8	10.8
Slovakia	−5.9	−0.5	−31.5	−43.5	19.3	27	–	–	–	–		
Slovenia	–	–	–	–	–	–	36.9	20.3	2.7	0.7	1.8	8.9
Switzerland		16.4	20.2	16.2	16.9	22.6	24.7	18.7	20.5	15.3	17.2	24.4
Sweden	–	–	–	–	–	–	–	–	–	5.7	5.7	26.2
Hungary	–	–	−5.7	−32.9	−6.3	−13.5	4.4	5.7	17.6	19.6	18	10.7
Great Britain	–	–	–	–	5.4	9.6	7.4	2.8	–	–		
Italy	−7	−2	−7.7	−0.6	6.2	7	14.7	11.8	8.4	7.7	7.5	9.7
Median	2.4	7.35	9.2	7.07	14.82	8.84	11.23	10.41	9.47	10.98	8.8	12.25

Source: Own compilation based on OECD reports, Global Insurance Market Trends for 2011–2019.

institutions and the crisis of 2007 negatively verified three basic ideas on which modern economics is based (Robbs, 2009):

1 Economic rationalism, which makes all economic decisions based on rational premises – measures of financial effects of decisions. The moral or ethical aspect of action is ignored.
2 Market reliability – in 2007 the 'invisible hand' of the free market failed, it turned out that the free market lacked self-regulatory features, and the lack of effective control over the financial market and its participants became evident.
3 The credibility of accounting and rating information was clearly undermined as a result of erroneous assessments by rating agencies. Financial engineering used to 'improve' financial information has allowed both investors and the market to be misled.[11]

We may not be talking clearly about the crisis of confidence in financial institutions, but the effect of this in the insurance sector is changes in the behaviour and expectations of insurance market participants. On the one hand, relationships, i.e. permanent relationships assuming trust, cooperation, and common interests, have been replaced by transactions, which are one-time acts, bringing measurable financial benefits (Dembinski, 2009). On the other hand, we can see more and more clearly the actions and interventions of the regulator (both the EU and the national one), supervisory authorities, and consumer protection institutions, the purpose of which is to protect the interests of consumers in the insurance market. However, the experience so far shows, unfortunately, that often this reaction consists in 'putting out the fire' and not in preventing its occurrence.

Conclusions

It seems that one of the most important effects of anomalies in the financial market related to their perception not as a sector serving the real economy, but as one that generates colossal profits, was the financial crisis of 2007. It affected the entire financial sector, including insurance companies. In the current situation, it is worth drawing lessons from it and re-evaluating the theories and concepts of financial institutions and financial intermediation. The erosion of social trust in financial institutions, including insurance companies, as well as the financial problems of clients who follow the recommendations of intermediaries and pseudo-advisers should be a challenge for the future, how to rebuild very low trust and what to base financial intermediation and activities of financial institutions on.

The concept of responsible finance seems to be a positive phenomenon. It is already implemented by legal regulations, including supervisory recommendations or institutions responsible for protecting the insurance client, and is also included in the EU regulations (MIFID II, MCD Mortgage Directive, IDD Insurance Distribution Directive). One would therefore like to believe that we are dealing with only temporary turbulences on the insurance market and the entire financial market, and perhaps, as Dembinski (2009) writes, disseminate, even if it still eludes a comprehensive diagnosis.

On the one hand, the actions of regulators, supervisory authorities, and insurance consumer protection institutions lead to the fact that the consumer is treated as a subject rather than as an object. However, the reactions of the regulator and consumer protection institutions are still delayed and consist in reacting only when large-scale irregularities have had a very negative impact on the market. On the other hand, post-crisis activities aimed at greater control of financial markets have not seemed to bring the expected effects of returning to the traditional role of insurers. Excessive regulation has led to an even greater concentration on the market, and yet it is small- and medium-sized enterprises that are perceived as 'closer to the client'. Strict barriers to entry into the market, high capital requirements, or, finally, limitations in the diversification of their activities sometimes have the opposite effect from the intended one.

Notes

1 The term financial advisor is not precisely defined and is often equated with the term financial intermediary (agent). Leaving aside issues related to the marketing implications of such a procedure, this is due to the fact that financial advice can be treated as a component of the intermediary service, or as a separate, fee-based service. According to definitions created by the European Federation of Financial Advisors and Intermediaries, an advisor represents only the interests of the client and is only remunerated by the client, while an intermediary is remunerated by the provider of financial products and therefore represents both the interests of the client and the institution commissioning the sale of financial services (https://www.fecif.eu/html/objectives.html).

2 Leaving aside the problem of misselling, which will be presented in the next part of the article in these places, it is worth showing the problems with the design of these products.

3 In the case of Italian case law, the relevant date is January 25, 2007 (i.e. after Legislative Decree No. 303 of December 29, 2006, came into force), all unit-linked contracts entered into after that date are automatically considered an investment product, while earlier contracts, according to a Supreme Court ruling, must be interpreted individually and analysed due to demographic (death) risk. Life insurance with insurance capital fund, Financial Ombudsman Report Part II, Warsaw, March 2016.

4 The recommendations mandate that before concluding an insurance contract for insurance with UFK, the insurance company obtains from the policyholder, in the form of a questionnaire, information on his needs, knowledge, and experience in the field of life insurance and his financial situation, so that the insurance company can assess what insurance contract is suitable for the policyholder's needs.

5 In the bancassurance market, more than 97% of insurance products during this period were sold in the form of a group contract in which case the bank acts as both – the policyholder and the insurance intermediary at the same time.

6 This was analysed in detail in the Insurance Ombudsman's 2007 report 'Basic problems of bancassurance in Poland' and its 2012 addendum.

7 In Continental Europe, until the mid-1990s, the practice of Stakeholders Value associated with the theory of the so-called social market economy, which attempted to maximise the value of companies to stakeholders (employees, customers, shareholders, and local communities), was common in the management practice of capital companies.

8 As a result, 'too big to fail' financial institutions were created. In a crisis situation, they are subsidized with taxpayers' money just so as not to cause panic in the market and avoid the so-called contagion effect. In this way, public money has been 'rewarded' by the completely irresponsible policies of the management of, among others, AIG, 80% of whose shares were taken over by the US government for a price of $85 billion in 2008 and another $30 billion in 2009, or in the banking sector of, among others, Bank of America, Goldman Sachs, Citygroup or JP Morgan Chase.

9 Similar phenomena could also be observed in other insurance markets. See more (Janowicz-Lomott & Łyskawa, 2011).

10 It is worth noting that in this period (after 2010), we are talking about the debt crisis in PIGS countries. See more (Śliwiński et al., 2019).

11 See more (Janowicz-Lomott & Śliwiński, 2017).

References

Allen, F., & Santomero, A.M. (1997). The theory of financial intermediation. *Journal of Banking and Finance*, 21, 1461–1485. https://doi.org/10.1016/S0378-4266(97)00032-0.

Barembruch, A. (2007). Pośrednicy finansowi w świetle teorii ekonomii. In: Bieliński, J. (ed.) *Kapitał intelektualny w realizacji celów strategii lizbońskiej*, FRUG, Gdańsk, 152–161.

Clemente, G. P., & Cornaro, A. (2022). A multilayer approach for systemic risk in the insurance sector. *Chaos, Solitons & Fractals*, 162, 112398. https://doi.org/10.1016/j.chaos.2022.112398.

Cummins, J. D., & Weiss, M. A. (2014). Systemic risk and the US insurance sector. *Journal of Risk and Insurance*, 81(3), 489–528.

Daszewski, A. (2019). *Commentary on Training for Insurance Distributors*, WIB, unpublished.

Dembinski, P. H. (2009). *Finance: Servant or Deceiver? Financialization at the Crossroads*, Palgrave Macmillan, London.

Epstein, G.A. (2006). *Financialisation and the World Economy*, Edward Elgar Pub, London.

Froud, J., Johal, S., & Williams, K. (2002). Financialisation and the coupon pool. *Capital & Class*, 26(3), 119–151. https://doi.org/10.1177/030981680207800106.

Greenbaum, S. I., Thakor, A. V., & Boot, A. (2019). *Contemporary Financial Intermediation*, Elsevier Inc, Amsterdam.

Hartwig, R.P. (2016). Overview & outlook for the P/C, insurance industry: trends, challenges, disruptors & opportunities. www.iii.org.

Janowicz-Lomott, M., & Łyskawa, K. (2011). Domestic insurers in Poland and the global crisis. *Scientific Bulletin - Economic Sciences, University of Pitesti*, 10(1), 81–92.

Janowicz-Lomott, M., & Ostrowska-Dankiewicz, A. (2011). Ubezpieczeniowe produkty strukturyzowane – wpływ na polski rynek ubezpieczeń życiowych. *Wiadomości Ubezpieczeniowe*, 4, 63–84.

Janowicz-Lomott, M., & Śliwiński, A. (2017). New role of mutual insurers on the insurance market. In: Goić, S., Karasavvoglou, A., & Polychronidou, P. (eds.) *Finance in Central and Southeastern Europe. Contributions to Economics*, Springer, Cham, 145–159. https://doi.org/10.1007/978-3-319-64662-6_9

Jarrow, R. A. (2011). The role of ABS, CDS and CDOs in the credit crisis and the economy. Working Paper. https://www.russellsage.org/sites/all/files/Rethinking-Finance/Jarrow%20ABS%20CDS%20CDO%202.pdf.

Liberadzki, K. (2015). Toxic currency options in Poland as a consequence of the 2008 financial crisis. Available at SSRN: https://ssrn.com/abstract=2669391 or https://dx. doi.org/10.2139/ssrn.2669391.

Magee, S., Schilling, C., & Sheedy, E. (2019). Risk governance in the insurance sector—determinants and consequences in an international sample. *Journal of Risk and Insurance*, 86(2), 381–413. https://doi.org/10.1111/jori.12218.

Manko, R. (2021). Unfair terms in Swiss franc loans overview of European Court of Justice case law. European Parliamentary Research Service, PE 689.361. https://www.europarl.europa.eu/RegData/etudes/BRIE/2021/689361/EPRS_BRI(2021)689361_EN.pdf.

Michalski, T. (2017). Paradygmat finansów na przełomie XX i XXI w. Ewolucja czy rewolucja? In: Szymańska, A. (ed.) *Ubezpieczenia i finanse. Rozwój i perspektywy*, Wydawnictwo UŁ, Lodz, 103–116. https://dx. doi.org/10.18778/8088-628-5.08.

Pawłowicz, L. (2017). Hazard moralny i konflikty interesów. In: Hausner, J., & Paprocki, W. (eds.) *Dewiacje finansjalizacji*, CeDeWu, Warszawa, 6–23.

Pietrzak, B., Polański, Z., & Woźniak, B. (eds.) (2004). *System finansowy w Polsce*, PWN, Warszawa.

Rego, M. L., & Carvalho, J. C. (2020). Insurance in today's sharing economy: new challenges ahead or a return to the origins of insurance? In: Marano, P., & Noussia, K. (eds.) *InsurTech: A Legal and Regulatory View*. AIDA Europe Research Series on Insurance Law and Regulation, vol. 1, Springer, Cham, 27–47. https://doi.org/10.1007/978-3-030-27386-6_2.

Robbs, A. (March 2009). Opportunities for mutuals and cooperatives. *Voice*, (64), 12–13.

Scholtens, B., & Wensveen, D. V. (2003). The theory of financial intermedia on: an essay on what it does (not) explain. Chapters in SUERF Studies, 7–53.

Shaikh, A. (2016). *Capitalism. Competition, Conflict, Crisis*, Oxford University Press, Oxford.

Sigma (2012). Understanding profitability in life insurance, Sigma No. 1/2012. S. 21, SwissRe.

Śliwiński, A., Michalski, T., & Janowicz-Lomott, M. (2019). Development of an insurance market in PIGS countries after the crisis. In: Sykianakis, N., Polychronidou, P., & Karasavvoglou, A. (eds.) *Economic and Financial Challenges for Eastern Europe*. Proceedings in Business and Economics, Springer International Publishing, Springer, 243–257. https://doi.org/10.1007/978-3-030-12169-3_15.

Słowik, P. (2019). Przełomowy wyrok w sprawie UFK: Tysiące ludzi mogą odzyskać utopione pieniądze, Gazeta Prawna.pl. https://serwisy.gazetaprawna.pl/finanse-osobiste/artykuly/1426486,polisolokaty-wyrok-niewaznosc-umowy-ufk.html.

Steindel, C. (2011). Implications of the financial crisis for potential growth: past, present and future. In: Pisani-Ferry, J., Posen, A., & Saccomanni, F. (eds.) *An Ocean Apart? Comparing Transatlantic Responses to the Financial Crisis*, Bruegel/PIIe, Brusells, 55–76.

Stockhammer, E. (2004). Finacialisation and the slowdown of accumulation. *Cambridge Journal of Economics*, 28(5), 719–741. https://doi.org/10.1093/cje/beh032.

Taft, J. G. (2012). *Stewardship: Lessons Learned from the Lost Cul ure of Wall Street*, John Wiley & Sons, Hoboke New Yersey.

Tobin, J. (1984). On the efficiency of the financial system, Lloyds Bank Review, No. 153, 1–15. https://economicsociology.org/wp-content/uploads/2014/12/tobin-on-the-efficiency-of-the-financial-system.pdf.

Trichet, J. C. (2005). Financial stability and the insurance sector. *The Geneva Papers on Risk and Insurance-Issues and Practice*, 30(1), 65–71.

Ülgen, F. (2019). Innovation dynamics and financialisation: is another regulation possible to re-industrialise the economy? *Journal of Innovation Economics & Management*, 2–29. https://doi.org/10.3917/jie.029.0133.

Williamson, O. E. (1985). *The Economic Institutions of Capitalism*, Macmillan, New York.

Zelizer, V. A. R. (2017). *Morals and Markets: The Development of Life Insurance in the United States*, Columbia University Press, New York.

13 Technology foresight and industrial strategy toward a green and digital future

Marek Dziura, Andrzej Jaki and Tomasz Rojek

Introduction

Technology foresight represents a systematic exercise aimed at looking into the longer term future of science technology and innovation (S&T) in order to make better informed policy decisions (Irvine & Martin, 1984). Since its early inception, pioneered in Japan, technology foresight has tried to help societies and economies to define strategic areas where the future of S&T would lead. During the last few decades, the practice of technology foresight diffused through a wide range of developed countries as well as regions, large companies, and other organizations. A growing number of developing countries have undertaken technology foresight exercises too. But to what extent does technology foresight really reflect their different condition of developing countries trying to catch up with more advanced ones? Given their scarcity of resources and lower levels of technological development, developing countries are facing remarkable constraints to catch up with developed countries. Industrial and technology foresight strategies are of crucial importance to this aim since they both pursue the same scope, which needs to be consistent with and help strengthen the National Innovation System (NIS). Thus, technology foresight needs to go beyond a pure speculation of where the future will lead and instead foster large-scale efforts to align stakeholders' interests toward the common agreed vision of the future. This chapter addresses this central question and analyzes to what extent technology foresight exercises are essential parts of wider industrial strategies in developing countries by first reviewing and discussing the theory and then analyzing three examples from three countries. First, we examine the case of a now-developed country, South Korea, where clever industrial policies combined with a foresighted national vision clearly contributed to achieve a well-defined and unprecedentedly fast economic growth. Second, we analyze the case of a developing economy, Poland, where the fusion and mutual reshaping between industrial strategies and technology foresight exercises is demonstrating the country's ability to fully understand the new dynamics of global value chains (GVC). Finally, we focus on the institutional development in Poland, especially in the face of sustainable development. The government set up an institutional framework embodied by the national bodies on innovation and competitiveness that would appear to favor the coherence and close connection between industrial strategy and technology foresight with a long-term perspective.

Technology foresight – characteristics

An essential fact characterizing today's economic development is the speed of technological change which brought about unprecedented levels of productivity growth (Baumol, 1986). As a consequence, industrial and trade structures are continuously being reshaped toward more complex sets of activities that often follow a logic of vertical and horizontal fragmentation within GVC, with room for outsourcing by multinational companies (MNCs) and foreign buyers that

DOI: 10.4324/9781003663539-14

drive the process and ensure its internal coherence (Baldwin, 2011; Cattaneo et al., 2013; Gereffi, 1999). This opens up a new window of opportunities in terms of strategic investments that developing countries may follow to move closer to the technological frontier. Technology foresight represents the concrete effort to overcome this emerging complexity since it systematically embodies a set of programs to study innovation plans and priorities to foresee, shape, and direct potential future orientation of technological change (Martin, 1995). Its essential feature stems from the active involvement of a variety of actors such as government, experts, industry, and civil society that gather together in order to define a joint vision of the future (Miles, 2010). Among technology foresight participants, the role of experts from science/academia and the private sector is of crucial importance since they might have better insights on technological issues with respect to policy makers and hence help reduce the uncertainty brought about by the unprecedented speed of technological change (Hilbert et al., 2009, p. 882). The rationale behind these "exercises" is to generate positive-sum games whose outcomes are expected to be more effective in terms of technological advancement but also more sustainable in terms of socio-economic benefit than those of isolated initiatives taken by each actor. Relevant literature refers to technology foresight as to an exercise encompassing a wide range of activities, including anticipation, forecasting, systematic looking ahead, forward looking activities, strategic intelligence, futures research, technology road-mapping, and prognostic among others (Miles, 2010; Phaal et al., 2004). The pioneering country in technology foresight was Japan that in the 1970s used to call its national technology planning studies "forecast activity" despite the fact that what it was actually performing was "technology foresight" and perhaps in one of the most refined manners (Miles, 2010). It was later in the mid-1980s thanks to Irvine and Martin (1984) seminal work inspired by the long Japanese tradition in S&T and technology foresight that we now call these "forecasting" activities "foresight". The difference is not trivial. On the one hand, forecasting activities, which are typically performed by closed circles of experts, provide a mere prediction of future contingencies founded on deterministic precision. Their outcome reflects a specific vision of the world, with a single point of view. On the other hand, technology foresight embraces a broader view of the world that is synergistically integrated with policy strategy. Its outcome sketches insights for forward looking S&T policies that "create" rather than "predict" the future (Miles, 2010) by placing emphasis on the learning processes (van Dijk, 1991) as well as the dialog among different disciplines and actors (Elzinga, 1983). Irvine and Martin's (1984) work did not only provide the definition and understanding of technology foresight as we conceive it today but also spurred the proliferation of technology foresight exercises around the world. Right after Japan, France started to perform foresight exercises during the 1980s, followed by Sweden, Australia, and Canada (UNIDO, 2005). However, it was during the 1990s that technology foresight gained momentum, expanding also within the United Kingdom, the United States, The Netherlands, and Germany: if one country engaged in foresight activity, others decided to pursue the same exercises too in order to remain competitive (UNIDO, 2005). Technology foresight in fact was appreciated as a valuable tool to identify fast, market-oriented, and forward-looking innovation policies agreed by the government and the private sector. Recently, foresight has also spread to developing countries as a strategic tool to narrow their competitive gap with the technological frontier. The narrow indication that cutting edge technology productions are only a concern to industrialized countries has gradually been overcome, and the literature in this regard has often used the language of "leap-frogging" (Perez, 1983). From our perspective, the most distinctive features of technology foresight are the following:

1 In its attempt to predict the future, technology foresight has the potential to influence technology direction and hence to "make the future happen" (Miles, 2010). In fact, by fostering a

participatory approach and boasting a strong legitimacy which helps building consensus, technology foresight increases awareness, accountability, transparence, and predictability of future technological developments and also provides ownership and responsibility (Elzinga, 1983).

2 At the same time, a participatory approach ensures the inclusion of new actors who can expand the range of possible strategies beyond the narrow interests of single individuals. For instance, technology foresight can significantly facilitate the strategic decision faced by stakeholders to "make or buy" new technologies considering the local knowledge endowments and organization (Lall, 2004).
3 Technology foresight can be pursued at various levels: organizational, local, regional, national, or supranational.[1] All these levels of foresight aim to manage both demographic and socio-economic heterogeneity faced by actors involved in the analysis.
4 For its effort to try to link and reorient science and innovation on a national and regional scale, technology foresight is inherently linked with the NIS. Technology foresight seeks to foster economic impact by "wiring up" the network between industries, university, governmental bodies as well as the society at large (e.g. aging societies, education, and training) (Martin & Johnston, 1999; Andersen & Andersen, 2014).

A number of "failures" intrinsic to innovation activities and S&T policies are usually tackled by technology foresight exercises, such as:

- coordination failures among NIS stakeholders that often have different views on the importance of S&T. The balancing of such interests is crucial to wipe out rent-seeking behaviors and bounded rationality (Schlossstein & Park, 2006);
- communication failures, especially when different actors from distinct disciplines (i.e. specialized in different subject-languages and forms of communication) express diverging interests and are convened together in order to define a common strategy;
- market failures, since usually S&T programs require a long-term investment that should be weighed against the possibility of temporary short-term losses; and
- political failures since governments too should adopt a long-term perspective on innovation, which might not coincide with the political perspective of maximizing consensus in the short-term political interest for the upcoming election (this is often called "dynamic inconsistency").

Technology foresight and industrial strategy

Nowadays globalization, increased complexity of manufacturing and services, stronger competition, and faster technical change have radically transformed the range of economic activities that developing countries can perform. Production is internationally fragmented and organized along GVCs. Dense flows of knowledge and technology are available, but need to be fully exploited and employed within coherent industrial strategies. A specialization by technology and learning is becoming the dominant paradigm and developing countries need to detect opportunities for future technological and productive specialization in order to catch up and forge ahead. Therefore, individual isolated responses cannot be sufficient to address these complexities and guarantee that countries develop and catch-up. The interdependencies emerging from a globalized competitive setting make it imperative to devise and follow an appropriate "strategy" to orchestrate responses from the Government, the private sector, and research organizations (Lall, 2004). However, technology foresight exercises often do not go hand in hand with the concrete identification and design of a policy strategy to promote catch-up.

The central argument it will be developed in this chapter is that technology foresight exercises need to be mutually consistent with industrial development strategies since both pursue essentially the same objective of industrial development via technological catching up. In the next part, it will be briefly described how the concept of industrial strategy has evolved over time, and how it needs to take into account the more recent changes to the international organization of industry, the emergence of GVCs, and the role of innovation.

Different conceptions on industrial policies

Industrial policies have been the object of vivid debates expressing radically diverging views both in the literature and political arena. Traditionally, the liberal approach argues that the best policy for all countries and in all situations is to liberalize, as free markets dynamics will let countries identify their comparative advantage. The underlying assumption behind this rationale is that products' markets provide the correct signals for investments to which actors respond accordingly. Governments' single duty would be to provide a stable macroeconomic environment with clear rules of the game along with the provision of essential public goods. Any further intervention is not required and would distort the already optimal allocation of resources. The weakest aspect of this approach is that it overlooks the existence of widespread market failures (Stiglitz, 1989), which tend to be especially pronounced in the field of knowledge and innovation and that in turn have a central influence on the long-term growth of productivity and income (Hall & Jones, 1999; Griliches, 1979). In stark contrast, the literature on technological capabilities maintains that technological change is crucial to emerging countries' economic development, but it is hindered by market failures (Bell & Pavitt, 1993; Katz, 1984; Lall, 1992, 1996, 2001; Westphal, 2002). According to this approach, countries' industrial success largely depends on their capacity to adopt and master existing technologies, even by not being at the technological frontier (Nelson & Winter, 1982). Due to market failures, technology is not freely available and cannot be absorbed without costs or risks. Conscious and purposive efforts to invest in technology-specific learning processes and building technological capabilities are essential for firms (Lall, 1992; Pietrobelli & Battisti, 2000; Lall, 2004, p. 12). The technological capability approach offers government a platform that indeed justifies policy action in a functional and selective manner. Selectivity is crucial, since the cost of offering uniform support to all industrial sectors would be too high and probably not effective given the fact that the learning processes differ by technology (Lall, 2004). Some simple activities require minimal protection and support if the learning period is relatively brief and the information is easily accessible. Conversely, within more complex activities characterized by high entry costs and externalities, newcomers might never enter unless specific policies are implemented to incentivize them to do so. However, the existence of market failures does not alone establish a case for intervention: interventions are costly and risky and a careful assessment of costs and benefits and long-term impacts is required. This policy learning and capacity development process requires interaction between government and firms involving mutual learning and experimentation within an institutionalized process (Rodrik, 2007; Rodrik et al., 2004; Morris, 2010; Kaplinsky & Morris, 2008; Sabel & Zeitlin, 2011). This process is essential both for industrial strategy and for technology foresight exercises and worked extremely well in the successful experiences of Poland economy.

Lessons from the East-Asian "tigers" countries

The experience of the East-Asian "Tigers" (i.e. Hong Kong, Singapore, Taiwan, and South Korea) offers a solid example of how an active industrial strategy mutually consistent with a

TF framework promoted fast industrialization and technological development. Even though the Asian Tigers are far from having followed the same development model, some major common features of their industrial strategy can be identified (Lall, 1996). First of all, selective and horizontal policies have been used interchangeably and simultaneously in each country (with the exception of Hong Kong). For example, all countries have been investing to create advanced human technical skills, whilst also selectively supporting some sectors with innovation and export subsidies and protection of the domestic market. Second, the capability development that they pursued actively took place within a long time frame. Third, FDI has been used differently by each country. The countries wanting to promote local capabilities' development restricted foreign entry and directed their activities to exploit spillover effects, and hence they favored indigenous companies over foreign ones (South Korea and Taiwan) (Shin & Kim, 1994). Conversely, those countries relying on MNCs to promote technology development targeted foreign investors to persuade them to engage in more complex and technology-intensive functions (Hong Kong and Singapore). The success of these policies may be explained by some significant principles guiding their implementation. East Asian tigers have been constantly selecting and targeting those activities offering better opportunities for learning, technological benefits, and linkages. The importance attributed to fostering learning (Lall, 1987; Lall & Pietrobelli, 2002) implied massive investment in skills generation through education and infrastructure. Learning also extended to strategy formulation and implementation in order to discover the lessons from past mistakes and improve upon them (Amsden, 1989). Such policy learning and flexibility in the strategic decision-making systematically endorsed the private sector, supported by an active role of public institutions to fill in gaps in unusually risky areas (Lall & Teubal, 1998). Finally, exports have been constantly used as a discipline to force early entry in the world markets. The role of industrial policies is changing with the emergence of GVCs. Since the early 1990s, the twin forces of technology and globalization have led to the geographic fragmentation of industries, where value is added in multiple countries together with vast improvements in the functional integration of these activities. This process created what is currently known as GVC. Today, it is difficult to imagine a production that is entirely carried out in just one country (Gereffi & Sturgeon, 2013; Milberg & Winkler, 2013). In 2009 world exports of intermediate goods surpassed that of the combined export values of capital and final goods (WTO & IDE-JETRO, 2011, p. 81). These developments pose remarkable challenges as well as opportunities for developing countries' firms and governments. A large body of evidence indicates that despite the potential presence of certain barriers in some markets and value chains, the interaction between global actors and local suppliers can be a conduit of knowledge and learning experiences that foster processes of learning and capability acquisition and spill over to other firms not engaged in the same value chain (Pietrobelli & Rabellotti, 2007). This, however, does not suggest that an initial contact between a local supplier and a global buyer is enough. For instance, a minimum of previous accumulation of skills is typically required for a supplier to engage in contract manufacturing with a global buyer (Morrison et al., 2008), and there are certainly cases in which existing contracts were terminated because the supplier was not capable to increase its capabilities to the levels initially expected. Therefore, various countries have developed different programs targeted at local firms to support their efforts to become suppliers of global firms. Within this new setting, the case for industrial policy and for technology foresight exercises got elevated to a great prominence (Gereffi & Sturgeon, 2013; Pietrobelli & Staritz, 2013; Sturgeon et al., 2013). The point is not only to find the country's competitive advantage, but also to tailor it to the requirements of these GVCs. In the challenge to define multifaceted policies and programs coherent with GVC organization and requirements, careful consideration of the systemic nature of GVCs is needed. In this regard, an explicit account of the local innovation system (IS) and its interaction with GVCs is necessary (Morrison et al., 2008; Pietrobelli & Rabellotti, 2011, 2012). Indeed, the relationship between IS and GVCs is two-way, as GVCs, and in particular lead firms, may support firm learning and innovation as well as improve local IS (Morrison et al., 2008) but may also block them. Similarly, the IS also influences the capabilities, performance and functions of local firms within GVCs. The effective combination of technological efforts and absorption capabilities of local firms and public support may in turn raise the interest of lead firms to support upgrading processes, locate higher value activities, and source higher value products locally (Pietrobelli & Rabellotti, 2011). What is the economic rationale for value chain-related policies? The debate on public policies in the context of GVCs is part of the broader debate on the role of states and markets in the development process, and the existence of market and coordination failures we discussed above. These issues are particularly problematic in the area of technology, innovation and learning where the contribution of internationalization through integration into GVCs may be most fruitful. The following policy justifications are especially relevant in the context of GVCs. First of all, externalities on other firms are likely to emerge once one firm signals the potential and the means required to integrate into a GVC. Second, in the presence of coordination failures, suppliers would not invest to upgrade their production, and lead firms would not support them either. In the absence of long-term contracts, coordination and trust lead-firms and suppliers may engage in learning and upgrading activities to a lesser extent than would be socially desirable. Third, the distribution of rents along GVCs is affected by substantial market failures and entry barriers in specific segments (e.g. branding and product conception) (Pietrobelli & Staritz, 2013). In sum, the existence of GVCs is raising and reshaping the need for cleverly-designed industrial policies and for their coherence with technology foresight and long-term planning exercises.

Coherence between technology foresight and industrial strategy in developing countries (Polish case)

In developing countries like Poland, the need for coherent technology foresight exercises, inherently coupled with industrial strategies, is especially strong. First of all, developing countries are often characterized by widespread market failures, poor institutional development (Rodrik, 2000), and a scarce coordination of society and science with public policies, which result in a missing sense of common purpose (Tavares & Wacziarg, 2001). As a consequence, it is unlikely to expect that in such context each actor would naturally and easily align with the vision outlined by the technology foresight. Information does not often flow smoothly and is marked by substantial asymmetries; the rules of the games are not often solid and enforceable as they would be needed, and inter-firm and inter-organization coordination is poor and occasional. In contrast, more developed countries are generally characterized by better aligned NIS and actors that are more likely to quickly respond to the incentives launched by the market or by government policies. The simple "signaling" effect of a technology foresight exercise is often sufficient to determine behaviors consistent with its long-term objective. Second, technology foresight exercises in developing countries need to be of a different nature. This is because they are seldom frontier innovators but rather users of technologies developed abroad that need to be adopted and adapted to local contexts and conditions. Provided that their final aim is to promote a catching up process, technology foresight should help searching for existing technologies that could be more appropriate to their needs and level of NIS development, and should be closely related to their industrial strategy to promote the improvement of technologies. Thirdly, a major issue identified in the literature inherent to developing countries' technological development is the forecast of the timing of technology realization. Developing economies are generally lagging behind in technology development, and the adoption of a new technology, either through domestic firms' efforts or through technology transfer, might be retarded by several constraints that can delay the time of the technology realization. These constraints can include the lack of appropriate regulation and policy standards, human and financial resources, and research infrastructure (Chan & Daim, 2012). Fourth, when technology foresight is mutually consistent with the industrial strategy, this can help limit the extent of the dynamic inconsistency, which is typically stronger in developing countries, whereby the urgency to achieve positive results in the short run prompts the tendency to overlook the benefits of long-term investments (Ascher, 2009). This shortsightedness can be mitigated and possibly solved through a shared private and public vision for the future and by turning common commitment into actions (Martin & Johnston, 1999). While investing in key strategic sectors of the future, technology foresight and industrial strategy should create, nurture, and strengthen the institutional and physical infrastructure that leads to innovation. This latter type of investments can guarantee a country enough flexibility to reorient its policies in the case of failures and mistakes.

Links and coherence between technology foresight and industrial strategy in Poland

A careful review of the literature points to some common characteristics between technology foresight exercises and industrial strategies that deserve to be highlighted. First of all, private sector involvement is key, and as such it should occur through a participatory approach. Its scope is twofold: on the one hand, it raises the relevance of these exercises by helping define the content that public policies should have that are often unknown a-priori from Government (Hausmann et al., 2008; Hausmann & Rodrik, 2006); and on the other hand, they guarantee ownership, responsibility, and accountability throughout the process. Second, it is widely acknowledged that well-organized, competent, and effective institutions are the backbone of successful innovation and industrial policies (Crespi et al., 2014). Participation of entities like the Ministries of Industry, Planning, Education, and S&T should encourage actors to adopt behaviors that are consistent with the long-term benefits of TF programs. "Innovation councils" for instance, can support long-term strategies whose duration exceeds that of the government, and help mitigate governments' tendency to overlook the benefits of long-term investments in favor of short-term gains. A third important condition for technology foresight and industrial policy's success is a thorough understanding of GVCs logic along with their underlying power relationships. Nowadays, GVCs represent one of the main sources of information and technology (as well as market access) for developing countries. With GVCs, countries can target specialization niches, but in order to do so, they need to develop the necessary skills and technologies to deal with powerful large chain leaders. In the next part, we examine the case of Poland's coherent coupling of technology foresight and industrial strategy, especially of sustainable development, which has been more evident.

The link between technology foresight exercises and industrial policies in Poland

The most striking aspect of Poland's industrial development is the quite radical shift of its economy from low- to high-tech value-added sectors in only a few decades. This would be made possible because, over time, technology foresight and industrial policies have become deeply intertwined via complex and at time overlapping measures. Their main aim has been to respond to the technological challenges raised by global competition.

One of the major challenges of technology foresight exercises and industrial policies is to overcome the dynamic inconsistency between short-term gains and long-term benefits, typically faced by governmental institutions. This is sometimes achieved through the establishment of a more permanent S&T policy body, able to overcome the political and economic cycles with a foresighted vision. The international experience of such S&T councils varies from country to country. Councils should be seen as a source of strategic intelligence for the innovation policy agenda. According to the extent of their influence on government policy planning, three types of councils can be identified: A joint planning model, which draws from the Japanese experience, where councils serve the government as horizontal ministries of innovation by bringing together different actors from different disciplines to pursue joint projects; A coordination model: based on the Finnish experience, in which the council's main goal is to advice the government by communicating across ministries to direct and align innovation policy. Such advice though is not always necessarily binding. An advice model: as the Canadian case, where the government proactively seeks the council's advice though it does not intend to be restricted from it.[2]

Formulation of an effective plan for Polish industrial policy, especially with realizing the technology foresight, is a complex task. On the one hand, it seems to be essential to focus on industries that promise the greatest development and determine the economic competitiveness of the country; on the other hand, the development of Polish industrial policy is determined by the European Union guidelines. In the case of Poland, this issue is so difficult, because strategic sectors of our economy do not fully correspond with the priorities of European Union policy. The authors of industrial policy as a guarantee of employment present three main factors of competitiveness of the Polish industry, which are relatively low labor costs, high absorbency of the internal market, and flexibility of the zloty exchange rate (Kiewra et al., 2011, p. 32). However, these are not assets that the state can use to compete in the long perspective and to develop economically and eventually to advance to the group of developed countries. So based on assets, we should create a program to adapt the Polish industry to changing conditions (and European Union requirements), in order to derive benefits from it. A deeper analysis of the state of Polish industry and possible ways of development requires a review of the overall Polish macroeconomic situation. According to the Central Statistical Office, in 2013 Polish GDP amounted to 1,662,052 billion PLN (per capita −43,168 PLN). The GDP compared to the previous year increased by 1.7%. The value of export in 2013 amounted to 766,344 million PLN and was about 38,373 million PLN higher than in the previous year. In 2013, the unemployment rate reached the average level of 13.4% – the rate remained at the same level as in 2012. The value of investment in 2013 in the Polish economy was 231,155 million PLN and was lower than in 2012 by 1.2%. It is worth to notice that investment in industry increased in 2013 as compared to the previous year by 4% (in industrial processing this index was 7%). Also, sold production of the industry increased in the analyzed period by 1.8%, with the largest increase in mining and extraction (3.3%) (Poland 2030, 2017).

The last economic crisis caused by speculations on financial markets has forced re-direction toward industry, which for many years was effectively pushed to the economy margins. However, this return to industry cannot be chaotic and must be based on specific assumptions and long-term goals, in order to activate economy and to recover from recession, which many countries suffer from. Industrial policy is an answer for these needs. If it will be well formulated and effectively implemented, it allows for economies regeneration by restoring the industry its meaning. However, this policy has to be adapted to the current reality and world economic situation. That is why, high-tech industry and widely understood innovation are so important. A new policy of the European Union with its priorities (advanced manufacturing technologies, key enabling technologies, bioproducts, sustainable policy in industry, construction and raw materials, environment-friendly vehicles, smart grids and digital infrastructure) is focused on these areas. As the EU statements largely determine the directions of national policies of Member States, Poland also has to adapt its industrial policy to these statements. Poland should focus on high-tech industry development, because then it will be able to successfully compete on the international arena and increase pace of economic growth. The strength of Polis' economy during the global economic crisis is the fact that so far it has not fallen into recession. One reason for this might be an optimal share of industry in GDP of approximately 23%. This value is close to the result that the EU wanted to achieve in 2020. However, in Poland, the issue of modernity and innovation of industry looks much worse. The share of high-tech production in export is about 7%, which is far below the EU average. Also investment in research and development in our country are far too low and amount less than 1% of GDP, while the EU average is 2% of GDP. As a result, Poland is in the 25th place in the ranking of innovativeness of EU countries, and it is called country of innovative stagnation. If Poland wants to have a competitive economy, it should formulate assumptions of industrial policy in such a way to support the development of modern industries and facilitate the implementation of innovative solutions, especially in the face of technological foresight realizing within the country.

Poland's economic success in recent decades sets a global precedent. But it is by no means certain that Poland can maintain its rapid pace of growth going forward. Whether it does so or not depends on a number of factors, such as the level of investment, innovation, human capital, and the country's resilience to external factors. Poland should beware of resting on its laurels – for two reasons at least. First, it would be well advised to prepare now for a less positive economic situation in the future. And second, the fact that Poland is rapidly becoming a developed economy will make it all the more difficult for it to keep up its heady growth pace. Up until now, the growth engines have been traditional sectors of the economy, consumption, falling unemployment with relatively low labor costs, and incoming funds from the European Union. But many of these engines are now gradually powering down.

If Poland wishes to continue along its path of rapid economic growth and increasing prosperity while avoiding the "middle income trap", it should consider redefining its development strategies and seeking out new sources of growth. Ideally, it should stop fixating on the idea of catching up with leading European economies and start carving out its own development path. This will enable it to compete effectively with the world's most dynamic economies. Analysis by McKinsey & Company shows that over the coming decade Poland has the chance to secure long-term rapid economic growth of as much as 5% a year, doubling the size of the Polish economy. Below, we outline our advice for achieving this ambitious goal. That includes the need to raise productivity, to adapt the labor market to new challenges (above all, demographic change and the need for a highly qualified workforce) and to create a positive environment for business and society as a whole.

Analysis by McKinsey suggests two potential paths of economic development. In the first scenario – the baseline scenario – Poland develops at around 3% a year, the natural continuation of a long-term slowdown in growth based primarily on demographic and productivity forecasts. In this scenario, real GDP grows by EUR 200 billion by 2030 and per capita GDP to EUR 18,500 (compared to EUR 12,400 today) – higher than Portugal's current per capita GDP. However, a number of risk factors could affect Poland's economic development, preventing it from realizing even this baseline scenario. The risks include a significant drop in the number of people of working age, EU funding being phased out faster than expected, a slump in foreign investment and a slowing down of productivity growth due to failure to improve the education system or poor cooperation between business and universities. However, McKinsey analysis also shows that Poland could set itself more ambitious goals, successfully competing on the global market. In a second, aspirational scenario, Poland grows at 5% a year in the period to 2030. This assumes that the difference between Poland and Western Europe in terms of participation in the labor market and productivity is halved (in other words, participation in the labor market reaches 70% and productivity rises by more than 20%) and the share of investments in GDP reaches 22.5%, which is halfway between the level of the European Union and the Visegrad Group, excluding Poland. If this happens, the Polish economy could potentially double in size, growing from EUR 477 billion in 2018 to EUR 890 billion in 2030 at constant prices. That would mean per capita GDP of EUR 24,300, on a par with Spain today. It could be argued that 5% GDP growth is actually not all that ambitious. After all, Poland has grown on average 4% a year over the last 15 years, and in 2018 it grew by more than 5%. But we must not forget that the economy is becoming larger and more developed, and such economies usually grow more slowly due to their size. For example, Germany experienced annual per capita GDP growth of 1.4% in 2004–2018, while France grew by less than 1%.

What steps can Poland take to achieve this ambitious goal of doubling the size of its economy by 2030 and maintaining its position as one of the fastest-growing countries in the European Union? What should entrepreneurs and policymakers focus on in order to achieve success? We identify five key areas for action on the basis of analysis by McKinsey and experience from other markets around the world, taking into account Poland's position within Europe. These five areas are consistent with the findings of the 2015 joint report by McKinsey and Forbes 5 opportunities for Poland:

1 Close the productivity and competitiveness gap between Poland and Western Europe;
2 Boost investment and secure capital;
3 Increase innovation;
4 Ensure an adequate supply of skilled workers;
5 Support business, enhance public services, and improve the natural environment.

In each area, despite the passage of last years, much remains to be done.

Conclusion

In this chapter, it was argued that the link between technology foresight and industrial development strategy needs to be taken seriously in light of its role to shape technological change and economic growth. Since technology foresight and industrial strategy essentially pursue the same goal and are two sides of the same coin, they need to be coherently designed and implemented. When technology foresight began to be adopted in industrial countries, it tended to be still somewhat of a marginal activity in developing countries. It was then believed that technology foresight and its prediction of the future was a matter that only highly industrialized countries could endeavor, being more engaged and interested in frontier and "new to the world" innovation. Today globalization, increased complexity, competition, and fast technical change make it imperative for countries to specialize in technology and learning. This new competitive setting offers a window of opportunities for developing countries that need to devise an appropriate industrial strategy to address these complexities and interdependencies. In addition to providing insights about critical technological areas, technology foresight can prove a valuable instrument to add coherence to S&T policy in developing countries but needs to be designed and implemented together with the country's industrial strategy. The experiences were explored from Poland, where this coherence has been sought successfully, provide preliminary support to our argument.

Acknowledgements

The publication presents the results of the Project financed from the subsidy granted to the Krakow University of Economics – Project nr 040/ZIE/2025/POT.

Notes

1 For a comprehensive review of the various methodologies that can combine both quantitative and qualitative methods of technology foresight, see Ciarli et al. (2013).
2 Source: Adapted from OECD (2009).

References

Amsden, A., (1989). *Asia's Next Giant: South Korean and Late Industrialization.* Oxford University Press, Oxford.

Andersen, A.D., & Andersen, P.D., (2014). Innovation system foresight. *Technological Forecasting and Social Change 88*, 276–286.

Ascher, W., (2009). *Bringing in the Future: Strategies for Farsightedness and Sustainability in Developing Countries*. The University of Chicago Press, Chicago, IL and London.

Baldwin, R., (2011). Trade and industrialisation after globalisation's 2nd unbundling: how building and joining a supply chain are different and why it matters. NBER Working Paper 17716, Cambridge, MA, December. Available from https://www.nber.org/papers/w17716.

Baumol, W., (1986). Productivity growth, convergence and welfare: what the long run data show. *American Economic Review 76* (5), 1072–1085.

Bell, M., & Pavitt, K., (1993). Technological accumulation and industrial growth. *Industrial and Corporate Change 2* (2), 157–209.

Cattaneo, O., Gereffi, G., Miroudot, S., & Taglioni, D., (2013). Joining, upgrading and being competitive in global value chains: a strategic framework. World Bank Policy Research Working Paper No. 6406.

Chan, L., & Daim, T., (2012). Exploring the impact of technology foresight studies on innovation: case of BRIC countries. *Futures 44* (6), 618–630. https://doi.org/10.1016/j.futures.2012.03.002.

Ciarli, T., Coad, A., & Raffols, I., (2013). Quantitative analysis of technology futures. Part I: technique, context and organizations. NESTA Working Paper 13/8.

Crespi, G., Ortiz, E., Vargas, F., (2014). Innovation for Economic Performance: The Case of Latin American and Caribbean Firms. *Eurasian Economic Review,*

Elzinga, A., (1983). *Foresight as Anticipatory Intelligence.* Science Council of Canada, Ottawa.

Gereffi, G., (1999). International trade and industrial upgrading in the apparel commodity chain. *Journal of International Economics 48* (1), 37–70.

Gereffi, G., & Sturgeon, T., (2013). Global value chains and industrial policy: the role of emerging economies. In: Elms, D. K., & Low, P. (Eds.), *Global Value Chains in a Changing World*, pp 329–360. WTO Geneva. Available from https://www.cggc.duke.edu/pdfs/201307_Elms&Low_ eds_GlobalValueChains_in_a_ChangingWorld_WTO.pdf#page=354.

Griliches, Z., (1979). Issues in assessing the contribution of research and development to productivity growth. *The Bell Journal of Economics 10* (1), 92–116.

Hall, R., & Jones, C., (1999). Why do some countries produce so much more output per worker than others? *Quarterly. Journal of Economics 114* (1), 83–116.

Hausmann, R., & Rodrik, D., (2006). Doomed to choose: industrial policy as a predicament. Harvard Kennedy School Working Paper.

Hausmann, R., Rodrik, D., & Sabel, C., (2008). Reconfiguring industrial policy: a framework with an application to South Africa. Harvard Kennedy School Working Paper No. RWP08-31.

Hilbert, M., Miles, I., & Othmer, J., (2009). Foresight tools for participative policy making in intergovernmental process in developing countries: lessons learned from the eLAC Policy Priorities Delphi. *Technological Forecasting and Social Change 76* (2009), 880–896. https://doi.org/10.1016/j.techfore.2009.01.001.

Irvine, J., & Martin, B.R., (1984). *Foresight in Science*. Pinter Publishers, London.
Kaplinsky, R., & Morris, M., (2008). Do the Asian drivers undermine export-oriented industrialization in SSA? *World Development 36* (2), 254–273. https://doi.org/10.1016/j.worlddev.2007.06.007.
Katz, J., (1984). Domestic technological innovation and dynamic comparative advantage: further reflections on a comparative case study-program. *Journal of Development Economics 16* (1), 13–38. https://doi.org/10.1016/0304-3878(84)90100–7.
Kiewra, D., Darteyre, P., Jakubowski, A., Januszkiewicz, T., Portet, S., Towalski, R., Ulianiuk, A., & Morvannou, P., (2011). *Industrial Policy as a Guarantee of Employment (Polityka przemysłowa gwarantem zatrudnienia)*. S. Partner sp. z o.o, Warsaw.
Lall, S., (1987). *Learning to Industrialize: The Acquisition of Technological Capability by India*. Macmillan, London.
Lall, S., (1992). Technological capabilities and industrialization. *World Development 20* (2), 165–186. https://doi.org/10.1016/0305-750X(92)90097-F.
Lall, S., (1996). *Learning from the Asian Tigers Studies in Technology and Industrial Policy*. Macmillan, London.
Lall, S., (2001). *Competitiveness, Technology and Skills*. Edward Elgar, Cheltenham.
Lall, S., 2004. Reinventing industrial strategy: the role of government policy in building industrial competitiveness, G-24 Discussion Paper, 28. United Nations.
Lall, S., & Pietrobelli, C., (2002). *Failing to Compete: Technology Development and Technology Systems in Africa*. Edward Elgar, Cheltenham.
Lall, S., & Teubal, M., (1998). Market stimulating technology policies in developing countries: a framework with examples from East Asia. *World Development 26* (8), 1369–1385. https://doi.org/10.1016/S0305–750X(98)00071–0.
Martin, B., (1995). Foresight in science and technology. *Technology Analysis and Strategic Management 7* (2), 139–168. https://doi.org/10.1080/09537329508524202.
Milberg, W., & Winkler, D., (2013). *Outsourcing Economics: Global Value Chains in Capitalist Development*. Cambridge University Press. New York, NY.
Miles, I., (2010). The development of technology foresight: a review. *Technological Forecasting and Social Change 77* (9), 1448–1456. https://doi.org/10.1016/j.techfore.2010.07.016.
Morris, M., (2010). Industrial policy, politics and state capacity building. Discussion Note for Presentation at the Workshop State Building in the Developing World, May 7–8, 2012. Available from https://www.cssr.uct.ac.za/sites/cssr.uct.ac.za/files/pubs/Industrial%20Policy%20MM%20discussion%20paper.pdf.
Morrison, A., Pietrobelli, C., & Rabellotti, R., (2008). Global value chains and technological capabilities: a framework to study learning and innovation in developing countries. *Oxford Development Studies 36* (1), 39–58. https://doi.org/10.1080/13600810701848144.
Nelson, R.R., & Winter, S.J., (1982). *An Evolutionary Theory of Economic Change*. Harvard University Press, Cambridge, MA.
OECD, (2009). Chile's national innovation council for competitiveness. Interim Assessment Outlook, April, 2009. Available from https://www.cincel.cl/documentos/Recursos/ CHILE_COUNCIL_FINAL.pdf
Perez, C., (1983). Structural change and assimilation of new technologies in the economic and social systems. *Futures 15* (5), 357–375.
Phaal, R., Farrukh, C.J., & Probert, D.R., (2004). Technology road-mapping—a planning framework for evolution and revolution. *Technological Forecasting and Social Change 71* (1), 5–26.
Pietrobelli, C., & Battisti, G., (2000). Intra-industry gaps in technology and investments in technological capabilities: firm-level evidence from Chile. *International Review of Applied Economics 14* (2), 253–269.
Pietrobelli, C., & Rabellotti, R., (2007). *Upgrading to Compete. Global Value Chains, SMEs and Clusters in Latin America*. Harvard University Press, Cambridge, MA.
Pietrobelli, C., & Rabellotti, R., (2011). Global value chains meet innovation systems: are there learning opportunities for developing countries? *World Development 39* (7), 1261–1269.

Pietrobelli, C., & Rabellotti, R., (2012). Innovation systems and global value chains. In: Pietrobelli, C., & Rasiah, R. (Eds.), *Evidence-based Development Economics: Essays in Honour of Sanjaya Lall*. University of Malaya Press, Kuala Lumpur.

Pietrobelli, C., & Staritz, C., (2013). Challenges for global value chain interventions in Latin America. IDB, Technical Note No. IDB-TN-548, May. Available from https://www.iadb. org/projectDocument.cfm?id=38815216.

Poland 2030. A chance to join the economic big league. (2017). McKinsey & Company in cooperation with Forbes. https://www.mckinsey.com/pl/en/~/media/mckinsey/locations/europe%20and%20middle%20east/polska/raporty/polska%202030/poland%202030%20report.pdf.

Rodrik, D., (2000). Institutions for high-quality growth: what they are and how to acquire them. *Studies in Comparative International Development 35* (3), 3–31. https://doi.org/10.1007/BF02699764.

Rodrik, D., (2007). Industrial development: stylized facts and policies, in United Nations. Industrial development for the 21st century, New York. Available from https://www. un.org/esa/sustdev/publications/industrial_development/1_1.pdf.

Rodrik, D., Subramanian, A., & Trebbi, F., (2004). Institutions rule: the primacy of institutions over geography and integration in economic development. *Journal of Economic Growth 9* (2), 131–165. https://doi.org/10.1023/B:JOEG.0000031425.72248.85.

Schlossstein, D., & Park, B., (2006). Comparing recent technology foresight studies in Korea and China: towards foresight-minded governments? *Foresight 8* (6), 48–70. https://doi.org/10.1108/146366806 10712531.

Shin, T., & Kim, H., (1994). Research foresight activities and technological development in Korea. Science and technology policies in National R&D programs. *Technological Forecasting and Social Change 45* (1), 31–45. https://doi.org/10.1016/0040-1625(94)90061–2.

Stiglitz, J.E., (1989). Markets, market failures, and development. *American Economic Review 79* (2), 197–203.

Sturgeon, T., Gereffi, G., Guinn, A., & Zylberberg, E., (2013). Brazilian manufacturing in international perspective: a global value chain analysis of Brazil's aerospace, medical devices, and electronics industries. Brazil's Confederação Nacional da Indústria (CNI), September. Available from https://www.cggc.duke.edu/pdfs/CNI_Brazil_GVC_Report_Final_2013–09-05.pdf.

Tavares, J., & Wacziarg, R., (2001). How democracies foster growth. *European Economic Review 45* (8), 1341–1378. https://doi.org/10.1016/S0014-2921(00)00093–3.

United Nations Industrial Development Organization (UNIDO), (2005). *Technology Foresight Manual, Organizations and Method*, vol. 1. United Nations, Vienna.

van Dijk, J.W.A., (1991). Foresight studies: a new approach in anticipatory policy making in The Netherlands. *Technological Forecasting and Social Change 40* (3), 223–234.

Westphal, L., (2002). Technology strategies for economic development in a fast changing global economy. *Economics of Innovation and New Technology 11*, 275–320.

WTO & IDE-JETRO, (2011). *Trade Patterns and Global Value Chains in East Asia: From Trade in Goods to Trade in Tasks*. World Trade Organization, Geneva and Tokyo, Institute for Developing Economies-Japan External Trade Organization. Available from https://www.wto.org/english/res_e/booksp_e/stat_tradepat_globvalchains_e.pdf.

14 Environmental tax policy and R&D innovation networks

Pascal Billand, Christophe Bravard, Kenneth Ky and Sudipta Sarangi

Introduction

Pollution, defined as the introduction of contaminants into the natural environment, can cause serious damages. For instance, in a recent report, the World Health Organization estimates that 7 million people died – one out of every nine of total global deaths – as a result of air pollution exposure (World Health Organization, 2016, p. 15). Air pollution, the world's single largest source of health risk is largely caused by industrial activity. Thus, countries, like China and India, facing sudden and rapid growth of such activities are finding the resulting pollution to be a serious negative externality that has to be brought under control in order to save millions of lives.

There are several *tools* that public authorities can use in order to limit pollution, such as norms, quotas, or taxes. Taxing the emissions of industrial firms is a commonly used strategy to tackle pollution. These taxes, also called Pigouvian taxes, aim at inducing firms to internalize the external damages associated with polluting activities. Because of these taxes, firms are incentivized to incur expenses developing projects that allow them to limit pollution and thereby reduce the amount of the tax they pay.

One strategy that firms can use to reduce pollution is to engage in R&D projects with other firms for developing cleaner production processes.[1] However, there can exist strong impediments for a firm to engage in collaboration with other firms for pollution abatement. In particular, such collaborations are costly. Moreover, to be efficient, collaborations should typically involve firms that operate on the same market, use similar technologies, and face similar environmental challenges. In that case, the collaborations of a given firm with competitors can have an adverse effect on the firm itself. Indeed, while on one hand, such collaborations can reduce taxes; they also allow competitors to develop cleaner production processes, making them stronger rivals on the market.

Keeping these facts in mind, the purpose of the current chapter is to examine the formation of R&D collaboration networks, where firms collaborate to reduce pollution before competing on the market and to find the optimal pollution tax policy schemes under oligopoly markets.

To this end, we set up a three-stage game. In the first stage, public authorities impose a Pigouvian tax t per unit of pollution so that firms internalize the external damages associated with polluting activities. Given this tax, in the second stage, firms establish their collaborative links. A link between two firms is costly and is established if and only if there is mutual consent. Each link leads to a reduction of pollution per unit produced. In the third stage, given the per unit tax and the distribution of the firms' production processes with regard to pollution (which results from collaborative links), firms compete in quantities on the market.

We begin by examining pairwise equilibrium networks in our framework. We find that such networks always exist. Moreover, we show that only three types of architectures can be pairwise

DOI: 10.4324/9781003663539-15

equilibrium: the *empty network*, the *complete network*, and the *k-group-dominant networks*. The last architecture, which can be viewed as an intermediate network between the two polar extremes of the complete and empty network, contains two types of firms: k firms that have formed links together (a completely connected component), and other firms with no links (like the empty network). This result is due to the fact that the firms' payoff functions satisfy strategic substitutability and convexity in own links. It is worth noting that in k-group-dominant-networks, firms obtain different profits even though they are *ex ante* identical. It follows that when public authorities aim to reduce the amount of pollution, this policy has very asymmetric consequences: *ex ante* identical firms find themselves in different positions with regard to clean technologies and profits.

Next, we examine the relationship between the tax and the different architectures that emerge as pairwise equilibrium networks. First, we establish that there is ambiguous relationship between the tax and the incentive of firms for maintaining the complete network as a pairwise equilibrium network. Also, we show that an increase in the tax does not always induce firms to form a link in the empty network. However, there exist parameters such that in a k-group-dominant network, an increase in taxes increases the incentive for firms to establish a $k+1$-group-dominant network.

Finally, we look at the optimal, *i.e.* welfare maximizing emission tax, given the equilibrium architecture that this emission tax induces. Due to tractability problems, we restrict our attention to the simple case with three firms in the market. In this part of the chapter, we show that there exist parameters such that each potential pairwise equilibrium network, the empty network, the complete network, and the two dominant-group network, is an efficient network. Moreover, the higher the cost of link formation, the lower the environmental tax. Interestingly, we also observe that there exist situations where the optimal tax increases with the number of links in an efficient network.

Let us now relate our chapter to the existing literature. Indeed, there exists a large literature on efficient environmental policy under different market structures. The first studies dealt with the polar cases of perfect competition and monopoly. Baumol and Oates (2015) have established that under perfect competition, emission taxes can result in complete internalization of external damages by firms. Buchanan (1969) has shown that complete internalization is not possible under monopoly. In the latter case, optimal taxes deviate from external damages, since complete internalization will impose additional social cost by further restricting the already suboptimal monopolist's output. In recent years, there has been a growing interest in the analysis of environmental policy under conditions of oligopoly (see e.g. Levin, 1985; Ebert, 1991; Carraro & Soubeyran, 1996; Requate, 1993; Katsoulacos & Xepapadeas, 1995). Under oligopoly, the optimal degree of internalization of external damages due to pollution depends on the oligopoly structure of the market. To our knowledge, in the context of this literature, our study is the first to introduce collaboration between oligopoly firms as a means of lowering pollution in the analysis of tax emission schemes.

Our chapter also relates to the large theoretical literature on strategic R&D network formation between competing firms. This literature was initiated by Goyal and Joshi (2003) who consider a homogeneous oligopoly setting in which firms form pairwise collaborative links with other firms before competing on markets. These pairwise links lead to a reduction in marginal (and unit) costs of production for firms that form links. Goyal and Joshi (2003) deal with pairwise equilibrium networks, that is, networks that should be formed by firms maximizing profit, as well as efficient networks, that is networks which maximize social welfare, both under quantity and price competition. Some authors (Westbrock, 2010; Billand et al., 2014) introduce product differentiation in the model and examine its impact on efficient networks. Other authors (Billand et al., 2015) examine how multi-market competition has an impact on equilibrium and efficient networks. In all these models, collaborative R&D leads to lower production costs or higher product quality. Our chapter examines situations in which R&D collaborations have an impact on the amount of pollution and the emission fees paid to public authorities. Moreover, when we introduce the choice of a per unit tax by public authorities, we add a third stage to the game. In this stage, public authorities choose the per unit tax that maximizes the social welfare, given the choices of firms that result from this tax in the other two other stages, *i.e.* their choice of collaborations with competitors, and the quantity of output they put on the market. This third stage adds to this literature by being the first to explicitly examine the policy dimension.

The rest of the chapter is organized as follows. In the Model setup Section, we present the model setup, and in the Homogeneous Cournot game Section, we analyze the impact of tax emissions on market equilibrium in the homogenous Cournot game. In the Network analysis Section, we provide the network equilibrium results associated with the tax emission policy, and in the Tax policy and incentives for innovation Section, we examine how the tax emission policy modifies the possibility of obtaining the complete network, the empty network as well as the *k*-group dominant network as a pairwise equilibrium networks. In the Social welfare Section, we deal with the tax that maximizes social welfare.

Model setup

Network definitions

We consider an industry with a set of $N = \{1, \ldots, n\}$ firms. In the game we consider, every firm first announces its intended R&D collaboration links: $s_{i,j} = 1$ means that firm i intends to form a collaborative link with firm j, and $s_{i,j} = 0$ otherwise. Following the networks literature, we assume that firms only play pure strategies. Thus a strategy of firm i is given by $s_i = \{\{s_{i,j}\}_{j \in N \setminus \{i\}}\}$. Let S_i denote the strategy set of firm i. The set $S = \times_{j \in N} S_j$ is the set of strategy profiles of firms. A link ij between two firms i and j is formed *if and only if* $s_{i,j} = s_{j,i} = 1$. A strategy profile $s = \{s_1, s_2, \ldots, s_n\}$ therefore induces a network $g^{[s]}$. For expositional simplicity, we will often omit the dependence of the network on the underlying strategy profile. A network g is a formal description of the pairwise links, representing R&D collaborations, that exist between the firms. If firms i and j are linked in g, we say $ij \in g$, and $ij \notin g$ otherwise. Let $|g(i)|$ denote the number of links in which i is involved; $|g(i)|$ is called the degree of firm i. We denote by $N(g)$ the set of firms that are involved in at least one link in g. We define g_{-i} as the network formed when firm i and its links are deleted.

Network architectures

Three types of architectures play a crucial role in our model. The *empty network* is the network with no links.

The *complete network* is the network where every firm i is linked with each other firm. In a *k-group-dominant network*, there is a set of firms that are all linked together and there are no other links. Moreover, the size of the set of firms that are linked together is k. We illustrate all these networks in Figure 14.1.

Structure of the game

The game played by the firms consists of three stages.

Stage 1: Public authorities set the value of the environmental tax, t, per unit of pollution, so that firms internalize the external damages associated with polluting activities.

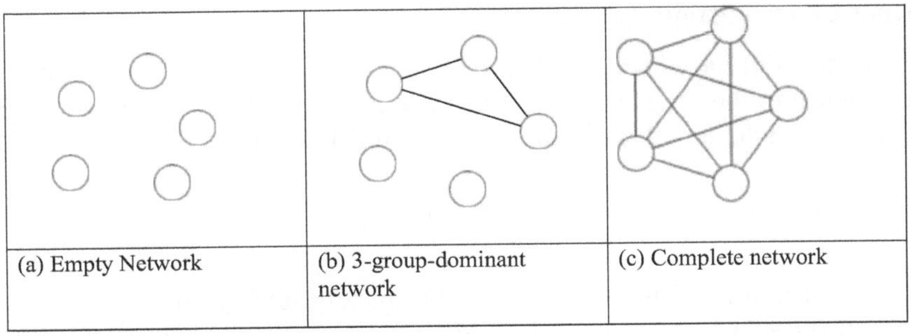

Figure 14.1 Network architectures.

Stage 2: Given the value of the environmental tax, firms simultaneously choose the R&D collaborative links they intend to form. The links are costly, but they allow firms to reduce the amount of pollution per unit of production, and for a given quantity produced, to pay lower environmental taxes.

Due to Stages 1 and 2, the environmental tax and the amount of pollution per unit produced are given when firms compete on the market at Stage 3.

Stage 3: Firms play a simultaneous oligopoly game by choosing the quantities they produce on the market.

Pairwise equilibrium network

We use the notion of pairwise equilibrium network defined by Goyal and Joshi (2006) to characterize the architectures of the networks formed by profit-maximizing firms.

First, we define a Nash equilibrium. Let $S_{-i} = \times_{j \in N \setminus \{i\}} S_j$ be the joint strategy set of all firms except i, with s_{-i} a typical member of S_{-i}, and let $\pi^*\left(g^{[s_i, s_{-i}]}\right)$ be the reduced oligopoly equilibrium profit function of firm i in the second stage[2] given the strategy profile $s = (s_i, s_{-i})$ played by the firms in the first stage.

The strategy $s_i \in S_i$ is said to be a best response of firm i to $s_{-i} \in S_{-i}$ if $\pi_i^*\left(g^{[s_i, s_{-i}]}\right) \geq \pi_i^*\left(g^{[s'_i, s_{-i}]}\right)$, for all $s'_i \in S_i$. The set of firm i's best responses to s_{-i} is denoted by $BR_i(s_{-i})$. A strategy profile $s \in S$ is said to be a Nash equilibrium if $s_i \in BR_i(s_{-i})$, for all $i \in N$. In the following, to simplify notation, we replace $\pi_i^*(g^{[s]})$ by $\pi_i^*(g)$. It is now possible to define pairwise equilibrium networks.

Definition 1

(Goyal & Joshi, 2006, p. 324) A network g is a pairwise equilibrium network if the following conditions hold:

1 There is a Nash equilibrium strategy profile that supports g.
2 *For* $g_{i,j} = 0, \pi_i^*(g + ij) - \pi_i^*(g) > 0 \Rightarrow \pi_j^*(g + ij) - \pi_j^*(g) < 0.$

Observe that a pairwise equilibrium network is a refinement of Nash equilibrium: it is a Nash equilibrium where there does not exist a pair of firms with an incentive to form a link.

Homogeneous Cournot game

Our analysis of the third stage begins with the textbook oligopoly model. To simplify the analysis, following much of the literature, we assume that the marginal cost function is $c_i(q_i) = cq_i$. Moreover, we assume the following linear inverse demand function:

$$p = \alpha - \sum_{i \in N} q_i, \alpha \geq 0,$$

where p is the market price of the good and q_i is the quantity sold by firm i.

We assume that each unit of production yields an amount of pollution $\eta_i(|g(i)|) = \gamma_0 - \gamma|g(i)|$, with $\gamma < \gamma_0/(n-1)$. It is worth noting that collaborations between firms reduce the amount of pollution per unit of production. The regulatory authorities impose a Pigouvian tax $t > 0$ on firms for each unit of pollution they create. We also assume that R&D collaborations are costly, and each firm incurs a cost $f > 0$ for each link in which it is involved. The profit function of firm i is

$$\pi_i(|g(i)|) = \left(\alpha - \sum_{i \in N} q_i - c - t\eta_i(|g(i)|) \right) q_i - f|g(i)|$$

To ensure the existence of a market, we assume that[3]

$$\alpha - c - t(\gamma_0 + \gamma(n-1)(n-2)) > 0 \tag{14.1}$$

Finally, we assume that there exists a damage function, $D\left(\sum_{i \in N} \eta_i(|g(i)|) q_i \right)$, which measures the external social damages, or the loss in social welfare/consumers surplus, due to pollution:

$$D\left(\sum_{i \in N} \eta_i(|g(i)|) q_i \right) = \left(\sum_{i \in N} \eta_i(|g(i)|) q_i \right)^2$$

Let us now provide the equilibrium Cournot output for each firm i, q^*, for any given network g. By straightforward computations, we obtain:

$$q_i^*(g) = \frac{\alpha - c - t\gamma_0 + nt(\gamma|g(i)|) - t\gamma \sum_{j \in N} |g(j)|}{n+1}$$

That is,

$$q_i^*(g) = \frac{\alpha - c - t\gamma_0 + (n-1)(t\gamma|g(i)|) - t\gamma L(g_{-i})}{n+1}$$

with $L(g_{-i}) = \sum_{j \in N} |g_{-i}(j)|$.

Moreover, the equilibrium Cournot profit for any given network g is

$$\pi_i^*(|g(i)|, L(g_{-i})) = \left(a_1(t) + (n-1) a_2(t)|g(i)| - a_2(t) L(g_{-i}) \right)^2 - f|g(i)| \tag{14.2}$$

with $a_1(t) = \dfrac{\alpha - c - t\gamma_0}{n+1}$ and $a_2(t)\dfrac{t\gamma}{n+1}$.

We need some additional notations in order to proceed. First, for $|g(i)| \in \{1, \ldots, n-1\}$,

$$\Delta_{11}\left[\Pi_i^*\left(|g(i)|, L(g_{-i})\right)\right] = \Delta_1\left[\Pi_i^*\left(|g(i)|, L(g_{-i})\right)\right] - \Delta_1\left[\Pi_i^*\left(|g(i)|-1, L(g_{-i})\right)\right]$$

is the marginal profit obtained by firm *i* when she forms an additional link. Second, for $|g(i)| \in \{2, \ldots, n-1\}$

$$\Delta_{11}\left[\Pi_i^*\left(|g(i)|, L(g_{-i})\right)\right] = \Delta_1\left[\Pi_i^*\left(|g(i)|, L(g_{-i})\right)\right] - \Delta_1\left[\Pi_i^*\left(|g(i)|-1, L(g_{-i})\right)\right]$$

is the variation of the marginal profit obtained by firm *i* when it varies its number of collaboration links by one. Third, for $|g(i)| \in \{1, \ldots, n-1\}$, and $L(g_{-i}) \in \{1, \ldots, (n-1)(n-2)\}$,

$$\Delta_{12}\left[\Pi_i^*\left(|g(i)|, L(g_{-i})\right)\right] = \Delta_1\left[\Pi_i^*\left(|g(i)|, L(g_{-i})\right)\right] - \Delta_1\left[\Pi_i^*\left(|g(i)|, L(g_{-i})-1\right)\right]$$

is the variation of the marginal profit obtained by firm *i* when the total number of links in which *i* is not involved increases by one.

Based on this, we now introduce two useful definitions.

Definition 2

The payoff function is convex in own links if $\Delta_{11}[\Pi_i^*(|g(i)|, L(g_{-i}))] > 0$.

Definition 3

The payoff function satisfies the strategic substitutes property if $\Delta_{12}[\Pi_i^*(|g(i)|, L(g_{-i}))] < 0$. In other words, the payoff function is convex in own links if the marginal payoff of firm *i* increases in the number of links formed by *i*. Similarly, the payoff function satisfies the strategic substitutes property if the marginal payoff of firm *i* decreases with the total number of links formed by the other firms.

In our model, given the equilibrium Cournot profit in (14.2), we obtain the following values:

$$\Delta_{11}\left[\Pi_i^*\left(|g(i)|, L(g_{-i})\right)\right] = 2\left(a_2(t)\right)^2(n-1)^2 > 0,$$

and

$$\Delta_{12}\left[\Pi_i^*\left(|g(i)| > 0, L(g_{-i})\right)\right] = -2\left(a_2(t)\right)^2(n-1) < 0.$$

Network analysis

Here we examine the second stage of the game described in the model setup. First, we present a result from Goyal and Joshi (2006).

Proposition 1

(Adapted from Proposition 3.1 Goyal & Joshi, 2006, p. 327) Suppose $\Pi_i^*(|g(i)|, L(g_{-i}))$ *is convex in own links. A pairwise equilibrium network is empty, complete, or is a k-group-dominant*

network. There exists a pairwise equilibrium if $\Pi_i^*(|g(i)|, L(g_{-i}))$ *satisfies strategic substitutability property.*

This result allows us to obtain the following proposition.

Proposition 2

Suppose the profit function satisfies Equation (14.2). Then there exists a pairwise equilibrium. Moreover, a pairwise equilibrium is empty, complete, or is a k-group-dominant network.

Proof We know that the Cournot profit equilibrium in (14.2) satisfies both convexity in own links and strategic substitutes properties. The result follows.

One of the most interesting architectures in our framework is the complete network. Indeed, in this architecture, the number of collaborations is the maximum possible. Consequently, the quantity of pollution per unit produced is minimized. In the following result, we provide a condition for obtaining the complete network as a pairwise equilibrium. Let $\zeta(t) = (n-1)a_2(t)(2a_1(t) - a_2(t)(n-1)(n-3))$. It is worth noting that since $\alpha - c - t\gamma_0 > 0$ by (14.1), we have $\zeta(t) > 0$.

Corollary 1

Suppose that the profit function satisfies Equation (14.2). The complete network is a pairwise equilibrium if $0 \le f < \zeta(t)$.

Proof First, we show that the complete network is a pairwise equilibrium if $\zeta(t) > f$. Due to the convexity of the profit function, if a firm has no incentive to maintain its $(n-1)$th link in the complete network, then it has an incentive to remove all its links. Hence, to ensure that the complete network is a pairwise equilibrium network, we have to compare $A_{n-1} = \Pi_i^*(n-1, (n-1)^2 - (n-1))$ and $A_0 = \Pi_i^*(0, (n-1)^2 - (n-1))$. We obtain that $A_{n-1} - A_0 \ge 0$ if and only if $\zeta(t) > f$.

Tax policy and incentives for innovation

In this section, we examine how the environmental tax modifies the possibility of obtaining different pairwise equilibrium network architectures. We begin with the complete network. Let

$$\omega = \frac{\alpha - c}{2\gamma_0 + \gamma(n-1)(n-3)}.$$

Straightforward computations show that $\zeta'(t) > 0$ if and only if $t \to \omega$. Hence, we have the following remark.

Remark 1

Suppose the profit function satisfies Equation (14.2).

1 *An increase in the tax encourages firms to form the complete network if* $t < \omega$.
2 *A decrease in the tax encourages firms to form the complete network if* $t \ge \omega$.

This remark establishes that again there is an ambiguous relationship between the tax and the incentive of the firms for maintaining the complete network as a pairwise equilibrium network.

We now examine how the tax modifies the possibility of obtaining the empty network. The difference between the payoff obtained by firm i when it forms one link and when it forms no link, given that other firms form no link, is equal to

$$\psi(t)=\frac{-\gamma t(n-1)(-2\alpha+2c+2\gamma_0 t-\gamma nt+\gamma t)}{(n+1)^2}-f$$

Let

$$\omega'=\frac{\alpha-c}{2\gamma_0-\gamma(n-1)}.$$

Straightforward computations allow us to obtain that $\psi'(t)>0$ if and only if $t<\omega'$. Hence, we have the following remark.

Remark 2

Suppose the profit function satisfies Equation (14.7).

1 *An increase of the tax encourages firms to form a link in the empty network if* $t<\omega'$.
2 *A decrease of the tax encourages firms to form a link in the empty network if* $t\geq\omega'$.

This remark establishes that there is an ambiguous relationship between the tax and the incentive of the firms for forming a link in the empty network. In the next proposition, we examine how the incentive of the isolated firms to form links varies when the pairwise equilibrium network is a k-group-dominant network.

Let us introduce three values that allow us to simplify the presentation.

$$\kappa(t)=\frac{\gamma t(n-1)\left(2(\alpha-c)-2\gamma_0 t-\gamma t\left(n-\kappa-2k^2+1\right)\right)}{(n+1)^2}$$

$$v=\frac{\alpha-c}{2\gamma_0+2\gamma k^2-2\gamma\kappa-\gamma n+\gamma}$$

and

$$\xi=\frac{2\gamma(n-1)\left(\alpha-c-\gamma_0 t+\gamma t\left(n+2k-2k^2-1\right)\right)}{(n+1)^2}$$

Proposition 3

Let g be a k-group dominant network. If $t<v$, *then the higher the tax, the higher is the incentive of an isolated firm to form a link in g.*

Proof Straightforward computations show that an isolated firm has an incentive to form a link in g if

$\kappa(k,t)>f$. We have $\kappa'(t)=\xi$. Consequently, if $t<v$, then the result is obtained.

Social welfare

We now have to establish the tax that maximizes social welfare, defined as the sum of the total profits and the consumers' surplus. In other words, given the two last stages of game, we consider the first stage of the game described in the model setup.

We first define the notion of efficient pair $(g; t)$. Let $PE(t)$ denote the set of pairwise equilibria given the tax rate t. To simplify the presentation, we use a slight abuse of notation: We write $q_i^*(g; t)$ and $\Pi_i^*(g; t)$ instead of $q_i^*(g)$ and $\Pi_i^*(g)$. Let us now define the social welfare function $W(g; t)$.

$$W(g;t)=\frac{1}{2}\left(\sum_{i\in N} q_i^*(g,t)\right)^2+\sum_{i\in N}\left(q_i^*(g,t)\right)^2-\left(\sum_{i\in N}\left(1-\gamma|g(i)|\right)q_i^*(g;t)\right)^2$$
$$+t\left(\sum_{i\in N}\left(1-\gamma|g(i)|\right)q_i^*(g;t)\right)-f|g(i)|$$

Recall that $\left(\sum_{i\in N}\left(1-\gamma|g(i)|\right)q_i^*(g;t)\right)^2$ is the cost associated with the damage from the pollution.

Definition 4

A pair (g; t) is efficient if

1 $g \in PE(t)$;
2 $W(g; t) \geq W(g'; t')$ *for every pair* $(g'; t')$ *such that* $g' \in PE(t')$.

We say that a network g is efficient if it is associated with an efficient pair (g, t).

Because of tractability issues, in this section, we restrict our attention to the simple case with three firms.

Proposition 4

Suppose $n = 3$. Then, for every equilibrium network g, there are parameters α, c, γ_0, $\gamma > 0$ for which there exists $f > 0$ such that g is efficient.

Proof We show this result through an example. Suppose $n = 3$, $\alpha - c = 1.5$, $\gamma = 0.5$, $\gamma_0 = 2$. Let $z_1 = 1/72$, $z_2 = 9/242$. We have:

1 If $f < z_1$, then the optimal tax is $t = \frac{5}{6}$ which leads to the complete network as equilibrium network.
2 If $f \in (z_1, z_2]$, then the optimal tax is $t = \frac{8}{11}$ which leads to the network where there is only one link between firms as equilibrium network.
3 If $f > z_2$, then the optimal tax is $t = \frac{23}{36}$ which leads to the empty network as the equilibrium network.

By Proposition 2, we know that a pairwise equilibrium network is either a k-group-dominant network, or the complete network, or the empty network. The above proposition establishes that there exist parameters such that each potential pairwise equilibrium is an efficient network. Interestingly, the example shown in Proposition 4 suggests that there exist situations where the optimal tax is increasing in the number of links in an efficient network. Finally, we observe a straightforward relationship between the cost of formation links and the number of links in an efficient network: *the higher the cost of links formation, the lower the number of links in an efficient network.*

Conclusion

In this chapter, we have examined the role played by an environmental tax on collaborations between firms for innovation in clean production processes.

First, using a result of Goyal and Joshi (2006), we have shown that there are only three types of networks that can emerge as equilibrium: the empty network, the complete network, and the *k*-group-dominant network. The latter network is interesting since it implies that a public policy that has the reduction of pollution as its objective leads to "unequal connections" (see Goyal & Joshi, 2006). In other words, when the public authorities try to decrease the amount of pollution using Pigouvian taxes, there exist situations where some firms will obtain higher profits than others, even though all firms are *ex ante* identical. To sum up, in this situation, the public authorities face a trade-off between the amount of pollution and equity between firms.

Second, we have examined the relationship between the environmental tax and the incentives for firms to add collaborative links. We have established that there is ambiguous relationship between the changes in the environmental tax and the incentives to form collaborative links for green innovations. More precisely, the level of environmental tax plays a crucial role in this relationship. If the environmental tax is sufficiently low (resp. high), then firms have more (resp. less) incentives to form collaborative links when the tax increases.

Finally, we have examined the optimal tax that the public authorities should impose in order to maximize social welfare. Note that here we have restricted our attention to the situation where only three firms exist on the market. We have established that the optimal environmental tax depends on the cost of link formation. The higher the cost of link formation, the lower the environmental tax.

Clearly, there exist several interesting research directions for the future. The main one consists of examining the optimal tax policy taking social welfare into account when there are more than three firms. The difficulty in this task comes from the fact that the optimal tax value may not always lie in the interior. Indeed, the tax value that solves for the optimal condition using social welfare for a given network g may imply that g itself is not the equilibrium network. In this case, we have to consider corner solutions for the optimal tax level. Obviously, such technical difficulties have to be dealt with in order to obtain new results. Another direction of research that could be explored concerns the introduction of uncertainty in the innovation. Again this possibility introduces important technical problems that are beyond the scope of this chapter.

Notes

1 There are several examples of collaborations aimed at curbing pollution. For instance, in the textile industry, Parkdale Advanced Materials, Inc., the innovative fibers and yarns division of Parkdale Inc., the world's leading manufacturer of spun yarns, and Intrinsic Textiles Group, LLC, have announced the formation of Intrinsic Advanced Materials, a joint venture to bring CiCLO Sustainable Textile Technology to market. Moreover, in the transport sector, six harbor trucking firms operating in the Ports of Long Beach and Los Angeles have collaborated to design new engines and fuel for trucks to slash transportation emissions. Sources: Gastonia, N. C. and Hayward, C. A., September 12, 2018, Green Car Congress, May 2018.

2 The reduced oligopoly equilibrium profit function of firm i associates with each potential network g the profit of I when firms produce the Nash equilibrium quantities, given the level of pollution that results from g.

3 Note that this is equivalent to the $\alpha - c > 0$ condition in the standard Cournot oligopoly model.

References

Baumol, W. J., & Oates, W. E. (2015). *The Theory of Environmental Policy*. Cambridge University Press.

Billand, P., Bravard, C., Chakrabarti, S., & Sarangi, S. (2014). A note on networks of collaboration in multi-market oligopolies. *The Annal of Regional Sciences*, 53, 325–335. https://doi.org/10.1007/s00168-013-0577-x

Billand, P., Bravard, C., Durieu, J., & Sarangi, S. (2015). Efficient networks for a class of games with global spillovers. *Journal of Mathematical Economics*, 61, 203–210. https://doi.org/10.1016/j.jmateco.2015.06.019

Buchanan, J. M. (1969). External diseconomies, corrective taxes and market structure. *American Economic Review*, 59(1), 174–177.

Carraro, C., & Soubeyran, A. (1996). Environmental policy and the choice of production technology. In: Carraro, C., Katsoulacos, Y., & Xepapadeas, A. (eds.) *Environmental Policy and Market Structure. Economics, Energy and Environment*, vol 4, pp. 151–180. Springer. https://doi.org/10.1007/978-94-015-8642-9_9

Ebert, U. (1991). Pigouvian tax and market structure: The case of oligopoly and different abatement technologies. *FinanzArchiv/Public Finance Analysis*, 49, 154–166.

Levin, D. (1985). Taxation within Cournot oligopoly. *Journal of Public Economics*, 27, 281–290. https://doi.org/10.1016/0047-2727(85)90052-0

Goyal, S., & Joshi, S. (2003). Networks of collaboration in oligopoly. *Games and Economic Behavior*, 43(1), 57–85. https://doi.org/10.1016/S0899-8256(02)00562-6

Goyal, S., & Joshi, S. (2006). Unequal connections. *International Journal of Game Theory*, 34(3), 319–349. https://doi.org/10.1007/s00182-006-0023-8

Katsoulacos, Y., & Xepapadeas, A. (1995). Environmental policy under oligopoly with endogenous market structure. *Scandinavian Journal of Economics*, 97, 411–420. https://doi.org/10.2307/3440871

Requate, T. (1993). Pollution control under imperfect competition: Asymmetric Bertrand duopoly with linear technologies. *Journal of Institutional and Theoretical Economics (JITE) / Zeitschrift Für Die Gesamte Staatswissenschaft*, 149(2), 415–442. https://www.jstor.org/stable/40751615

Westbrock, B. (2010). Natural concentration in industrial research collaboration. *The RAND Journal of Economics*, 41(2), 351–371. https://doi.org/10.1111/j.1756-2171.2010.00103.x

World Health Organization. (2016). *Ambient Air Pollution: A Global Assessment of Exposure and Burden of Disease*. World Health Organization. https://iris.who.int/handle/10665/250141

Index